Keynes and the Cambridge Keynesians

What was the Keynesian revolution in economics? Why did it not succeed to the extent that Keynes and his close pupils had hoped for? *Keynes and the Cambridge Keynesians* addresses these and other questions by tracing the historical development of Keynesian economics. This volume consists of three parts, which the author calls Book I, Book II and Book III. Book I contains the author's Caffè Lectures on Keynes's 'unaccomplished revolution'. Book II is a series of biographical essays where the author, himself a witness and participant of the group on which he writes, presents the successful and unsuccessful endeavours of Keynes's most important Cambridge pupils: Richard Kahn, Joan Robinson, Nicholas Kaldor, Piero Sraffa and Richard Goodwin. Book III looks to the future. It develops a conceptual analytical framework that makes sense of the Cambridge group as a whole, discussing the many aspects in which the Keynesian way of doing economics, as opposed to the neoclassical way, brings forward the more permanent and fertile features of Keynes's 'revolution in economics'.

Luigi L. Pasinetti was Reader in Economics and Official Fellow of King's College, Cambridge, up to the mid-1970s, then Professor of Economic Analysis (now Emeritus) at the Università Cattolica del Sacro Cuore, Milan, Italy. He was a student of Goodwin, Kahn, Kaldor and Sraffa, and is a leading member of the second generation of Cambridge Keynesians.

Federico Caffè Lectures

This series of annual lectures was initiated to honour the memory of Federico Caffè. They are jointly sponsored by the Department of Public Economics at the University of Rome, where Caffè held a chair from 1959 to 1987, and the Bank of Italy, where he served for many years as an adviser. The publication of the lectures will provide a vehicle for leading scholars in the economics profession, and for the interested general reader, to reflect on the pressing economic and social issues of the times.

Keynes and the Cambridge Keynesians

A 'Revolution in Economics' to be accomplished

Luigi L. Pasinetti

CAMBRIDGE
UNIVERSITY PRESS

CAMBRIDGE UNIVERSITY PRESS
Cambridge, New York, Melbourne, Madrid, Cape Town, Singapore, São Paulo, Delhi

Cambridge University Press
The Edinburgh Building, Cambridge CB2 8RU, UK

Published in the United States of America by Cambridge University Press, New York

www.cambridge.org
Information on this title: www.cambridge.org/9780521872270

First published 2007

Printed in the United Kingdom at the University Press, Cambridge

A catalogue record for this publication is available from the British Library

ISBN   978-0-521-87227-0 hardback

Contents

x   Contents

Plates

Preface

The winning ideas in scientific work are not necessarily those that promptly succeed but those that endure. In this respect, Keynes's ideas are tricky to assess. In terms of economic policy their success was immediate. In terms of economic theory Keynes's original ideas failed to achieve wide acceptance. Economic science, essentially, continued to do 'business as usual', i.e. with a Walrasian engine at its core. The 'Keynesian revolution' thus succeeded halfway – it did from an economic policy point of view; it did not on a theoretical level. This book deals mainly with the half that has not succeeded – at least, not yet.

This work on 'Keynes and the Cambridge Keynesians' therefore bends backwards but aims forwards. It considers the origins of Keynes's theoretical revolution, the accidents that made it fail (or rather, that kept it unaccomplished), the reasons why it has remained incomplete and what justifications there are in all efforts aiming to pull it out of the darkness into which it has admittedly fallen.

To assert that Keynes did not succeed in shaping dominant economic theory as he intended may sound unusual to many professional economists, since the so-called 'Keynesian' theories appear to have spread again to all sorts of places, including those firmly ingrained in neoclassical mainstream economics. In spite of the monetarist 'counter-revolution' of the 1970s, I think very few macroeconomists nowadays would seriously deny that their profession has been directly or indirectly influenced by Keynes's concepts and ideas. Samuelson's post-World War Two reported statement, 'We are all Keynesians now' (1970), has largely become part of the economists' conventional wisdom.[1]

In the following pages I shall dispute this widespread feeling. The great majority of those theories that we now call 'Keynesian' have in fact little to do with the theoretical 'revolution' that Keynes had in mind in the 1930s when, right in the middle of the deepest economic slump that had ever hit the industrial world, he wrote his *General Theory*. It may well be that an economic model that shows some market imperfections, some unemployment of labour and of existing resources, or that hints at the role of uncertainty in investment decisions or at the non-neutrality of money or at the inherent instability of financial markets may contain some strands of Keynesian thought. But Keynes's *General Theory of Employment, Interest and Money*, as the title suggests, was not aimed at patching up existing, deficient theories, it was aimed at refounding economic theory on different bases altogether.

Which bases? The present work started from the conviction that, in order to resume the original theoretical framework that inspired Keynes's 'revolution in economics', one needs to go back to the place and environment where he conceived and fostered his 'revolutionary' ideas. That place was Cambridge. There, he chose to put the dominant economic theories, including those he had presented in his previous works, to the test of the discussions and criticisms of a group of unusually bright pupils, brought together from different backgrounds. The reliance he placed on this group of talented young scholars was extraordinary, all of them being fascinated by his personality and at the same time being admired by him, in an intellectual process of understanding and developing his intuitions. It was this group of scholars that

[1] Samuelson (1948, 8th edition 1970, p. 193).

came to form what I call here the Cambridge School of Keynesian Economics.

Good historians are well aware that to acquire a sound knowledge of what has happened in any particular circumstance – in our case the event under investigation is the 'Keynesian revolution' – one must first of all grasp the context within which such an event took place. Precisely for this reason, the members of the Cambridge School of Keynesian Economics, the environment in which they moved, the theories from which they started and from which they all took inspiration are to be submitted to careful scrutiny.

Within such a context, the essential feature of the School was to take Keynes's ideas, in conjunction with those of the early Classical English School, and to develop them without any compromise, i.e. without making any concession to the dominant theories prevailing at the time. Thus its members were determined to break away from orthodoxy. Coherently, the School followed a line of theoretical development alternative, not complementary, to the theoretical core of mainstream economics. This sharp opposition to current economic theory is in fact rather well known; probably too well known. It is a feature so often used as a *j'accuse* platform against them for being far more prone to and *capable* of criticising and destroying than of building up a viable alternative theory.

In this work, even though I could not avoid mentioning this destructive attitude, I shall devote my major efforts to highlighting the opposite aspect – i.e. the constructive part – of their efforts. I shall therefore argue that the relevant message that should be extracted from the works of the Cambridge School of Keynesian Economics is, in fact, positive – not negative. In essence, my conviction is that essentially the 'revolution in economics' that Keynes proposed is bound to have a future in economic theory, simply because the 'monetary production economies' that he singled out for investigation are precisely the kind of economies that have increasingly been emerging since the industrial revolution. In other words, history is on the side of Keynes's theory, not against it. And if this is so, the consequences are far reaching.

The course of normal science – and in this economics can be no exception – may resist many intellectual challenges, but it cannot persistently resist an irreversible change of reality. Under this light, Keynes and the Cambridge Keynesians emerge as having something far more relevant to say about the economic developments of the world around us than Walras and his neoclassical followers.

Of course, any scientific paradigm is not a monolithic and static block of human knowledge; it is normally open to self-adjustment in the face of necessity. By this token, mainstream economics nowadays is clearly not a mere copycat of the original Walrasian theory. However, it must also be admitted that the process of reformulating the same theory, though with different sets of analytical tools, almost *ad infinitum* does not seem to be the most efficient way of doing creative research. Sometimes it may be easier, and much more fruitful, to scrap the papers altogether and start anew, with fresh ideas in an entirely novel approach.

That was the intention of the Keynesian theoretical 'revolution'. Why did it not succeed? My arguments will be developed in a two-fold direction. The first has to do with the type of reaction that the economic profession adopted towards Keynes's theoretical proposals. Contrary to what one might presume, his opponents did not always reject Keynes's ideas entirely. More often, they adopted (consciously or unconsciously) a subtle and insidious attitude of taking bits and pieces of Keynes's theory, here and there, and conveniently adapting them to fit orthodoxy, without however accepting the *generality* of his theoretical framework.

A second reason – which will be stressed particularly in the final part of this work – may be summarised as follows. The theory that Keynes proposed, though *general*, was incomplete, in some directions even to a considerable extent. Not only did it miss the polish and finish that all great constructions lack at the beginning (this would hardly be surprising for such an original work and would pose no great problem), it also lacked some essential (building) blocks. Perhaps in the urgency of publication, Keynes neglected some important pillars at the very foundational level.

Understandably enough, nobody would be willing to abandon a dominant theory – no matter how imperfect it may be – if no other alternative theory were to be seen around the corner, at least with the same degree of apparent solidity. There is no reason to believe that economists should be an exception to this 'risk-averse' attitude. If this is so, it becomes imperative to examine what needs to be done to strengthen the economic paradigm that lies behind the Keynesian revolution. Is this paradigm ready for prime time or not?

Once again, it appears extremely important to go back to the features of the Cambridge School of Keynesian Economics and to the lives of the (individual) members. What does emerge is that Keynes's pupils, perhaps themselves facing urgency, were driven to pressing immediately for further developments of Keynes's ideas rather than for strengthening the foundations of the alternative paradigm behind them. Sraffa was the notable exception in this respect. He devoted his efforts to a search for coherence and for avoiding inconsistencies, thus strengthening the merits of the Classical foundations of their alternative way of thinking. But conversely, he could not devote appreciable efforts to analysing Keynes's construction, thus neglecting much of the richness of Keynes's ideas. The result is that Keynes's pupils, taken all together, appeared more cohesive as a group of critical thinkers than as a group of theoretical founders. And it is probably true that the external glue that appears to have held them together during their academic life had a dominant flavour of criticism rather than of construction.

In the final part of the present work, I attempt to reverse this attitude. I shall try to find a cohesive framework for unifying the whole of Keynes's and the Cambridge Keynesians' theories under a single (scientific) umbrella. I shall do this precisely by placing Sraffa's approach to economics, duly integrated by an apparatus of (structural) economic dynamics, at the very heart of the whole theoretical construction. And in order to render the foundations clear and solid in the face of factual complexity, I am proposing a novel two-stage methodological approach to economic analysis. I shall suggest, first, concentrating on the essentiality of *pure theory*, just as Sraffa did in his masterpiece, where the fundamental and natural (i.e. permanent) sectoral and macroeconomic features of the economic system are clearly singled out. Then I shall suggest (logically, not necessarily chronologically) proceeding to a second stage of investigation, which I have called the *institutional* stage, where social and individual types of behaviour may be explored in their variety and interaction and where economic analysis is opened up to suggestions and hypotheses and behavioural models coming from the other social sciences. This attempt at unifying the whole theoretical framework of the Cambridge School of Keynesian Economics is not of course intended to be self-contained. In a book like the present one, I do not pretend to be so over-ambitious as to show precisely each step that should be taken. But I do try to show the direction in which this process of unification may be pursued. I hope this will be fruitful enough to allow Keynes's theoretical ideas to endure – a necessary condition to make them *ultimately* successful.

* * *

The scheme of the whole work reflects the succession of arguments as presented above. It is subdivided into three distinct parts, which I call Books One, Two and Three. Book One is an account of Keynes's radical decision to break with orthodoxy. It gives an account of the stumbling blocks that prevented the accomplishment of the 'revolution', after publication of *The General Theory*. The expository layout is the one I used in my 'Caffè Lectures', which I have left here practically as they were delivered at La Sapienza University in Rome in October 1994.

Book Two contains a series of biographical essays on Keynes's closest pupils and on the Cambridge School of Keynesian Economics that they formed. I happened to become, at a certain point, part and witness of this School. The inevitable emotional involvement of a participant may well have influenced my judgements, for better or worse. But I hope this will be counter-balanced by those insights that only insiders have the privilege to perceive. I hope the details may help to keep high the torch of an alternative way of doing economics. All the biographical essays (on Kahn, Joan Robinson, Kaldor, Sraffa and Goodwin) have appeared previously. But I have taken the freedom to insert some minor changes wherever I felt it appropriate or useful. Moreover, I have interwoven them with three new pieces (Prelude, Interlude and Postlude), aimed at clarifying the interpretative keys that I have used for giving a unitary sense to otherwise apparently puzzling, scarcely understood and to some extent unwise behaviour of the protagonists, besides reporting on their scientific works.

Finally, Book Three discusses openly the incompatibility of the Keynesian way, as compared with the neoclassical way, of doing economics. It is aimed at attempting – constructively – to develop a framework of economic analysis within which Keynes's original ideas may not only be kept alive but also continue to bear fruit in the long run. Most of this constructive part takes advantage of other works of mine. The purpose is obviously not that of presenting them on their own but of placing the whole of the Cambridge School of Keynesian Economics into a coherent methodological framework, where a series of concepts and logical (inter)relations may at last help to revive the message and substance of a fully fledged Keynesian 'revolution in economics'.

L.L.P.
Milano, May 2006

Acknowledgements

In opening a book which has been in progress for fifteen years, with interruptions, resumptions, rewritings, but always with a definite aim to uncover and stress fundamental principles, the temptation is strong to begin by expressing one's gratitude to one's teachers. I refer especially to those who formed the Cambridge School of Economics, under whose influence I have been during the sixteen years I spent at the Faculty of Economics and Politics of Cambridge, England. And, of course, also to those with whom I had endless discussions in Oxford, England, in Cambridge, Massachusetts and in Italy. But I shall resist emotional feelings on this occasion.

My explicit thanks will be confined here to those who have, at some point or another, read and expressed remarks, criticisms or suggestions on excerpts that have actually ended up in this volume, with one exception, to express my boundless gratitude to Siro Lombardini, without whose determined care and encouragement my career as an economist would probably never have started.

Among those who commented (or criticised) the early draft of my Caffè Lectures, I must thank: Nicola Acocella, Mario Tiberi, Andrea Boitani, Terenzio Cozzi, Siro Lombardini, Ferruccio Marzano, Alberto Quadrio Curzio, Luigi Spaventa and Paolo Sylos Labini. On the biographical essays collected in Book Two, I am most grateful, for careful and useful comments, to Marco Dardi, Cristina Marcuzzo, Nerio Naldi,

Ferdinando Targetti, Tony Thirlwall, and (on the Richard Goodwin essay) to Paul Samuelson and Robert Solow.

The drafts of the last part of the book have attracted the most concentrated and detailed comments and criticisms, simply because I distributed personalised drafts of parts of Book Three in specifically organised meetings, in Milano (Università Cattolica) and in Porto (at the 2006 Annual Meeting of the European Society for the History of Economic Thought). I am grateful for such comments and criticisms to Enrico Bellino, Antonio D'Agata, Domenico Delli Gatti, Davide Gualerzi, Giorgio Lunghini, Giandemetrio Marangoni, Cristina Marcuzzo, Ferdinando Meacci, Piercarlo Nicola, Daniela Parisi, Pier Luigi Porta, Pippo Ranci, Angelo Reati, Alessandro Roncaglia, Moshe Syrquin, Paolo Varri and Stefano Zamagni.

Exceptional and very special thanks must be reserved for Geoffrey Harcourt, Mauro Baranzini, Heinrich Bortis and Roberto Scazzieri, who have been nearest to me in my efforts to bring this book to completion. Their keen attention to the development of my ideas has accompanied me from beginning to end, throughout the gestation of this work.

In the very last phase of preparation of the manuscript, I have benefited from the undeserved attention of Will Baumol, who – besides interacting on comparisons with the alternative views that are to be expressed in a forthcoming book of his – has unexpectedly told me that he has taken up some of my points and seems to be very keen on starting discussions on aspects of agreement and disagreement on the basic features of the 'monetary production economies' – as Keynes called them – that are the latest evolutionary stage of the industrial societies in which we live. I am eager to see the extent to which our respective points of view may be alternative or complementary, or both.

I cannot end these personal acknowledgements without mentioning the profound gratitude I have for GianPaolo Mariutti, who, for the final stages of this work, has been my precious, and far-from-passive, research assistant. Without his help, his keen telematic sense of bibliographical enquiry, his (indeed critical) comments, his alternative suggestions, this publication would have taken an even longer time and might even, perhaps, never have come to fruition. I must also express my thanks to the Catholic University of Milano for providing me with the necessary research facilities (project D.3.2).

In closing, I must mention the original venues of those essays, which, though with some amendments and integrations, are republished here (in Book Two), namely:

- 'Richard Ferdinand Kahn: 1905–1989', originally published in *Proceedings of the British Academy, Lectures and Memoirs*, vol. 76, London, 1991, (pp. 423–443).

- 'Robinson, Joan Violet', as an item of *The New Palgrave Dictionary of Economics*, Eatwell, John, Milgate, Murray and Newman, Peter, eds., The Macmillan Press Ltd., London, vol. IV, 1987 (pp. 212–217).

- 'Kaldor, Nicholas', an item in 'Biographical Supplement', vol. 18 of *The International Encyclopedia of the Social Sciences*, New York: The Free Press and London: Collier Macmillan Publishers, 1979 (pp. 366–369); and 'An introduction' to: Nicholas Kaldor, *Economia senza equilibrio* (Italian version of Kaldor's Yale Lectures), Bologna: Il Mulino, 1985 (pp. 9–21).

- 'Sraffa Piero', an item in 'Biographical Supplement', vol. 18, *The International Encyclopedia of the Social Sciences*, New York: The Free Press, a division of Macmillan Publ. Co., 1979 (pp. 736–739).

- 'Continuity and Change in Sraffa's Thought', in Cozzi, T. and Marchionatti, R., eds., *Piero Sraffa: a Centenary Estimate*, London: Routledge, 2000 (pp. 139–156).

- 'Richard Murphey Goodwin (1913–1996)', *The Cambridge Journal of Economics*, vol. 20, 1996 (pp. 645–949).

I renew my thanks to Pierangelo Garegnani (Sraffa's literary executor) for allowing me, in my third essay on Sraffa, to reproduce unpublished material from the *Sraffa Papers*, held in the Wren Library of Trinity College. My expression of thanks also goes to John Eatwell and Alessandro Roncaglia for their permission to publish their exchange of letters with Piero Sraffa. Finally, let me say how grateful I am to Jonathan Smith and Peter Jones, the librarians of Trinity College and King's College, Cambridge, respectively, for helping me on many occasions to get access to unpublished material concerning all the authors who are the subject of the present work.

Last, but not least, I must express my affectionate gratitude to my family, especially to Carmela, my wife, for the generous patience and graciousness with which she endured the time I stole from my most elementary family duties. Indeed: thanks, and love.

L.L.P.
Milano, May 2006

Book One   Keynes's Unaccomplished Revolution

Keynes's Unaccomplished Revolution

The Federico Caffè Lectures, 1995

A note on Federico Caffè

Federico Caffè (born 1914) was a Professor of Economic Policy at the University of Rome and a National Member of the Accademia Nazionale dei Lincei.

He learned his basic economics from the most representative Italian economists of the inter-war period, who included both liberist, laissez-faire enthusiasts (such as Luigi Einaudi) and more interventionist proponents (such as Enrico Barone). Caffè was among the early economists in Italy to absorb and teach the economic theories and policies of John Maynard Keynes.

His main interests were in the fields of welfare economics, history of economic thought and economic policy at large. Thanks to deep concern with economic policies he was asked for advice by an influential (albeit small) group of post-war politicians (Partito di Azione). For some years he was also in charge of some economic studies on behalf of the Bank of Italy.

As a bachelor, he devoted the whole of his life primarily to teaching, lecturing and supervising his university students, instilling in them a deep sense of devotion and admiration.

After retirement, in May 1984, he happened to go through dramatic personal vicissitudes. He lost, in quick succession, the most beloved members of his family and almost at the same time, in tragic circumstances, a number of his most brilliant pupils and affectionate colleagues (Ezio Tarantelli and Fausto Vicarelli being among the most well known).

But those were also years in which he had to face the strongest attacks on the whole conception of economic theory and policy that he had been teaching consistently, particularly the welfare economics of Keynesian inspiration, of whose correctness and relevance he remained profoundly convinced. He upheld his views vigorously, both in his lectures and in his writings, openly stressing what he called 'autonomy of thought', even 'against reality', claiming that the latter may not always be rational or acceptable. (Defending the Welfare State was his last book.)

His last contact was a brother, who lived with him. They bid each other good night on the evening of 14 April 1987. Early the following morning, one may presume, he silently slipped out, unnoticed, leaving his watch, passport and wallet on his bedside table. Nobody has seen him or heard of him since.

Chapter I

A decision to break with orthodoxy

> L'apporto del pensiero keynesiano riceve [qui]
> un rilievo prevalente . . . come rivoluzione
> intellettuale incompiuta . . .[1]
> Federico Caffè
> (from: The Foreword to *In Difesa del 'Welfare State'*)

1. Introduction

The subject which I have chosen for these lectures, in honour
of Federico Caffè, concerns events that led to the formation
and development of the Cambridge School of Keynesian Economics. I hope it will not be taken as presumptuous to link
them with the preoccupations that characterised the very last
years of the person whom we are honouring. They may not
even be extraneous to his disconcerting disappearence.

The 'Keynesian revolution', as it was instantly called in
Cambridge, England, did not come easily to Italy, at least until
the postwar period. But there were precursors and Federico
Caffè was one of them. He was also one of those who remained
faithful to Keynes's scientific revolution to the end, steadily
defending Keynesian theories and policies even when, in the
1980s, they came under heavy attack from many sources,

---

[1] *Transl.*: 'The contribution of Keynesian thought is [here] brought into
relief . . . as an unaccomplished intellectual revolution . . .'

while at the same time the major protagonists of that intellectual drama, which characterised the cultural environment of Cambridge during and after the Keynesian period, were disappearing one after another. I am obviously referring to the 'indestructible' Joan Robinson, as Caffè defined her in his farewell article (Caffè, 1990), to Nicholas Kaldor, to Richard Kahn, and to Piero Sraffa, all of whom disappeared in the 1980s. In this frame of reference, it is by no means surprising that Federico Caffè himself chose to disappear in 1987.

I shall try to investigate the intellectual inheritance that this group of economists has left to us, and to trace their endeavours since its origin. This may well help to indicate new directions. People inevitably disappear, but ideas remain, and may become fruitful at a distance, even in directions which their authors originally would not have suspected.

2.   Alternative interpretations

I shall begin by recalling the essential features of the intellectual crisis that took place in Cambridge in the very early 1930s and led Keynes to abandon the positions stated in what had been his major scientific work, the *Treatise on Money*, and to write a new, 'revolutionary' book (*The General Theory of Employment, Interest and Money*). The drama connected with this crisis continues to attract attention. Not only does it appear as one of the most fascinating events in the history of economic thought, but it has become one of those events, the correct interpretation of which may have far-reaching implications for the way economics itself is to be intended and pursued today. The interpretations have become many.[2]

If one looks back from the end of the twentieth century, one realises that – in comparison with the plurality of radically different strands of economic theories that took shape in the nineteenth century (notably, Classical economics, Marxian economics, Marginalist economics) – the really new theories

---

[2] See, on this subject, Patinkin, 1990.

proposed in the twentieth century were remarkably few. There has been an extraordinary and unprecedented proliferation of models, devices and applications of statistical and mathematical tools, but proposals of originally and fundamentally new theories have been undeniably scarce. Thus Keynes's theories risk emerging almost as the only really novel strand of economic theory that is going to characterise the twentieth century.

But even this is not uncontroversial. Were they really a novelty? The answer, which seemed so obvious immediately after World War Two, does not appear so obvious today. The enormous amount of material that has come to light, with the publication of thirty volumes of 'Collected Writings of John Maynard Keynes', with the recent voluminous new biographies of Keynes (Moggridge, 1992, Skidelsky, 1983, 1992, 2000) and with the full availability of all Keynes's papers, has had a curiously ambiguous effect.[3] On the one side, a mass of material has become available that documents the steps through which, in a very short time, Keynes changed his mind from economic tradition to economic 'revolution'. On the other side, the sheer number of Keynes's pre-*General Theory* publications (indeed the majority of them), and the many documents that have become available on how he was educated as a (traditional) economist, inevitably direct attention towards the enormous number of writings that preceded his conversion to the *General Theory* and to the way in which he learned to think. A human being, even of extraordinarily flexible mind, may change opinion on many problems, but more rarely is he or she able to change his/her way of thinking. It is not inconceivable that one may be able to claim that, within an inevitably incomplete new theoretical framework, Keynes reached solutions to many new problems by applying to them methods of reasoning that he had formed many

---

[3] Keynes's papers are available to scholars in the King's College Library, Cambridge. Of course, not all of them are included in the thirty published volumes of collected writings, but they have been produced in micro-film form by Chadwyck-Healey Ltd.

years earlier and had applied to various problems in his previous (traditional) works. This may be shown sometimes even
against his statements, or even against his determined will.

Curiously enough, at the same time as putting together
statements, arguments and pieces of evidence showing the
'revolutionary' character of *The General Theory*, one can easily carry out an assembling exercise of pre-*General Theory*
pieces that may be used to fill gaps that one finds in *The General Theory*. One may assemble (perfectly orthodox) arguments that Keynes had used earlier in similar contexts. In
this way, one may even conclude that, essentially, there was
nothing new, in spite of the claims to the contrary. In a nut-
shell, 'it was all in Marshall', whose othodoxy was, after all,
on many points not unambiguous.

In the present work I shall use an external interpretative
clue to claim that a genuine effort was made to break with tradition. The effort was real and radical. It was strongly aimed
at a 'scientific revolution'. It may not have been successful.
But this is the source of so many other questions.

3.   To 'revolutionise the way the world thinks about economic problems'

It was Keynes himself who, at a certain point, began to talk
of his change of mind as a 'revolution'. In a much-quoted
passage from a letter to George Bernard Shaw, dated 1 January
1935, slightly more than a year before the actual publication
of *The General Theory*, he was writing:[4]

> To understand my state of mind, however, you have to know that
> I believe myself to be writing a book on economic theory which
> will largely revolutionise – not, I suppose, at once but in the
> course of the next ten years – the way the world thinks about
> economic problems. (Keynes, 1973a, p. 492)

---

[4] Moggridge (1992, p. 567) reports that especially in 1934, Keynes talked
very often of his work as 'revolutionising economics'.

The turnabout that caused this state of mind was in fact quite dramatic. Keynes had been, in all his career as a university teacher at Cambridge, what we today would call a 'monetary' economist. He lectured on the pure theory of money. He had written a lucid and successful *Tract on Monetary Reform*. He had completed a *Treatise on Money*, on which he unsparingly bestowed his efforts for eight years. His colleagues had been waiting for this work, which was expected to be the crowning of his career. The work appeared, at last, in two volumes, in October 1930. Quite extraordinarily, only a few months after publication, when Keynes had not even seen all the book reviews, he began to entertain acute doubts. He stimulated the formation of a discussion group among the most brilliant young economists he could put together at Cambridge – the well-known *Cambridge Circus*, led by Richard Kahn and composed of Joan Robinson, Austin Robinson, Piero Sraffa, and – as a temporary visiting member – James Meade.[5]

The vicissitudes of those months must have been excruciating for Keynes, as he became convinced that the othodox theory he had learned, and had actually been teaching for many years, since the beginning of his career, was flawed; in fact so irremediably flawed that his *Treatise on Money* could not be corrected. It is important to realise that this cannot have been a pleasant experience for a man of Keynes's stature, at the age of fifty. Among other things, it caused him a break of personal friendships with many of his colleagues. Only a deep convinction of the enormous importance of a new discovery can justify the way he acted.

It was quite different for the young people around him, among whom the excitement suddenly grew to a high pitch. All the indications we have, all impressions that are conveyed by the correspondence among the members of the

---

[5] Austin Robinson (1947) also mentions C. H. P. Gifford, A. F. W. Plumptre and L. Tarshis as other participants in the '*Circus*'.

Circus and Keynes, and by all documents of that period now published in Keynes's 'Collected Writings' are of an extraordinary excitement, of a deep conviction of having reached a great discovery. Keynes and his pupils give the clear impression of being convinced of living through an exceptional, unique experience of great importance to the future of economics. They use a language that implies the achievement of a new vision rather than the realisation of a single, even important, scientific contribution. They talk of at last 'seeing the light'. To take just one example, it is interesting to read the account that Richard Kahn gave, four decades later, of a weekend which was arranged for discussion with London School of Economics (LSE) graduate students, in the summer of 1933. He tells us of how Abba Lerner changed his mind and was at last brought to understand (Kahn, 1984, pp. 182–183). To indicate what was to be understood, Kahn uses the words 'the General Theory', even in his recent reminiscences, for lack of a better term.

At that time, the members of the group themselves were not quite sure of what 'the new thing' ultimately implied. They were unable to give it clear expression. It appeared to be so fundamental, so much of a break with established thinking, that it was almost impossible to express it in a few words.

But what really was it? And when did it exactly happen? The answers to these questions have remained controversial to this day. Curiously enough, it seems less controversial to narrow down to a short period of a few months the time at which the great event happened than to state what exactly the event was.

I therefore face, first of all, the less controversial part of the question.

4.   A review of a well-established chronology of events

Many efforts have been put into specifying the succession of the key events that characterised those early years of the

1930s in Cambridge (see, as notable examples, Moggridge, 1973, Patinkin, 1993). I may recall them synthetically.

Keynes's *Treatise on Money* was published in October 1930 (the Preface is dated 14 September). We know that, by that time, discussions had been going on for more than a year on the effects of public works. These discussions had followed the (unsuccessful) proposals made by Keynes (and Hubert Henderson) in the pamphlet *Can Lloyd George Do It?* (1929). In July 1930, Keynes had made Richard Kahn the joint secretary (with Colin Clark) of a Committee of Economists (on the Economic Advisory Council) and Kahn had begun to work on these problems. The following month (August 1930, see Kahn, 1984, p. 91), while on holiday in the Alps, Kahn discovered the *multiplier*. On his return, Kahn passed on his notes to Keynes. An early draft of the multiplier paper was presented to the Committee of Economists in October 1930. This means that, in the autumn of 1930, almost simultaneously with the publication of the *Treatise on Money*, Kahn's early arguments on the multiplier began to circulate. (Kahn's multiplier paper was then published in the June 1931 issue of the *Economic Journal*[6]).

The Cambridge *Circus* was precisely formed at the end of that year (1930) as a consequence of these discussions. The purpose was explicitly that of discussing Keynes's just-published book and of suggesting improvements. But very soon things went far beyond that. It is not easy to reconstruct the events of those months when the Circus effectively met (end 1930 to June 1931). Donald Moggridge, in the process of editing Keynes's *Writings*, has made a remarkable effort to put together reminiscences of the surviving members of the group (see Keynes, 1973a, pp. 337 and ff.). This account is extremely valuable but must be approached with caution: human memories are faulty and may play curious tricks. Moreover, the method used is not without defects – it is inevitably bound

---

[6] Further notes on the multiplier device were then drawn a few months later by James Meade in the discussions of the Cambridge *Circus*. Kahn referred to them as 'Mr Meade's relation' (Meade, 1993).

to give more relevance to those people who have been prepared to talk more. Yet, though with qualifications and caution, what emerges is remarkable.

At the same time, a connected, parallel drama was unfolding. Keynes had been delivering a regular course of lectures to Cambridge undergraduates on 'the pure theory of money'. This had been going on for many years, always in the Michaelmas (i.e. autumn) term. In 1930, the lectures were cancelled. This appeared to be due to the extra efforts Keynes had to undertake in order to bring his major book, the *Treatise on Money*, to publication in the middle of his usual heavy engagements in London (though the book was actually finished by September, i.e. *before* the beginning of term). The presumption was that the course of lectures would be resumed the following year. But that was the year of the *Circus* discussions! When Autumn 1931 came, the lectures were *not* given; they were postponed to the Easter (i.e. spring) term, 1932.

Spring 1932 came, Keynes did resume, at last, his course of lectures, with the usual title, 'The pure theory of money'. But the young economists who had formed the Cambridge *Circus* did not remain passive – they attended those lectures. Keynes was apparently taken by surprise. He reported to his wife, Lydia, in a note, mentioned by Moggridge [Keynes, 1979, p. 35], that Kahn, Sraffa, Joan and Austin Robinson had come to 'spy' on him! And that audience did react. Not only did they argue (see Keynes, 1979, p. 35), but they did something rather unusual. Kahn, Joan and Austin Robinson decided to write a manifesto (dated May 1932) addressed to Keynes. They made a series of objections, which quite clearly related to arguments that had been submitted to Keynes already, but were only partly accepted. The objections concerned problems relating to the mechanisms of adjustments in terms of quantities rather than in terms of prices, but they reveal a diffused uneasiness. The writing of a manifesto by itself reveals that there was some strong disagreement on fundamentals.

It had all the character of a decision to take a collective stand, as if Keynes was dragging his feet and was reluctant to take some fundamental step. The manifesto brought a sort of showdown.

Keynes must have been shaken; no doubt he was in a sort of intellectual impasse.[7]

In the *Preface* (dated April 1932) to the Japanese edition of the *Treatise on Money*, Keynes had already admitted that he was dissatisfied with the book; that he had abandoned the idea to correct it. One must say that it is rather astounding that in presenting the *Treatise* in translation he should announce the intention to write another 'short book' [1971, C. W., V, p. XXVII]. In June 1932, after the Cambridge *Circus* 'manifesto' had been discussed, he wrote to Sir Ralph Hawtrey that he was 'working it out again' (Keynes, 1973a, p. 172).

In that summer, many excruciating thoughts, and doubts, must have gone through Keynes's mind. In the Michaelmas term 1932, Keynes's lectures were indeed resumed, regularly, but with a complete change of title. The title that had characterised them for many years – 'the pure theory of money' – was abandoned. It was replaced by a new title: 'The monetary theory of production' [Keynes, 1979, p. 49]. The change was explicitly aimed at carrying a strong message. We have confirmation, from all witnesses who have been able to report, that Keynes announced in his first lecture that the change of title meant 'a significant change', 'a change of attitude' (Rymes, 1989, p. 47).

A moment's reflection is enough to make one realise that something quite extraordinary must have taken place behind the scenes.

---

[7] One can speculate endlessly on who was ahead and who was behind in considering the path to be taken. Joan Robinson, talking of those events forty years later, could write provokingly: 'There were moments when we had some trouble in getting Maynard to see what the point of his revolution really was' (Robinson, 1979, p. 170). But the positions of Keynes and of his pupils were profoundly asymmetrical. The young had no past to repudiate; Keynes had a whole career behind him.

Keynes had devoted the best years of his mature activity as an economist – almost a decade – to writing what everybody expected to be his *magnum opus*; in a field, monetary theory, in which he was world renowned. In less than a year and a half after publication, he had decided to repudiate the book – the result of many years' work. Clearly, only a great discovery could justify such an abrupt decision, in a man of world reputation, at the age of fifty. Only by imagining the realisation of an extraordinary event can one make sense of such a decision. As his pupils said, the light had struck.

And he did start writing a new book with extraordinary involvement. The first surviving table of contents, drawn in autumn 1932, carries precisely the title *The Monetary Theory of Production*. This is the first originally conceived title of Keynes's new book [Keynes, 1979, p. 49]. From that point on, all efforts were applied to unfolding the new theory. The work went on with unprecedented richness of discussions, exchanges and correspondence, with as many economists as Keynes could manage to entertain useful discussions with, in Cambridge and outside.

This, too, is extremely significant. It is indeed unprecedented in Keynes's own procedures. He was not a young, inexperienced economist. The fact that he decided to open up an as-wide-as-possible discussion shows clearly that he was not entirely sure he was always pursuing the right track. The 'new thing' was obviously so great as to make him feel he needed continuous checks and criticisms. He felt compelled to rely on all the brilliant minds he could possibly put together.[8]

Inevitably, there were many changes and modifications, following upon endless, excruciating discussions and exchanges of notes and letters. However, by that stage, the

---

[8] In the Preface to the *General Theory* he confessed: 'It is astonishing what foolish things one can temporarily believe, if one thinks too long alone' (Keynes, 1936, p. vii).

Rubicon had been crossed and the changes began to take place in a gradual way. The title of the book itself underwent a slow metamorphosis, as is revealed by the successive drafts of tables of contents that Donald Moggridge has been able to recover and publish in Keynes's 'Collected Writings'. In early autumn 1933, the title became *The Monetary Theory of Employment* [Keynes, 1979, p. 62]. In December 1933, it became *The General Theory of Employment* [Keynes, 1973a, p. 421]. In autumn 1934, it settled down to *The General Theory of Employment, Interest and Money* [Keynes, 1973a, p. 423], which was the definitive title under which the great work was published, in February 1936.

5.   The principle of effective demand

Whatever the extraordinary event was that led Keynes to abandon his master work (the *Treatise*), it seems quite clear that the point of no return in Keynes's mind must be placed sometime in 1932. Biographers and historians of economic thought have paid enormous attention to defining the exact moment at which the *General Theory* was born. Their differences of opinion are surprisingly small (see Skidelsky, 1992, p. 443, Moggridge, 1992, p. 562).

But what was it?

Don Patinkin has played a major role in driving the attention, even of Keynes's biographers, to the importance of effective demand in Keynes's analysis.[9] It seems to me that this is not incorrect, but at the same time it is too reductive.

In too many discussions among Keynes's exegetes the 'principle' of effective demand is simply reduced to a

---

[9] See especially Patinkin, 1990. The arguments are based on Keynes's own ex post account of the way his mental process proceeded. This account is taken from an often-quoted letter to Harrod of 30 August 1936, in which Keynes explicitly indicates effective demand as 'one of the most important transitions', the sudden realisation of which brought him to abandon the *Treatise* (see Keynes, 1973b, p. 85). The point of this important letter will be resumed further down (see p. 224).

quantity-adjustment market mechanism. Now, it is certainly true that for a monetary production economy, Keynes's claim was that when there is an imbalance between demand and available productive capacity, a mechanism of adjustment is at work, which acts through the adaptation of physical quantities rather than (as it was traditionally held) through the adaptation of prices. But surely the *General Theory* cannot simply be reduced to this market-adjustment mechanism. If it were simply so, then such a quantity-adjustment mechanism could quite easily be inserted into a scheme of demand and supply functions of a suitably adapted Walrasian macroeconomic model, which is in fact the gist of what Hicks, implicitly, and Patinkin, quite explicitly, have been claiming (Hicks, 1937, Patinkin, 1987, 1990).

But this sounds highly inplausible to me. Can we really believe that the whole Cambridge drama of the early 1930s, that Keynes's traumatic break with his colleagues, that his repudiation of a whole career as an economist, that all the excitement of that new generation of brilliant economists could all take place simply due to the discovery of a quite simple and theoretically innocuous mechanism of market adjustment through quantities rather than through prices?

Indeed, this does not sound credible.

Of course, that adjustment mechanism was placed at the centre of heated discussions. The 'Kahn-Meade relation', which then became the multiplier, originally referred to employment, then to output, then to both, and was a major analytical piece of the 'revolution'. But surely it must itself have been much more than a market-adjustment mechanism. Even if we simply concentrate attention on the multiplier, to reduce it to a simple device of how the market reacts when it is out of equilibrium seems to me an unwarranted and extremely reductive conception. Indeed, there must be much more to it.

I have done some work to investigate how the principle of effective demand cannot but be a far more fundamental and

profound principle, that goes much deeper into the characteristics of an economic system of an industrial type; a principle
that descends far below the superficial level of a particular
institutional mechanism (i.e. far below what simply appears
from the operation of the market).

In my investigation, I have made an effort (Pasinetti, 1981,
1993, 1997) to show that one must distinguish between
Keynes's 'point' of effective demand, which is explicitly
defined as 'the point of the aggregate demand function, where
it is intersected by the aggregate supply function' (*General
Theory*, p. 25) and the 'principle' of effective demand, which
Keynes has put as the title of his crucial Chapter 3 of the
General Theory, but has not explicitly stated. The 'principle'
lies much deeper, below any behavioural function connected
with any particular institutional set-up. In other words, the
principle of effective demand belongs to those profound
characteristics that mark the 'production' economic systems.
What is more, the theoretical schemes behind the Walrasian
model are not even capable of detecting it, while, on the contrary, in production systems, such characteristics are so profound as to precede even the institutional set-up that is considered. If this is so, it is precisely the traditional theoretical
schemes which have been used that are irretrievably lacking
and that remain at the surface of the more basic investigation
that Keynes had decided to attempt.

The efforts – initiated by Hicks and Modigliani and then
pursued with determination by Don Patinkin – to reduce
Keynes's analysis to no more than a variant of the Walrasian
model of general equilibrium may in fact give us a measure of
the inadequacy of such a reductive way of interpreting what
Keynes has done. Patinkin refers to the quantity-adjustment
market mechanism as the new Keynesian 'paradigm'
to be inserted into the Walrasian general equilibrium model
in place of the more traditional price-adjustment market
mechanism, which according to him represented the earlier
'paradigm'.

The concept of a paradigm is indeed very appropriate in characterising a 'scientific revolution', but the use made of it by Don Patinkin is hopelessly short of the mark and, in the end, misleading. The term has recently not been used appropriately, it seems to me; it has even been abused, especially by economists.[10]

It may well be useful to devote some attention to this concept and to the seminal ideas that are behind it. The concept of a paradigm will precisely represent in the following pages the external clue, mentioned at the beginning, that may help us to better understand what the Keynesian revolution was aimed at.

6.   Scientific revolutions and alternative paradigms

As is well known, it is only relatively recently that Thomas Kuhn, in a well-known and seminal work (1970a), has been able to set out clearly and convincingly the essential features of what may be termed a 'scientific revolution.'[11]

Kuhn has pointed out that in the history of (natural) sciences, any great discovery that marks a sharp change in established thought never emerges as the outcome of a smooth evolution of the prevailing way of thinking. It generally comes about as a traumatic break with the past; as he puts it, as a 'scientific revolution'. What normally happens is that the whole prevailing set of concepts, making up a coherent framework of reference – in his terminology, a 'paradigm' – is

---

[10] One recent example of inappropriate use (or rather abuse) of the term is the one made by Ned Phelps (1994), with reference to what is no more than a version of the general equilibrium model. He inappropriately calls it a 'structuralist paradigm'.

[11] Kuhn's work has been followed by numerous discussions (see especially Lakatos, 1970, Kuhn, 1970b). Many methodologists think of Lakatos's more complex concept of a research programme as a more satisfactory framework in which to insert the scientific revolutions. For our purposes, we might just as well refer to Lakatos's research programmes, but it is easier to stick to Kuhn's original concepts.

at a certain point found to be unsatisfactory and is discarded, while a new paradigm is put into its place.

According to Kuhn, a paradigm is a basic comprehensive theoretical framework that essentially allows scientists to carry out a whole process of problem solving. Most of what is going on as 'normal science' is precisely a problem-solving process within a basic frame of reference (a 'paradigm'), which is taken as commonly known, accepted and given.

When new evidence, i.e. when new empirical observations, conjectures or analytical discoveries, come to light, they may be either compatible or incompatible with the prevailing paradigm. When they are incompatible, they do *not* cause, for that reason only, the abandonment of the prevailing paradigm; they rather set in motion a series of attempts to *adapt* the prevailing paradigm so as to accommodate, in some way, the new evidence. In the extreme, if adaptation of the prevailing paradigm turns out to be impossible and the new evidence does not fit in, the evidence itself is set aside as an 'anomaly', an 'exception', or is even simply ignored (at least for the time being).

Of course, this sort of adaptation (or patching-up) process is bound to make the prevailing paradigm itself less and less satisfactory. This may help stimulate new ways of thinking. But the paradigm itself will not be abandoned only because it has become less and less satisfactory in explaining the new evidence. It is only when a new paradigm, a new more satisfactory and comprehensive frame of reference that explains the anomalies, becomes available that the old one is discarded and the new one is accepted. A scientific revolution thus takes place.

There is no reason why one should not expect this logical scheme to apply to the case of the social sciences as well. If at all, the succession-of-paradigms scheme seems an even more appropriate way of interpreting the development of thought in the social than in the natural sciences. But it is not inconceivable that the process may take a more complex and roundabout way, simply because, for various reasons (among them the possible failures in the development of appropriate analytical tools), a paradigm may at a certain point be set aside *before* it has given all the contributions it is capable of generating so that the same paradigm may come back later on and be successfully resumed. Furthermore, in the social sciences, alternative paradigms may well be carried on simultaneously, and separately, for quite a time, by different groups of social scientists, each group developing a frame of reference which is accepted within the group and looks, or is considered, extraneous to the others.

It is within this framework, it seems to me, that it is possible to argue that, in the historical evolution of economic ideas since Adam Smith, all economic theories may be reduced to either of two very broad, alternative paradigms – one focusing on exchange (and more fundamentally on utility and subjective value), the other focusing on production (and more fundamentally on labour and objective value).[12]

In the 'exchange' paradigm, to which what has come to be known as Walrasian economics belongs, the basic role is played by a pure exchange (or pure individual utility) model, in which, given a set of original resources with which a community of individuals is supposed to be arbitrarily endowed, single individuals maximise their utilities by exchanging the resources they have been endowed with, on the basis of the set of prices they find on the market. Thereby – if they are left free to exchange their resources without impediments – the market prices themselves will turn out to be such (in equilibrium) as to produce the unintended result of leading the economic system to a better (actually an optimum) allocation of the (at origin arbitrarily distributed) resources. The set of market prices (equilibrium prices) generated by all individuals' interactions take up an absolutely central role in the whole

---

[12] I have had an opportunity to stress this on various occasions, especially in Pasinetti, 1981, 1986, 1993.

model. They are indexes of relative scarcities and they carry with them all information that is needed in order to achieve optimal positions. All theorems, all elaborations, are normally developed first for this minimal model. Other features (including production) are introduced later, *after* theorems have been proved for that minimal pure exchange (utility) model. The pure exchange model thereby emerges as absolutely essential, in the sense that it contains those analytical features, and *only* those features, which the theory cannot do without.

One can single out another, alternative paradigm – a production paradigm – that has generated a whole series of economic investigations since the Classical economists of the end of the eighteenth/beginning of the nineteenth centuries. The 'pure production model', which is at the basis of this paradigm, has not been the subject of so many investigations as those that have dealt with the 'model of pure exchange'. Recently, I have tried myself to give it a formalisation (see Pasinetti 1986, 1993).

The economic phenomenon which is at the very basis of the pure production model is the technological process of production, with division and specialisation of labour. Prices and costs arise from the fact that each individual specialises in producing only one (or even a fraction of one) good or service, but at the same time needs the goods and services of the whole economic system, which must therefore be obtained through exchange. Production and exchange are inherently linked by labour specialisation. In this context, costs and prices express the Smithian 'toil and trouble' of production. They represent indexes of costs. But they do not carry all the information that is needed to achieve equilibrium in the economic system. The model, at the level of its basic relations, is characterised by a separation between a price equation system and a physical quantity equation system. And it requires additional, explicit and specific institutional relations in order to give answers to the problems arising from

the inter-relations between the two (price and physical quantity) equation systems. This means that there is no automatic
mechanism one can envisage – especially when the technology of the system is changing – for ensuring a complete utilisation of the available resources, particularly labour.

Here again it is interesting to note how all these features
are inherent in the pure production model at its origin. They
are all there at the beginning, without the need to consider
anything else or to introduce any other phenomenon. They
are all there in that minimal and basic model that contains
the very essential features of the 'production' paradigm, to
which Classical economics belongs. The pure production
model thus contains those analytical features, and only those
features, which Classical economic theory cannot do without.

The basic characteristics of the two paradigms are strikingly different. For example, with respect to time, the pure
exchange model is inherently timeless. The problem which
is posited is a once-and-for-all problem (how to allocate optimally given resources); and the solution which is provided
is a once-and-for-all solution (optimum allocation of given
resources, sometimes even reinterpreted over time). Once the
solution has been obtained, there is nothing more to be done,
except to investigate the mathematical conditions that make
it meaningful (existence, uniqueness and stability) or to illustrate the elegant properties it possesses (Pareto-optimality).

The problem which is posited by the pure production
model is inherently sequential in time. Production and labour
services are flows, that is to say, they have a time dimension.
The model naturally leads to the investigation of movements
through time (that is, to *dynamic* analysis).

It might also be said that the theoretical choice that is
implied in the formulation of the pure exchange model
springs from a rather specific way of looking at society; it
springs, so to speak, from a particular 'social philosophy',
that relies on each individual's self-interest as the basis of
rational behaviour; on the idea of the consumer's sovereignty

over the whole economy; on a great faith in the market as an institutional mechanism that brings about the utilisation of all resources, leaving none of them unemployed; and on the private property of all goods, as the principal institution, that must in fact be taken as a basic postulate of the theory.

By contrast, the pure production model springs from another particular way of looking at society; from another (alternative) social philosophy so to speak, that, through division of labour, stresses the necessarily *cooperative aspects* of any organised society; that looks for responsibility of society as a whole in bringing about situations that are considered as socially desirable. On this, the fulfilment becomes necessary of a macroeconomic condition, which concerns overall effective demand: the latter must be sufficient to ensure full employment. And it is important to realise that this condition is there, right at the initial and essential stage. Postulates concerning private ownership, or for that matter public ownership, are not made, and the problem of how the net product is distributed, both at a given point in time and through time, is thrown wide open for investigation.

These are basically the essential features that appear fundamental to the two paradigms (based on the pure exchange model and on the pure production model, respectively) that have been characterising our economic theories.

This completes the frame of reference into which I should like to insert the extraordinary events that took place in Cambridge in the early 1930s – the events that gave birth to *The General Theory*. Within such frame of reference, it should become easier, I hope, to understand what the 'Keynesian revolution' meant to its protagonists, as well as the nature of the events that followed.

7.   Keynes's break with orthodoxy

If the frame of reference of the previous section is accepted, the extraordinary, unique event that took place around

Keynes in Cambridge in the early 1930s becomes astonishingly clear. We may well put it very directly, as follows.

Shortly after the publication of the *Treatise*, mainly, but not only, as an effect of a combination of factual events (such as, in all industrial economies, massive unemployment) and theoretical breakthroughs, such as the emergence of a series of new analytical tools (e.g. the multiplier and the principle of effective demand), Keynes suddenly realised that all the discussions he was entertaining with the young economists of the Circus and with his colleagues, both in government circles and at the university, suffered from being laid on the wrong foundations. Their elaborations had been laid on a Marshallian version of the pure exchange paradigm. These foundations were inadequate. Maybe the realisation of this situation was helped by the fact that the Marshallian version of neoclassical economics is itself rather ambiguous and, to a certain extent, eclectic: it lacks the purity of the Walrasian model. Marshall had endeavoured to 'reconcile' Marginalist economics (which he had embraced) with the economics of the English Classical economists, trying all the time to smooth out or cover up the contradictions. (This may also help to explain why the 'revolution' found its more favourable humus in Cambridge rather than elsewhere).[13] Marshall's arguments had been subjected to criticisms, his contradictions and inconsistencies had been laid bare: indirectly by the works of Keynes's pupils themselves; explicitly by Piero Sraffa, whom Keynes had induced to emigrate to Cambridge. Suddenly, somewhat unconsciously, and in the case of Keynes no doubt as a result of deep intuition, it was

---

[13] The case of Michal Kalecki was quite different. Roughly at the same time as Keynes, he found himself working on the macroeconomics of business cycles and, quite independently, he came across the principle of effective demand. (Kalecki himself mentions his three papers – written in Polish in 1933, 1934, 1935 – contained in Kalecki, 1971, as expressing ideas close to Keynes's.) But he was basically moving from, and developing, a Marxian approach. In his case, one cannot talk of an intellectual 'revolution'.

realised that all the elaborations of current economics were relying on inadequate foundations, which had to be changed.

The hard decision – a hard decision indeed – was taken to break with orthodoxy. The change could not have been but traumatic: it consisted in shifting the whole body of economic elaborations away from the traditional 'exchange paradigm' foundations on which they had been laid to the alternative foundations of a 'production paradigm'.

The production paradigm had been elaborated by Smith, Malthus, Ricardo and the Classical economists of the beginning of the nineteenth century and even by earlier economists. But it was not such a clear-cut paradigm. Keynes saw distinctly the affinities with Malthus, less distinctly the affinities with Smith and Ricardo, for whom he did not spare criticisms. He also did his best to uncover roots and fragments that went further back, even to under-consumptionists and mercantilists. Smith and Ricardo were guilty of excessive reliance on the market institutions and of not realising that within a pure production model, Say's Law is *not* automatically satisfied.

In any case, it seems reasonable to think that Keynes, thanks to his peculiarly strong power of intuition, realised more fully than the young economists around him – drawn by enthusiasm – how deep the break with orthodox economics was going to be.[14] This is another reason that may help to explain why, to the members of the Cambridge Circus, he appeared to hesitate or to be reluctant to accept the implications of their arguments. Keynes, perhaps, more profoundly than the younger pupils around him, intuitively realised that the subject of their discussions concerning the output adjustment mechanism was merely the tip of a large iceberg. The principle of effective demand as such goes much deeper indeed than any specific detail concerning

---

[14] Keynes's remarkable power of intuition is a trait that is stressed by all his biographers; see in particular Moggridge (1992, pp. 551 and ff.)

any market-adjustment mechanism. It was its being laid on the foundations of a 'production scheme' that made it so revolutionary.

If this is so, it emerges quite clearly how radical the change was that Keynes announced in October 1932,[15] when he gave his course of lectures the newly framed title 'the monetary theory of production'.[16] The details had not yet been worked out, but the decision to break with orthodoxy had irretrievably been taken. A discontinuity had taken place. A wide breach had been opened. This was a 'significant change' indeed.

In the words of Thomas Kuhn, we may well say that a change of paradigm had occurred: precisely what he has termed a 'scientific revolution'. All the events that took place around Keynes clearly indicate this deep conviction: the conviction of setting a scientific revolution into motion. And the tension remained at a very high pitch, up to the publication of Keynes's great work.

[15] Against the depth of the break that must have taken place in Keynes's mind, the minute details that the 'Keynesiologists' (to use Patinkin's expression) have been pursuing – trying to single out the precise moment at which Keynes succeeded in expressing clearly the output-adjustment process inherent into the multiplier – appear quite secondary. In Keynes's mind the change had indeed taken place at a much deeper level, when he realised that the whole of his investigations had to be laid on the foundations of a monetary theory of production.

[16] This title expresses much better, and certainly more vividly, the paradigm which Keynes decided to go over to than the title he finally decided to give to his book, which emerged as a consequence of his concentrating on the functioning of a monetary production economy in an inevitably more specific, and thus more restrictive, institutional framework.

Chapter II

The 'revolution' after Keynes

1. Foreword

In my first lecture, I tried to recall the essential stages of an event of great relevance for the history of economic thought; a unique and extraordinary event which took place in Cambridge in the early 1930s. I have tried to show how, from the behaviour of the protagonists of that event (John Maynard Keynes and a group of younger pupils and collaborators), it is reasonable to infer that they were struck, so to speak, by a deep conviction of having discovered something radically new, something which convinced them of being in the process of giving birth to a scientific revolution in economic theory. They themselves began to talk in such terms, although they were not able to pin down clearly the detailed features of their discovery. Rather than follow their complicated, incomplete, sometimes ambiguous discussions as they have more recently come to our attention, especially through the publication of the 'Collected Writings of John Maynard Keynes', I think that for a better understanding one may insert that fascinating historical event into a more general theoretical-methodological scheme, concerning the characteristics and nature of scientific revolutions, taking advantage of a well-known recent work in the philosophy of science by Thomas Kuhn (1970a).

According to this work, the most important advances in science take place not through a continuous, smooth process but rather through *breaks* with previous conceptions. Improvements in knowledge do of course occur slowly within any established conceptual scheme, but the really great advances take place through radical breaches with the past – precisely, through scientific revolutions. A whole set of coherent theories – a scientific 'paradigm', in Kuhn's words – is at a certain point discarded and a new, alternative paradigm is put in its place.

I am prepared to argue that the *social* sciences introduce peculiarities into this scheme, which sometimes may give rise even to the simultaneous co-existence of different paradigms for quite a time, even if one of them may be prevailing over the other. Accordingly, I have contended that the economic theories of the past two centuries may well be looked at as belonging to two alternative paradigms: one based on a pure exchange model and the other based on a pure production model. Within this scheme, the events that took place around Keynes in the 1930s, and those that followed, can find an appropriate interpretation. They can be seen as the sudden realisation, by Keynes and his pupils, of the necessity of shifting the whole emphasis of economic elaborations from the prevailing paradigm based on the pure exchange model to a paradigm based on a model of pure production.

The basic conception of Keynes's *General Theory* thereby appears as a *break* with the traditional economic theory inherited through Marshall from the economists of the latter part of the nineteenth century/early part of the twentieth century, and an attempt to give substantiation to and establish an alternative economic theory based on the pure production model paradigm. Indeed, very appropriately, following his intuition, Keynes originally defined the work he intended to write as a 'monetary theory of production'.

2. 1936

Keynes's work was published, as *The General Theory of Employment, Interest and Money*, on 4 February 1936.

The frame of reference of Kuhn's scientific revolutions explains rather well the way in which the community of economists reacted to the publication of this 'revolutionary' work. The economists of Keynes's generation took Keynes's radical claim literally and, quite naturally, rejected it. Cecil Pigou, Dennis Robertson, Ralph Hawtrey, Lionel Robbins, Friedrich Hayek, in England, all did precisely this. In the United States, major reviewers of Keynes's generation, such as Frank Knight, Joseph Schumpeter and Jacob Viner, were all equally critical and negative. Schumpeter's review (1936) is significant – extraordinarily caustic and sarcastic.[1]

Not basically different was the establishment's reaction elsewhere. In Italy, for example, the reception was generally critical and hostile. One must stress that Keynes was a well-known economist. Up to and including the publication of his *Treatise on Money*, his books had been translated into Italian almost immediately. In the case of the *General Theory*, nobody showed any haste. From leading Italian economists – such as Luigi Einaudi, Costantino Bresciani Turroni, Giuseppe Ugo Papi, Giovanni Demaria – Keynes's 'revolutionary' work received disappointed and critical comments. Only after the war and after the author's death was the

---

[1] By a caricature of Keynes's principle of effective demand, Schumpeter goes as far as stating:

> Let him who accepts the message there expounded rewrite the history of the French *ancien régime* in some such terms as these: Louis XV was a most enlightened monarch. Feeling the necessity of stimulating expenditure he secured the services of such expert spenders as Madame de Pompadour and Madame du Barry. They went to work with unsurpassable efficiency. Full employment, a maximum of resulting output, and general well-being ought to have been the consequence. It is true that instead we find misery, shame and, at the end of it all, a stream of blood. But that was a chance coincidence. (Schumpeter, 1936, p. 795)

General Theory at last translated (rather badly) into Italian (1947).

Yet the rejection of Keynes's contemporaries, no matter how authoritative, did not work. A really fascinating phenomenon took hold almost instantly. In striking contrast with the criticism and scepticism of Keynes's colleagues and contemporaries, the response of the younger generation was enthusiastic. One may look at the reviews, almost all written by young economists, that appeared in England. They are all permeated by the conviction of being in the presence of an exceptional, extraordinary work – a conviction, among the young, that became widespread, both in Great Britain and in the United States.[2]

In a world unable to get out of a persistent, deep slump, the younger generation were looking for something dramatically new and saw in Keynes's work the much-awaited answer. As James Meade often put it, his generation was 'taken by a spell'. In Samuelson's words: 'The *General Theory* caught most economists under the age of thirty-five with the unexpected virulence of a disease' (1964a, p. 316).

There were some parallel and concomitant favourable features. For some time, practical men had been instinctively looking with some favour to public expenditure in time of depression. The Keynesian recipes were found congenial to their instinctive feelings and in fact reasonable on matters of strict economic policy. John Kenneth Galbraith (1956) expressed quite well this aspect of the Keynesian measures when he pointed out that, whatever revolution there was in theory, in practice the Keynesian recipe for public

---

[2] The Italian case was characterised by the same pattern, but with a ten-year delay, as it was compounded by another event. It coincided with the opening up of the postwar generation of Italian economists, after many years of closure towards the outside world, to the cultural developments that had taken place elsewhere. As already mentioned, Caffè was a precursor. Other early Keynesians were Ferdinando di Fenizio and Vittorio Marrama (see Bini, 1984 and the related proceedings of the 1983 conference 'Keynes in Italy').

expenditure in times of depression was not at all upsetting. Keynes – unlike Marx – did not appear a divisive figure to American businessmen. 'General Motors still decided what cars to produce, what prices to charge, how to advertise and sell them, when to build a new assembly plant and how many workers to employ' (p. 79). Hence Keynes moved 'in the Anglo-American tradition of compromise which seeks progress by reconciling . . . conflicts of interest' (p. 83).

Thus, for the young generation of economists, and for the business community at large, Keynes's theory and policies came exactly at the right moment; they appeared to be precisely what was required.

3.   'Bastard' Keynesianism (or neoclassical synthesis?)

The frame of reference of Kuhn's scientific revolutions can also help us to understand what happened in the years that followed. Keynes concentrated his immediate efforts on counteracting the objections of his contemporaries, but on this field the battle had already been won. He neglected the developments of the theory, which was the open field where the battle was still to be fought.

Once simple rejection had not worked, it was quite natural to expect that the obvious instinctive attitude would be that of aiming at inserting the most attractive innovations of Keynes's elaborations into the traditional way of thinking. The normal reaction to the appearance of any inconsistency or anomaly in the prevailing paradigm – as Kuhn points out – is to ignore it. When this becomes impossible, the next move is to try to reshape in some way the prevailing theoretical framework in order to accommodate the anomaly.

It was quite natural to expect the theorists to be eager to transcribe Keynes's arguments into simple, possibly algebraic and diagrammatic terms, suited for didactical purposes. Keynes and his pupils did not devote many efforts to this task.

Perhaps they thought they had other, much more urgent, and in any case more fundamental, problems to pay attention to. They did not do much after publication either. This situation, not surprisingly, led to encouraging the use of the traditional analytical tools and to trying to insert the Keynesian innovations into the prevailing paradigm.

The most successful of all devices in this direction was the IS-LM model of J. R. Hicks (*Econometrica*, 1937), to which contributions were also made by some of the more conservative-minded young economists of the Keynesian group, especially Harrod and Meade.[3] Hicks more recently (1980–81) stated quite plainly that there was no attempt on his part to convert himself to Keynes, but exactly the opposite.[4] As he writes, the 'IS-LM was in fact a translation of Keynes' nonflexprice model into my terms . . . the idea of the IS-LM diagram came to me as a result of the work I had been doing on three-way exchange, conceived in a Walrasian manner' (pp. 141–142). A few years later, Franco Modigliani (1944), starting from Hicks's model, proceeded to a well-known formalisation of Keynes's theory that had the explicit purpose – as he put it – of 'digesting' Keynes's hard tools or 'difficult' concepts into traditional economic analysis.

This whole process went on, without much opposition from the 'genuine' Keynesians. It was later crystallised by the expression, attributed to Paul Samuelson, of a 'grand neoclassical synthesis'.[5]

Don Patinkin (1987, 1990) represents perhaps, more recently, a typical example of this tendency. He reduces Keynes's innovations to a version not of the principle but of

---

[3] See footnote 7.
[4] It may be of interest to point out that in 1935, Hicks was in Cambridge, as a Fellow of Gonville and Caius College. But he took no part in the discussions surrounding the *General Theory*. He was working by himself (in isolation) on his *Value and Capital*. His attention to the *General Theory* started *after* publication of Keynes's work and was directed to accommodate the new ideas into his Walrasian way of thinking.
[5] See Samuelson, 1948, pp. 360–361.

a 'theory' of effective demand, which is simply conceived as consisting in an output-adjusting mechanism at sticky prices, inserted into a macroeconomic Walrasian model.

Quite clearly, the direction followed by this accommodating interpretation of Keynes's work is precisely the opposite of the one which the evidence mentioned above would reasonably indicate as intended to break with orthodoxy, such as took place in Keynes's mind in 1932.

Within Kuhn's framework, sketched out in the previous lecture, this process is perfectly understandable. One might even say that it is precisely what one should have expected. But the first relevant question to ask is: how did Keynes himself react?

It must be stressed that the attempts at reconciling *The General Theory* with tradition had quite obviously started very early, long before publication. We know that Keynes reacted against them very harshly. Among Keynes's colleagues, a firm believer in reconciliation was Dennis Robertson, who was not, after all, hostile to Keynes's economic policies. On practical matters of supporting public works in times of depression, he had even anticipated Keynes. But Keynes's reaction against his attempts at reconciliation was so harsh that it caused the break-up of their long-standing friendship. Among the young economists, James Meade, to a certain extent, but especially Roy Harrod were the ones who, in their exchanges with Keynes, took up the role of pleading the cause of reconciliation with orthodoxy. But again Keynes consistently reacted in very strong terms. There is an oft-quoted letter to Roy Harrod in which Keynes rejects explicitly any attempt at reconciliation. He expresses preoccupations at Harrod's suggestions and even goes on to say that such a tendency to find some sort of accommodation makes him feel that his assault on tradition should be made not weaker but stronger.[6]

---

[6] '... the general effect of your reaction ... is to make me feel that my assault on the classical school ought to be intensified rather than abated ... I am

What appears a much harder question to answer – as, after all, Skidelsky (Keynes's biographer, 1992, p. 611) points out – is why Keynes did not react with equal vehemence against the attempts at reconciliation that were made after the publication of *The General Theory*.

More specifically, the question that remains open to discussion is: why did he not react to Hicks's interpretation of his scheme? Hicks's was later to become the most widespread version of Keynes's theory to be propagated by the textbooks.[7] Perhaps Keynes was too busy having to fight on too many fronts for the affirmation of his theory, so that it is understandable that he paid less attention to the attempts of the young economists. He may also have been misled by the fact that they were in any case trying to find ways (even if he did not approve them all or did not approve them entirely) to express his theory.

He also became physically much weaker than before; in 1937 his health suddenly deteriorated.

No doubt he underestimated the potentialities of Hicks's IS-LM model.[8] And so did his closest pupils – especially Joan Robinson and Richard Kahn. Both of them did later react, very strongly, to Hicks's formalisation, but it was too late to alert Keynes to the danger.

To characterise Keynes's underestimation of Hicks's IS-LM model, Richard Kahn – in his Mattioli Lectures, delivered in Milan in 1978 – used the term 'tragic' – 'It is tragic that Keynes

frightfully afraid of the tendency, of which I see some signs in you to appear, to accept my constructive part and to find some accommodation between this and deeply cherished views which would in fact only be possible if my constructive part has been partially misunderstood' (Keynes, 1973a, p. 548).

[7] See the fascinating account, given by Warren Young (1987), of the Econometric Society Conference, held in Oxford in September 1936, in which Harrod, Meade and Hicks all presented simplified versions of *The General Theory*, that were then crystallised in Hicks's 1937 *Econometrica* article. Very unwisely, neither Richard Kahn nor Joan Robinson participated in that conference – a too-obvious mistake on their part.

[8] In Skidelsky's colourful expression: 'He let Hicks's 'generalisation' of the *General Theory* through on the nod' (1992, p. 616).

made no public protest when . . . the IS-LM and related diagrams and algebra . . . began to appear' (1984, p. 116). Joan Robinson, as usual, though reacting equally late, was crisper and more effective. She hit right at the centre of the problem: the reconcilers were not really Keynesians; at best, they were 'bastard' Keynesians.

The expression is polemical. Yet it goes precisely to the heart of the matter. To bring Keynes's elaborations back into the traditional, Walrasian paradigm was the negation of Keynes's revolution; it meant reducing Keynes's intended revolution to be no revolution at all.

4.   The Cambridge School of Keynesian Economics

Keynes's biographers alert us that, from shortly after the publication of *The General Theory*, Keynes was no longer the fighting polemist he had been before. For a year, he was too busy to reply to criticisms, answer questions and counter various attacks. But his physical health had been deteriorating.[9] He was not well at all in the winter 1936–37. In May 1937 (only slightly more than a year after publication of *The General Theory*) he suffered a heart attack that crippled him permanently, practically confining him to bed for the whole morning as a normal rule every day. It was a fatal blow to his fighting attitude. Yet his precarious health condition notwithstanding, he kept on doing a remarkable amount of work for a government in difficult times, just before, during and immediately after the war. It would clearly be unreasonable to pretend he could have done more than he actually did.

He died on Easter Sunday (21 April) 1946.

In the ten years from the publication of *The General Theory*, the really absorbing event was World War Two. Very little was

---

[9] See Skidelsky, 1992 (ch. 17: 'My breathing muscles were so wonky'); Moggridge, 1992 (ch. 23: 'Fertile of mind, frail of body').

done to carry ahead the Keynesian revolution. The last word on the matter of didactical presentation of Keynesian theories thus remained with Hicks's IS-LM scheme.

But immediately after the war, Keynes's closest pupils came to form a tight and powerful group in Cambridge, while from Oxford Roy Harrod, with the publication of his *Towards a Dynamic Economics* (1948), seemed to open up new horizons towards that long-run analysis which Keynes had not faced. In Great Britain, in the USA and in the Western world, Keynesian economics had achieved astounding success. It must be stressed, however, that this was essentially in the field of economic policy. The 1950s and the 1960s were characterised, in the whole industrialised world, by government demand management, low interest rates, low unemployment and unprecedented economic growth. No doubt: these were precisely the sorts of practical results the Keynesian policies were aimed at. All this may have created a superficially misleading euphoric atmosphere. But in the field of economic theory the Keynesian theory that was propagated by the textbooks did not come from *The General Theory*. It was rather the one conveyed by Hicks's IS-LM model, which – as already pointed out above, quoting Hicks himself – came from an attempt to translate Keynes's analysis into Walrasian terms. No other version of Keynes's theory made a permanent bridge-head into the prevailing textbooks.

Nevertheless, in Cambridge, Keynes's revolution seemed to go on. Joan Robinson, Richard Kahn and Piero Sraffa, reinforced by the acquisition at King's College of Nicholas Kaldor (a convert to Keynesian economics, who moved to Cambridge permanently from the LSE in 1947), made up a powerful group of direct pupils of Keynes who made a remarkable effort to carry Keynes's revolution to a reasonably advanced stage.

The scientific work done by this unusual group of intellectually powerful people is remarkable. At a certain point, in the late 1950s/early 1960s, their seminal contributions to the theories of economic growth, income distribution, capital accumulation and technical progress – placed on a surprisingly strong revival of Classical economic theory that led to a devastating critique of neoclassical economics – gave the impression that they had risen to a major leading school of economics on the world scene.

Yet this remarkable Cambridge School of post-Keynesian economics at a certain point ceased to spread. It produced few off-shoots outside Cambridge and even fewer in Cambridge itself. Essentially, and eventually, it has remained isolated from the rest of the world, even in Cambridge. The American post-Keynesians, such as Minsky (1986), Davidson (1972) and Weintraub (1959, 1966), represent a group of their own, springing up from that part of Keynes's analysis that dealt with uncertainty, money and financial instability. They have found more affinities with the analyses of Shackle (1952, 1967, another isolated 'Keynesian') than with those of the Cambridge group.[10] The scientific revolution that was supposed, or intended, to be carried out, did not in fact proceed. With the natural process of retirement of the whole group of Keynes's pupils in the early 1970s and, even more, with the death of all of them in the 1980s, the whole Cambridge School of Keynesian Economics seems to have lost contact – albeit with some exceptions – with today's generation of economists.

What happened? Whether it was all a failure may still be too early to say. But the point is relevant. If it has been a failure, this has not been merely the failure of the Cambridge

[10] There has always appeared to be enormous difficulty in communication between the American post-Keynesians and the Cambridge post-Keynesians; most of all, there have been very few efforts on either sides to try to integrate with the others. The only economist who, on the American side, made a serious and explicit effort to try to bridge the gap was Alfred Eichner (1979, 1991; see also Eichner and Kregel, 1975). Unfortunately, Eichner died prematurely (1988).

post-Keynesians. As the previous analysis should make clear, the failure is that of the Keynesian revolution.

It may be useful to try, for the time being – though the question is by no means simple – to single out at least *some* of the reasons why the economic theories of the Cambridge Keynesians have failed to take off and to be followed and developed.

There certainly is more than one reason. To begin with, the economists of the Cambridge Keynesian School wildly underestimated the enormous amount of work that was still to be done. To work out the foundations and then to erect, on them, the edifice of a monetary theory of production was a truly gigantic task that would have required the determined effort of many researchers, acting within a unifying theoretical framework.

If my own perception of this problem is correct (see also Pasinetti, 1986, 1993), the production paradigm, by being essentially dynamic, is bound to be more complex than the competing exchange paradigm. I have argued that to render the analysis manageable, a separation is necessary between two distinct levels of investigation. There is first of all (in logical order, not necessarily in order of actual elaboration) the task of singling out the logical foundations of the whole construction. This task (which, it must be said, the Classical economists perceived very clearly, though being unable to carry it out in an entirely correct way) consists of the setting up of a complete theoretical scheme of an economic system on objective bases, at a level of investigation that appears largely pre-institutional. I have called this level of investigation 'natural', borrowing the term precisely from the Classical economists, even if they were not fully consistent as to the implications of their 'natural' concepts. Keynes's basic ideas about the characteristics of a monetary theory of production, when stripped down to their essential elements, belong to this level of investigation. And so does, at its deep roots, his principle of effective demand. Piero Sraffa's logical scheme of production of commodities by means of commodities also belongs to this fundamental, natural level of investigation.

There is, then, a second, separate level of investigation (which, in the actual process of carrying out economic analysis, may well be faced straightaway, taking the investigations at the more fundamental level for granted), which concerns the behavioural relations meant to represent and explain the effective working of actual economic systems, within a well-defined institutional set-up. It is at this second level of investigations that the objective bases on which the fundamental relations are laid have to be integrated by behavioural relations constructed on those hypotheses that turn out to be the most appropriate to represent individuals' subjective or group behaviour. Almost all of Nicky Kaldor's contributions were developed at this level of investigation, while those of Joan Robinson, Richard Kahn and Keynes himself were developed sometimes at the more fundamental level, sometimes at the behavioural level, sometimes at both. In the case of some analytical tools – to take the most significant example, the multiplier – or in the case of whole areas of analysis – for example that relating to money – there are some aspects that concern the more fundamental level and other aspects that concern the behavioural institutional level. It seems to me that a clear perception of the separation of these two levels of investigation would have meant a decisive step ahead, would have exerted a great stimulus and would have opened the way to the clear definition of the whole research programme. But Keynes himself, and then the Keynesian group, proceeded more on the basis of intuition than on the basis of a clear vision of the logical steps to take. The clarification of these concepts has remained widely unaccomplished. The major protagonists of that intellectual adventure, by paying too little attention to the positive aspects of each other's contributions, have not encouraged the search of a comprehensive theoretical framework. In this respect they have been ambiguous.[11] Yet on the basis of their own works, the task could have been carried out. My contention is that it can and still should be accomplished.

There was, then, a personal and temperamental component that exacerbated the situation. Perhaps as a consequence, on the one side, of an incomplete or partially incorrect grasp of the enormous work that was to be carried out and, on the other side, of the euphoric atmosphere generated by what appeared to be the worldwide success of Keynesian economic policies, a sort of overestimation spread among the Keynesian group as to the degree of acceptance of the Keynesian revolution. The behaviour (or misbehaviour) of each single member of the Keynesian group gave the impression, in the 1950s and 1960s, that they believed themselves to be the masters of the place and of the theory, as if anybody else (in Cambridge and in the outside world) had accepted their ideas and authoritativeness. It was indeed a bad sign when some of them began

---

[11] Take Joan Robinson as an example. On some occasion she indicated the existence of a general framework:

> We now have a general framework of long and short-period analysis which will enable us to bring the insights of Marx, Keynes, Kalecki into coherent form and apply them to the contemporary scene . . . (Robinson, 1979, p. 216)

On other occasions, she even denied the possibility of any comprehensive theory:

> It is often said that one theory can be driven out only by another; the neoclassicals have a complete theory . . . and we need a better theory to supplant them. . . . I think any other 'complete theory' would be only another box of tricks. What we need is a different habit of mind – to eschew fudging, to respect facts, and to admit ignorance in what we do not know. (Robinson, 1979, p. 119)

This can only be termed an ingenuous statement. Who could ensure that 'to eschew fudging, respect facts, and admit ignorance of what we do not know' would remain a prerogative of Keynesian economists?

Yet, she was clearly unjust to herself. Alfred Eichner saw so much in Joan Robinson's writings as to dedicate his major work: 'To Joan Robinson who, by first putting into a coherent whole the alternative post-Keynesian paradigm, showed us the path out of the Valley of Darkness that is neoclassical economics. (Eichner, 1991, p. 3)

to quarrel among themselves, disputing over who had which particular idea first. As it may be inferred, especially from the reactions of many unsympathetic witnesses in Cambridge in that period, their behaviour appeared rather arrogant. To those who disagreed with them, it even appeared doctrinaire. In any case, they did fail (and this was indeed a failure) to co-involve into a fruitful discussion process many talents (not prejudicially hostile) that were present in Cambridge itself.[12]

In addition, one must not ignore an important albeit hidden feature (at the time grossly underestimated by all) that characterised the whole world in which we lived up to a few score years ago. This was a world sharply divided into two opposed, redoubtable military blocs (a capitalist bloc and a communist bloc), capable of destroying each other many times over. It was inevitable that, sometimes even unconsciously, suspicions of an ideological nature should be generated, any time any criticism was advanced against established institutions. In the case of Keynes, his strong and explicit anti-communist stand placed him on safe ground.[13] But in the case of the Cambridge Keynesians, their positions, though varying for the different individuals, were less explicit and clear-cut. They certainly all belonged to the left. This generated a kind of impalpable opposition, of which of course they were aware but which they always underestimated.

[12] I am thinking, to give a few examples, of Richard Goodwin, who during the whole time he spent in Cambridge ended up by doing more painting than economics; of Richard Stone, who was left, isolated, in the Department of Applied Economics; of James Meade, who was pushed more and more into neoclassical analysis; of Maurice Dobb, on the opposite side, who was left to work by himself; even of Austin Robinson, who, himself isolated, was left at the *Economic Journal* (and at the International Economic Association) to carry out a policy of publications that had little connection with the Keynesian School.

[13] This was not the case with Michal Kalecki, who had developed, independently of Keynes, a rather similar theory of effective demand and unemployment, starting however from Marxist premisses. This origin may well explain a lot about his being constantly underrated and in any case always put in a secondary position with respect to Keynes.

In one important respect, they failed completely to follow Keynes, namely in the care in selecting, shaping, preparing and paying attention to the younger generation. Into this task, Keynes had put a considerable amount of effort and time. The Cambridge Keynesian group seemed not to care. Worse still, they seemed to compress, or even repress, the ambitions of the young.[14]

They did almost nothing to prepare their succession. When pressed to make choices among possible successors, they hesitated, they made no choices, or half choices, or compromise choices, rather than clear ones. This was fatal to the School, which disappeared from Cambridge with them. Except for a few exceptions (for whom, in any case, they did very little or even created a lot of difficulties), they left no post-Keynesian follower in Cambridge.

One may finally mention an astonishing lack of far-sightedness on the part of those who formally succeeded them. To what they considered the arrogance of their predecessors, they over-reacted by demolishing whatever the Keynesians had left. They awfully underestimated the powerful significance of the Keynesian ideas. Worse still, they lacked vision. They attached no weight or value to the significance of keeping alive a truly Keynesian (i.e. non-Marxist) alternative to the prevailing orthodox line of economic thought. They failed to realise that such an alternative was a source of theoretical potentialities that represented a treasure, not only for Cambridge but for the world community of economists. Alas, that treasure has been squandered.

The overall effect is impressive. The natural result of a scientific revolution should have been a bobbling abundance of initiatives, discussions, developments, attempts in various

---

[14] As significant examples, one may consider the emotional reactions of two of the most brilliant representatives of the younger Cambridge generation of the 1950s: Harry Johnson (Johnson and Johnson, 1978) and Robin Marris (1991). I am sure one might draw a long list of first-rate brains, educated in Cambridge in that period, who did not find sufficient stimuli to remain.

directions, even if not immediately successful. All this did not take place. Of course, it has not been completely absent. Kaldor's ideas (on increasing returns, on consequences of the impossibility of perfect competition in the manufacturing sector, on endogenous technical progress, etc.) have permeated much recent economic literature, even when the latest authors seem to have been too easily forgetful or simply unaware.[15] Joan Robinson's stands on capital theory continues to stimulate contributions; Sraffa's extraordinarily compact little book has generated a whole new stream of economic literature; etc. Yet one cannot avoid the impression of a fragmentary character of the whole, of a lack of obvious evidence of a unifying overall frame, of an imbalance towards the destructive rather than towards the constructive aspects. There is no doubt that, with all their remarkable features, the contributions of the Cambridge Keynesian group, as a whole, have failed to achieve the required critical impetus necessary for a take-off. The revolutionary process has ground to a standstill.

5. **Difficulties with absorbing odd facts (notably unemployment) into the 'normal-science' process of orthodox economics**

Keynesian economics, especially in its textbook version, was bound to come under attack the very moment any factual event was to put its short- run limitations to some severe test. This happened in the 1970s, when a dramatic external event – the oil crisis – triggered off, in all the industrialised world, a dynamic process (cost-push inflation), which fell outside the demand-dominated compound of Keynesian policies. It was indeed the outburst of inflation that strained the Keynesian

---

[15] Kaldor's work, by being mainly concerned with the specific behaviour of capitalist systems, seems to be the more easily approachable by non-Keynesian economists. The two recent major biographies of Kaldor (Thirlwall, 1987, Targetti, 1992) may be of help.

policies into difficulties. Keynes himself had not concentrated on this problem, as it had remained practically irrelevant in the 1930s (though he did face it explicitly in his remarkable leaflet *How to Pay for the War*, 1944). And the Keynesians had not anticipated the appropriate work that the event would have required. They were caught unprepared.

Not unexpectedly, with the Keynesians being thrown into disarray, a strong, radical attempt was made to revert everything to the *status quo ante*.

The rational expectations strand of economic thought and the 'new-classical' macroeconomics elaborations of the 1970s and the 1980s have been powerful attempts to discredit Keynes's analysis and revert economic theory in general to the pure orthodoxy of the earlier pre-Keynesian times. I think one may safely conclude by now that these attempts have not succeeded. Inconsistencies between the various strands of Keynesian economic theory may well have become apparent and may render understandable the powerful attempts that have been made to revert everything to orthodoxy. But there are much wider anomalies in the sheer facts observable in the real world that orthodox economics is unable to explain. The striking disparities in the material wealth of the various nations, the awkward, extraordinary instability of the world financial markets, the connected enormous size of rentiers' incomes, the disrupting effects of the astonishing movements of the technological frontier, the persistent, widely spread, dangerously increasing, involuntary unemployment of masses of working people, in most countries; all these phenomena, together, appear as a sort of plague affecting the whole of the industrial and industrialising world.

As against these powerful features of reality, the appeal of Keynes's theory, in spite of all, remains strong. But the majority of today's Keynesian theorists are less ambitious than Keynes was and even less ambitious than his pupils were in the early 1930s. Though acknowledging the powerfulness of Keynes's ideas, they seem to be convinced (perhaps unconsciously frightened by experience) that it is not necessary, or perhaps that it is too risky, to try to repudiate the traditional paradigm. In essence, they seem to think that it is not necessary to go so far as to undertake a scientific revolution. One can patch up the anomalies and remain with orthodoxy. This more recent development of Keynesian economics is in fact essentially all in the direction that was opened up by J. R. Hicks, that is in the direction of some sort of reconciliation with orthodoxy. The process is not easy. The Keynesian body of theories is too much of an anomaly within orthodox economics to allow a smooth re-absorption. This may explain why the attempts that have been made are various.

Of these attempts at reviving or re-interpreting Keynes's ideas and giving them a place among the economists' existing theoretical framework, I may mention at least three that seem to me worthy of attention because of their representativeness.

Clower (1965) and then Leijonhufvud (1968) have tried to re-interpret Keynesian unemployment as the product of a lack of coordination in the markets, which have nevertheless always been interpreted in a Walrasian manner, more realistically pointing out that the Walrasian search for the equilibrium position (the famous *tâtonnement*) does not operate instantaneously and the process may, on the way, fall into numerous difficulties, when one considers situations that are out of equilibrium.

A group of mainly French economists (Benassy 1976, Malinvaud, 1977, and others) has developed the idea of such markets in which, for some reasons, physical quantities of commodities and/or of labour may be 'rationed', so that equilibrium positions come into being with markets that are not completely 'cleared'. They have called these (I think inappropriately) 'non-Walrasian' equilibria, though they pertain to the equilibrium family of the General Economic Equilibrium scheme proposed by Walras.

Finally, a whole series of elaborations has been proposed recently, with the appellative of new-Keynesian models, aimed at giving rise to 'Keynesian results', i.e. unemployment situations, though adopting perfectly orthodox assumptions at the microeconomic level (i.e. individuals' maximising postulates, or at least rational behaviour) and without questioning the basic foundations of orthodox general equilibrium theory. This is obtained by postulating situations in which there is imperfect competition, increasing returns to scale, asymmetry of information, rigidities of various kinds, etc.

None of these attempts goes in the direction of shifting economic analysis towards the foundations of the production paradigm. In this sense, they are not revolutionary; they all very much accept being placed within the Walrasian exchange paradigm; they all are in the direction of reconciliation. They are attempts – very much on the lines originally set up by J. R. Hicks and Franco Modigliani – at absorbing, or 'digesting' to use Modigliani's favourite term, the new elaborations, the 'imperfections', or 'odd facts' into the normal science paradigm of orthodox economics.[16]

6.   Post-Keynesians, neo-Ricardians, evolutionists, institutionalists and others

There remains, of course, the whole, variegated group of those who are carrying on their research while trying to remain on the track of the Cambridge Keynesian group. They have ended up outside mainstream economics. They are scattered

---

[16] It must be mentioned, for the record, that on his part, Hicks became quite uneasy, at a certain point, with his IS-LM formulation. He kept rethinking his theory and slowly moving away from his so successful IS-LM model. In the late 1960s/early 1970s, he courageously criticised it and in fact he explicitly repudiated it (see Hicks, 1975, 1980–81). He went as far as openly declaring that he had ceased to be a neoclassical economist (in his words: 'J. R. Hicks, [is] a "neoclassical" economist now deceased'). What is more, in order to underline his change of mind, he even ceased to sign his articles with the name J. R. Hicks, instead using John Hicks (in his words: 'Clearly I need to change my name . . . John Hicks [is] a non-neoclassic who is quite disrespectful towards his "uncle" [J. R.]', Hicks, 1975, p. 365).

all around the world, but they remain a minority. Though of course more numerous than the economists of the original Keynesian group, they make up, as a whole, a less weighty part of the economics profession.

A major new aspect of the intellectual environment has become relevant. The economics profession has become more institutionalised than in the past and, as an effect of this, less tolerant of dissent. Especially through the procedures of refereeing and editorship of the major economic journals, non-mainstream economists are faced very often with their articles being rejected. What are reputed to be the prestigious economic journals rarely decide to publish non-orthodox articles, so much so that new journals (the most well known of which are *The Cambridge Journal of Economics* in England and *The Journal of Post-Keynesian Economics* in the USA) had to be set up – and keep on being set up – precisely for the purpose of giving non-mainstream economists a chance to achieve publication at all. In any case, their articles are scarcely read by the majority of the economics profession. This contributes to a sort of separate and non-communicating departmentalisation.

The heterogeneity of the group has been brought to evidence by many surveys. To take an example, Hamouda and Harcourt (1988) call them 'a heterogeneous group of economists who nevertheless are united not only by their dislike of mainstream neoclassical economics . . . but also by their attempts to provide coherent alternative approaches . . .' (p. 2). The word 'approaches' is written in the plural, as they are many and in many respects conflicting. Hamouda and Harcourt classify them into three main strands – American Post-Keynesians, neo-Ricardians and Kaleckian-Robinsonians – but they also find that 'some outstanding individual figures . . . defy classification within any one group or strand' (p. 3).[17]

---

[17] Not very different is the assessment of Malcolm Sawyer (1988), pp. 1–5.

What is not at all helpful is that economists following these different strands or approaches have so often attacked one another, stressing many times, even to the extreme, their differences and overlooking or rather refusing to investigate what they have in common. No doubt the Cambridge Keynesian group had not been helpful, but in this respect they should not be imitated.[18]

Inevitably – in discussions, congresses and more recently in associations (consider, for example, the European Association for Evolutionary Political Economy (EAEPE)) – they have come into contact with other non-orthodox economists of different provenance: evolutionists, institutionalists, former Marxists, etc.[19] These contacts and interchanges could, and should, generate cross-fertilisation and enrichment, when appropriately directed. So far they seem only to have contributed to increase heterogeneity.

It is indeed surprising to me how insensitive the whole heterogeneous lot of non-orthodox economists have been to the necessity – which appears to me an absolute necessity – of building up an overall, comprehensive, solid theoretical framework as an alternative to the prevailing orthodox stream.

Some efforts are, of course, being carried out all the time to stress characteristic differences of post-Keynesian from neoclassical economics. Paul Davidson mentions three features.[20] Malcolm Sawyer lists no less than seven

---

[18] Unfortunately, this has not happened. The autobiographies published by Arestis and Sawyer (1992) show quite well how widespread is what one might call the Cambridge *prima donna* syndrome.

[19] In his textbook, Sawyer (1988), trying his utmost to simplify, presents non-mainstream economics as being constituted by four 'alternative paradigms' (though the word *alternative* is, strictly speaking, inappropriate when referring to more than two possibilities and the word 'paradigm' is, in Kuhnian terms, inappropriate): the Post-Keynesian, the Sraffian, the Marxian and the Institutional (p. 3).

[20] They are 1) the economy being considered in an historical process, 2) expectations having significant effects on economic outcomes, 3) institutions playing a significant role (see Davidson, 1981).

characteristic implications of post-Keynesian economics.[21] My view is that these characterisations may well be accepted as classifications or as ex post descriptions, but they can hardly be accepted as a satisfactory way of presenting a new paradigm. Something much deeper is necessary: something more specific, exclusive of the approach, capable of originating those characterisations as consequences. In a veiled way, a few glimpses at wider horizons are not lacking. Marc Lavoie has written a book 'to provide a convenient synthesis of post-Keynesian economics, by showing that it constitutes a coherent set of theories that can provide an alternative [at last, in the singular!] to the dominant neoclassical paradigm' (Lavoie, 1992, p. 1). He goes on to specify four 'presuppositions' of this alternative paradigm: realism, organicism, procedural rationality and production (as against instrumentalism, individualism, substantive rationality, exchange, respectively, of neoclassical economics).[22] I find all this perfectly correct, yet widely insufficient. For once, Lavoie's presuppositions are not all equally fundamental and are not all independent of one another. As Schumpeter very perspicaciously perceived, a well-defined 'vision of the world' is more essential than any detailed specification to present the basic lines of any strand of economic thought; it must be comprehensive and simple enough to provide a solid background for the purpose of whole sets of economic investigations. Again I should like to underline that the focusing

---

[21] They are 1) cumulative causation relying on increasing returns, 2) learning by doing, 3) historical (rather than logical) time, 4) sectoral allocation of resources depending on demand, 5) the relevance of creation of resources, 6) the uselessness of equilibrium analysis, 7) the market mechanism being only one of many economic insitutions (Sawyer, 1989, pp. 448–450).

[22] Hamouda and Harcourt (1988) see a similar attempt in the methodological investigation of Sheila Dow (1985), whose efforts they summarise as follows: '. . . what post Keynesians have in common exclusively is a particular view of how capitalism functions, the importance of groups/classes in combination with individual action, and a focus on particular problems such as involuntary unemployment and financial instability. Thus post Keynesian theory is holistic in terms of world view, not in terms of technique' (p. 25, footnote).

on particular aspects or the stressing of characteristic pre-suppositions should *follow*, as a sort of natural consequence, rather than be stated as a preliminary feature. Otherwise, it becomes difficult to counteract assertions such as denoting non-mainstream economics as a sort of Tower of Babel (Beaud and Dostaler, 1995).

From yet a different angle, this may evince rather well why – as far as my own views are concerned – I have insisted on the need for a sharp separation between the more fundamental, pre-institutional level of economic investigation, that can indeed give unity to the whole production paradigm, and the more variegated and quite open level of behavioural analyses, that are specific to particular institutional environments. These may well show a variety of possibilities and may in fact take advantage of – and even incorporate – many of the analyses which are being carried out at the margin – or from a different point of view at the frontier – of mainstream economics. (I am thinking of the social applications of game theory, of much of what goes under the term of social choice and even of some contributions coming from the literature on property rights.) My contention has been that at the basic level, a solid, comprehensive framework of investigation does exist and that Keynes and his group originally did intuitively perceive its existence, though being bogged down by many obfuscating prejudices and, as Keynes explicitly warned, facing the major difficulty of being unconsciously prisoners of old modes of thinking.

It is about time that the whole heterogeneous group of non-orthodox economists should not spurn the necessity of a radical shake-up and carry out a serious process of severe self-criticism and self-re-examination.

7.   Conclusion

Let me venture a few remarks to conclude these two lectures. The economics of Keynes continues to remain a very powerful attractor, even through the multifarious and heterogeneous effects that we can observe. In this situation, the conception that for the time being remains by far prevalent still is not that of the original Keynes but that of the reconcilers. The basic idea among all the reconcilers – old and new – is that Keynes's original and radical attempt at shifting the basis of economics from the orthodox paradigm to the paradigm of a monetary theory of production was either too ambitious or unnecessarily radical. The consequence that has been drawn is that it did not succeed. But the conviction also is that, nevertheless, his attempts can survive in the form of a compromise with tradition and an absorption of his theories into the traditional paradigm.

Robert Skidelsky grasps this widespread conviction clearly when he ends his second volume of Keynes's biography precisely by concluding: 'In the work of the reconcilers there was more than one hint that [Keynes's] revolutionary assault on the orthodox framework had failed. Perhaps Joan Robinson was right to call it 'bastard Keynesianism'. But only in that form [i.e. actually with no revolution] could the 'Keynesian Revolution' survive and grow' (Skidelsky, 1992, p. 621). Yet the basic aim of any scientific endeavour is not to make anybody's theory survive; it is to give better and ever more satisfactory explanations of the facts.

The odd facts around us are mounting. Not surprisingly, they continue to cumulate.[23]

Indeed, in the end, it is the powerful driving force of the facts that is persistently bringing Keynes's intuitions and

---

[23] It seems to me significant that Kenneth Arrow, himself a major contributor to the clear formalisation of the present dominant paradigm based on the Walrasian exchange model of General Economic Equilibrium analysis, should write a short newspaper article (rather than an article in a scientific journal) called 'Problems mount in application of free market economic theory' (Arrow, 1994). While giving a proud statement of the exchange paradigm, Ken Arrow frankly gives at the same time a long list of its major points of weakness and downright failures, implying that the number and the seriousness of these failures are continually mounting.

hints and ideas back into the economists' discussions. If the result of all this is to continually modify the traditional framework so as to accommodate, in some way, the new elaborations and evidence, even though with an inevitable patching up and many analytical difficulties, the picture is bound to look more and more like the one that Thomas Kuhn describes, where he talks of the dominant theoretical framework becoming increasingly non-homogeneous, more and more precarious and thus ever more incoherent and difficult to maintain. Precisely the possibility of the collapse of an increasingly patched-up paradigm may turn out to become, in the end, the powerful stimulus to overcome our unsatisfactory modes of thinking, in spite of the sluggishness and confusions of present-day non-orthodoxy.

Perhaps, in spite of all, as a final consequence of the mounting difficulties in the attempts at reconciliations, it may well be the task of a new generation of economists to produce that break with orthodox economics that was started, genuinely attempted, strongly pursued, but not accomplished by Keynes and the Keynesian group. Many dramatic changes took place in the last two decades of the twentieth century on the economic and political scene. New minds – liberated from the prejudices that have been obfuscating our visions – may well have become better equipped to bring about that genuine Keynesian revolution which has so far remained unaccomplished.

References for Book One

Arestis, Philip and Sawyer, Malcolm, (1992), *A Biographical Dictionary of Dissenting Economists*, Aldershot: Edward Elgar.

Arrow, Kenneth, (1994), 'Problems Mount in Application of Free Market Economic Theory', in the rubric 'Debate' in *The Guardian*, 4 January.

Beaud, Michel and Dostaler, Gilles, (1995), *Economic Thought since Keynes*, Aldershot: Edward Elgar.

Benassy, Jean-Paul, (1976), 'Théorie du déséquilibro et fondements micro-économiques de la macro-économie', in *Revue Economique*, vol. XXVII, pp. 765–804.

Bini, Piero, (1984), 'Keynes in Italia e la trasmissione internazionale delle idee economiche', in *Annali dell' Economia Italiana – Istituto IPSOA*, pp. 97–133; 'Proceedings of a Conference on the centenary of Keynes's birth', University of Florence, 4–5 June 1983.

Caffè, Federico, (1986), *In difesa del 'Welfare State'*, Torino: Rosenberg & Sellier.

Caffè, Federico, (1990), *La solitudine del riformista*, in Acocella, N. and Franzini, M. eds, Torino: Bollati Boringhieri.

Clower, Robert W., (1965), 'The Keynesian Counterrevolution: a Theoretical Appraisal', in Hahn F. H. and Brechling, F. R. R., eds, *The Theory of Interest Rates*, London: Macmillan.

Davidson, Paul, (1972), *Money and the Real World*, London: Macmillan.

Davidson, Paul, (1981), 'Post Keynesian Economics', in Bell, D. and Kristol, I., eds, *The Crisis in Economic Theory*, New York: Basic Books.

Dow, Sheila, (1985), *Macroeconomic Thought: A Methodological Approach*, Oxford: Basil Blackwell.

Eichner, Alfred S., (1979), *A Guide to Post Keynesian Economics*, London: Macmillan.

Eichner, Alfred S., (1991), *The Macrodynamics of Advanced Market Economies*, Armonk, N. Y.: M. E. Sharpe.

Eichner, Alfred S. and Kregel, Jan, (1975), 'An Essay on Post Keynesian Theory: a New Paradigm in Economics', in *Journal of Economic Literature*, vol. 13, pp. 1293–1314.

Galbraith, John Kenneth, (1956), *American Capitalism – The Concept of Countervailing Power*, 2nd revised edition, Boston: Houghton Mifflin Co.

Hamouda, O. F. and Harcourt, Geoffrey C., (1988), 'Post-Keynesianism: From Criticism to Coherence?', in *Bulletin of Economic Research*, vol. 40, pp. 1–33.

Harrod, Roy F., (1948), *Towards a Dynamic Economics*, London: Macmillan.

Harrod, Roy F., (1951), *The Life of John Maynard Keynes*, London: Macmillan.

Hicks, J. R., (1937), 'Mr. Keynes and the "Classics" – a Suggested Interpretation', in *Econometrica*, vol. 5, pp. 147–59.

Hicks, John, (1975), 'Revival of political economy: the old and the new', in *Economic Record*, vol. 51, pp. 365–367.

Hicks, John, (1980–81), 'IS-LM: an explanation', in *Journal of Post Keynesian Economics*, vol. 3, pp. 139–155.

Johnson, Elizabeth S. and Johnson, Harry G., (1978), *The Shadow of Keynes*, Oxford: Basil Blackwell.

Kahn, R. F., (1931), 'The Relation of Home Investment to Unemployment', in *The Economic Journal*, vol. XLI, pp. 173–198.

Kahn, R. F., (1984), *The Making of Keynes's General Theory*, text of the 'Mattioli Lectures' (Milan, 1978), Cambridge: Cambridge University Press.

Kalecki, Michal, (1935), 'A Macro-dynamic Theory of Business Cycles', in *Econometrica*, vol. 3, pp. 327–344.

Kalecki, Michal, (1971), *Selected Essays on the Dynamics of the Capitalist Economy, 1933–1970*, Cambridge: Cambridge University Press.

Keynes, John Maynard, (1923), *A Tract on Monetary Reform*, London: Macmillan.

Keynes, John Maynard, (1930), *A Treatise on Money*, 2 vols, London: Macmillan.

Keynes, John Maynard, (1936), *The General Theory of Employment, Interest and Money*, London: Macmillan. *Italian transl.: Occupazione, Interesse e Moneta – Teoria Generale*, Torino: UTET, 1947.

Keynes, John Maynard, (1971), 'The Collected Writings of John Maynard Keynes', (Donald Moggridge ed.), vol. V, *A Treatise on Money*, I, London: Macmillan and Cambridge: Cambridge University Press.

Keynes, John Maynard, (1973a) 'The Collected Writings of John Maynard Keynes', (Donald Moggridge ed.), vol. XIII, *The General Theory and After – Part I Preparation*, London: Macmillan and Cambridge: Cambridge University Press.

Keynes, John Maynard, (1973b), 'The Collected Writings of John Maynard Keynes', (Donald Moggridge ed.), vol. XIV, *The General Theory and After – Part II Defence and Development*, London: Macmillan.

Keynes, John Maynard, (1979), 'The Collected Writings of John Maynard Keynes', (Donald Moggridge ed.), vol. XXIX, *The General Theory and After: A Supplement*, London: Macmillan and Cambridge: Cambridge University Press.

Keynes, John Maynard and Henderson, Hubert, (1929), 'Can Lloyd George do it?', in *Nation and Athenaeum*, 11 May; reprinted in 'The Collected Writings of John Maynard Keynes', (Donald Moggridge ed.), vol. IX, *Essays in Persuasion*, London: Macmillan and Cambridge: Cambridge University Press, pp. 86–125.

Kregel, J. A., (1973), *The Reconstruction of Political Economy: An Introduction to Post-Keynesian Economics*, London: Macmillan.

Kuhn, Thomas S., (1970a), *The Structure of Scientific Revolutions*, 2nd edition, Chicago: The University of Chicago Press.

Kuhn, Thomas S., (1970b), 'Reflections on my Critics', in Lakatos I. and Musgrave A., eds, *Criticism and the Growth of Knowledge*, Cambridge: Cambridge University Press, pp. 231–278.

Lakatos, Imre (1970) 'Falsification and the Methodology of Scientific Research Programmes', in Lakatos I. and Musgrave A.

eds, *Criticism and the Growth of Knowledge*, Cambridge: Cambridge University Press, pp. 91–196.

Lakatos, Imre and Musgrave, Alan, eds., (1970), *Criticism and the Growth of Knowledge*, Cambridge: Cambridge University Press.

Lavoie, Marc, (1992), *Foundations of Post-Keynesian Economic Analysis*, Aldershot: Edward Elgar.

Leijonhufvud, Axel, (1968), *On Keynesian Economics and the Economics of Keynes: a study in monetary theory*, Oxford: Oxford University Press.

Malinvaud, Edmond, (1977), *The Theory of Unemployment Reconsidered*, Oxford: Basil Blackwell.

Marris, Robin, (1991), *Reconstructing Keynesian Economies with Imperfect Competition*, Aldershot: Edward Elgar.

Meade, James, (1993), 'The Relation of Mr. Meade's Relation to Kahn's Multiplier', in *Economic Journal*, vol. 103, pp. 664–665.

Minsky, Hyman P., (1975), *John Maynard Keynes*, New York: Columbia University Press.

Minsky, Hyman P., (1986), *Stabilizing an Unstable Economy*, New Haven: Yale University Press.

Modigliani, Franco, (1944), 'Liquidity Preference and the Theory of Interest and Money', *Econometrica*, vol. 12, pp. 45–88.

Moggridge, Donald E., (1973), 'From the *Treatise* to *The General Theory*: an Exercise in Chronology', in *History of Political Economy*, vol. 5, pp. 72–88.

Moggridge, Donald E., (1992), *Maynard Keynes: An Economist's Biography*, London: Routledge.

Pasinetti, Luigi L., (1981), *Structural Change and Economic Growth – A theoretical essay on the dynamics of the wealth of nations*, Cambridge: Cambridge University Press.

Pasinetti, Luigi L., (1986), 'Theory of Value – A Source of Alternative Paradigms in Economic Analysis', in Baranzini, Mauro and Scazzieri, Roberto, eds, *Foundations of Economics – Structure of Inquiry and Economic Theory*, Oxford: Basil Blackwell, pp. 409–431.

Pasinetti, Luigi L., (1991), 'At the Roots of Post-Keynesian Thought: Keynes' Break with Tradition', in Adriaansen, W. L. M. and van der Linden, J. T. J. M., eds, *Post-Keynesian Thought in Perspective*, 'Association of Post-Keynesian Studies', Amsterdam: Wolters-Noordhof Publishers, pp. 21–29.

Pasinetti, Luigi L., (1993), *Structural Economic Dynamics – A theory of the economic consequences of human learning*, Cambridge: Cambridge University Press.

Pasinetti, Luigi L., (1997), 'The Principle of Effective Demand', in Harcourt, Geoffrey C. and Riach, Peter A., eds, *A Second Edition of Keynes's General Theory*, London: Routledge, pp. 93–104.

Patinkin, Don, (1987), 'Keynes, John Maynard', an item in *The New Palgrave Dictionary*, vol. 3, London: Macmillan, pp. 19–41.

Patinkin, Don, (1990), 'On Different Interpretations of the *General Theory*', in *Journal of Monetary Economics*, vol. 26, pp. 205–243.

Patinkin, Don, (1993), 'On the Chronology of the General Theory', in *The Economic Journal*, vol. 103, pp. 647–663.

Phelps, Edmund S., (1994), *Structural Slumps – The Modern Equilibrium Theory of Unemployment, Interest and Assets*, Cambridge, Mass.: Harvard University Press.

Robinson, A. E. G., (1947), 'John Maynard Keynes', in *The Economic Journal*, vol. 55, pp. 1–68.

Robinson, Joan V., (1972), 'What Has Become of the Keynesian Revolution?', Presidential Address, Section F, British Association, reprinted in Robinson, Joan, (1979), *Collected Economic Papers*, vol. V, Oxford: Basil Blackwell, pp. 168–177.

Robinson, Joan V., (1979), *Collected Economic Papers*, vol. V, Oxford: Basil Blackwell.

Rymes, Thomas K., (1989), *Keynes's Lectures, 1932–35 – Notes of a Representative Student*, London: Macmillan.

Samuelson, Paul A., (1964a), 'The General Theory', in Leckachman, Robert, ed., *Keynes's General Theory: Report of Three Decades*, London: Macmillan, pp. 315–347.

Samuelson, Paul A., (1948), *Economics – Introductory Analysis*, first and following editions, New York: McGraw Book Co.

Sawyer, Malcolm, (1988), 'Introduction' to Sawyer M., ed., *Post-Keynesian Economics*, Aldershot: Edward Elgar.

Schumpeter, Joseph A., (1936), 'Review of *The General Theory of Employment, Interest and Money*', in *The Journal of the American Statistical Association*, vol. XXXI, pp. 791–795.

Shackle, G. L. S., (1952), *Expectation in Economics*, 2nd edition, Cambridge: Cambridge University Press.

Shackle, G. L. S., (1967), *The Years of High Theory; Invention and Tradition in Economic Thought, 1926–1939*, Cambridge: Cambridge University Press.

Skidelsky, Robert, (1983), *John Maynard Keynes, a Biography*, vol. One: *Hopes Betrayed 1883–1920*, London: Macmillan.

Skidelsky, Robert, (1992), *John Maynard Keynes, a Biography*, vol. Two: *The Economist as Saviour 1920–37*, London: Macmillan.

Skidelsky, Robert, (2000), *John Maynard Keynes, a Biography*. vol. Three: *Fighting for Britain 1937–1946*, London: Macmillan.

Targetti, Ferdinando, (1992), *Nicholas Kaldor – The Economics and Politics of Capitalism as a Dynamic System*, Oxford: Clarendon Press.

Targetti, Ferdinando and Bogulslawa, Kinda-Hass, (1982), 'Kalecki's Review of Keynes' *General Theory*', in *Australian Economic Papers*, vol. 21, pp. 244–260.

Thirlwall, Anthony P., (1987), *Nicholas Kaldor*, Brighton: Wheatsheaf Books.

Weintraub, Sidney, (1959), *A General Theory of the Price Level, Output, Income Distribution, and Economic Growth*, New York: Chilton Books.

Weintraub, Sidney, (1966), *Employment, Growth and Income Distribution*, New York: Chilton Books.

Young, Warren, (1987), *Interpreting Mr. Keynes. The IS-LM Enigma*, Cambridge: Polity Press.

Book Two

The Cambridge School of Keynesian Economics

Prelude: the pupils of the first hour

Part Two is devoted to bringing to the fore achievements, accomplishments and missed accomplishments of the school of economic thought that, in Cambridge, England, after the disappearance of Keynes, pursued the scientific revolution started by the master. I shall present a series of essays, of a bio-bibliographical character, on Keynes's pupils of the first hour: Richard Kahn, Joan Robinson, Nicholas Kaldor and Piero Sraffa.

Keynes died in April 1946. But he had withdrawn from the front line of theoretical debates much earlier – practically since he suffered that heart attack (1937) which permanently crippled his ability for normal work. He had to concentrate his energies on advising the British government, at the Treasury, while a deadly war was approaching.[1] Very soon, the duties following the outbreak of World War Two also absorbed the whole young generation and this meant a forced interruption of the debates on the Keynesian revolution. But as soon as university activity resumed after the war, in Cambridge Keynes's pupils – as a direct consequence of their personal association with him – formed a unique school of 'Keynesian' economic thought, aimed at pursuing Keynes's

---

[1] It is nevertheless astonishing to go through, as Skidelsky (2000) does in detail in his third volume of Keynes's biography, the amazing amount of work that Keynes was able to do, up to the end of the Bretton Woods Conference (a few months before his death), whose results he considered a defeat for Britain.

'revolution in economics' in the literal sense of the word, i.e. as a break with orthodoxy.

Paradoxically, they found themselves at a disadvantage. The ten-year interruption of theoretical debates helped to give prominence to the only really relevant meeting, among the enthusiastic young Keynesians, that had taken place before the war, namely the session on 'Mr Keynes's System' at the Econometric Society Conference in Oxford in late 1936. This was precisely the meeting at which Hicks's IS-LM simple four-equation model was presented and widely discussed, as expression of Keynes's basic theoretical scheme. Neither Joan Robinson nor Richard Kahn took part in that meeting and they later regretted it bitterly. But the consequence of this was that, for ten years following Keynes's early defence of his position (which was in any case aimed at rebutting the criticisms of the economists of his generation, leaving aside the possible misinterpretations of the young generation, who seemed on the whole to be all on his side anyway), the actual teaching of *The General Theory* was propounded all around the world of economics by adopting Hicks's IS-LM model. This was a simple analytical tool, attractive and very convenient for didactical purposes, while Keynes's own work was – one must admit – rather unsuitable for teaching purposes. The consequence was that the version of *The General Theory* which was first absorbed by the new students of economics, returning to university after the war, was along the lines of those who preferred to adopt an accommodating compromise with the Walrasian tradition, as Hicks had openly stated, rather than on the lines of those who stressed the necessity of a sharp break with orthodoxy.[2]

Rather unwisely, the Cambridge group did not pay much attention to this circumstance. Besides underestimating, they spurned Hicks's IS-LM 'Keynesian' model, convinced, as they

---

[2] See above, p. 30. Modigliani, who worked during the war and published his famous 'Liquidity Preference' article in 1944, started precisely from Hicks's equations and developed them in the same direction.

were, that it was to them that the whole world would have looked as the genuine heirs and interpreters of John Maynard Keynes. With a typically nonchalant confidence, they pushed ahead on their own way.

One must recognise nevertheless that their role was prominent. In the immediate post-war period, not only did they dominate the Cambridge scene but their influence extended to the world of economics at large. It would have been impossible among economists, in the 1950s and 1960s, not to pay attention – in an approving or a disapproving mood – to what they were propounding and writing. Owing to them, Cambridge emerged as the most distinguished and original centre of British (and European) economic thought – a centre of national as well as international excellence. While Richard Kahn – Keynes's closest pupil – was active mainly behind the scene, Joan Robinson and Nicholas Kaldor, with the avowed aim of extending Keynes's economic theory to the long run, had no hesitation in launching their scathing attacks on neo-classical economics, in their writings and in their lectures, in Cambridge and abroad, during their numerous tours of universities and other places of research all over the world. Piero Sraffa, after a long period in which he had carried out his superb editorial work on Ricardo's writings, thereby reawakening interest in, and most of all positively inducing, a rediscovery of Classical economics – quite unexpectedly, in 1960, published his slim, disconcerting book, which created a stir in more than one field of economic thought.

There can be no doubt that this group of economists did form a powerful school on the track of Keynes's economic theory. Richard Kahn had been Keynes's closest pupil since the beginning of his studies in economics, which roughly coincided with the years of the greatest-ever economic disaster – the 1929 slump – which the Western industrialised countries had experienced. (And let it be remembered that Keynes's rethinking of economics had in any case widely been credited with the germinal ideas that contributed to overcome that disaster.) Joan Robinson had become the most outspoken world proclaimer of the Keynesian revolution. Nicholas Kaldor, the junior member of the group, had come into contact with Keynes in 1938, from the circles of Hayek's LSE. His conversion to Keynesian economics was, if sudden and striking, enthusiastic, full, vociferous and without the slightest shred of doubt. Piero Sraffa, the senior member of the group, was the only person whose contacts with Keynes dated back to pre-Keynesian revolution times. He remained a subject of reverence practically for all economists in Cambridge (and not only in Cambridge). In terms of the concepts associated with Keynes's *General Theory*, he was not as entirely involved as the others and remained the most critical member of the whole group. The evolution of his thought had started before *The General Theory* and proceeded more on parallel lines, rather than in succession, to the ideas of Keynes.

Paradoxically, if we were strictly to adhere to the sense that Schumpeter used in order to define an economics 'school', this group would not appear as a clearly homogeneous school of economic thought. They formed a group of many separate, sometimes even apparently discordant, voices. Yet to any external observer, they did appear as a 'school'. It has not been easy for anybody to spell out in detail what it was that conferred on them the mark of such unity and kept them together. They often quarrelled with one another. But at the same time, they kept among themselves a sort of strong cohesion that differentiated them, and kept them separate, from all the others. When they argued, sometimes bitterly among themselves, they did so within what was recognised, or appeared to be, a tight and exclusive intellectual circus. Their personal relations were extraordinarily strong and close. Nicholas Kaldor, in one of his reminiscences (see Kaldor 1986, pp. 67–8), claims that it was when the LSE had moved to Cambridge during (and because of) the war that they began to have regular discussions, resuming those of the 1931 Cambridge *Circus* and preceding those of the post-war 'Secret Seminar'. But all this could hardly be taken, by itself alone, to explain the closeness of their intellectual intercourse. One must look for something else, much deeper, that shaped their intellectual affinities or attractiveness and at the same time gave rise to their strong and stormy personal relationships.

The following essays, now gathered here in the form of separate chapters, are intended to illustrate the intriguing aspects of their partnership and the way in which they absorbed and brought forward the message of *The General Theory*, unambiguously intended as a break with orthodoxy and a reconstruction of economic theory on definitely alternative foundations. Each essay was written at a different time, separately and independently of the others, for different purposes and in different places. I have not tried to homogenise them, except that in the case of Nicholas Kaldor I have merged two separate essays. For all the others, I have left them in their original form, with few amendments concerning inaccuracies or omissions of no longer relevant details, and with an integration at the very end of the third essay on Sraffa. The reader may also find some repetitions here and there. It seemed to me wise not to try to eliminate them, when I thought they could help to stress the important aspects and features of this remarkable 'Keynesian' school of economic thought.

In presenting the essays here, it seemed appropriate to begin with Kahn – the convener of the 1931 Cambridge *Circus* – followed by his closest, life-long, most vociferous intellectual partner, Joan Robinson. Then I have placed the early convert (though by no means subordinate partner), Nicholas Kaldor. There follow three essays devoted to Piero Sraffa. In terms of space, he may thus appear as the scholar attracting most attention. But I had to leave them in their original form, as they are so different in approach and concerning such varied aspects of his contributions and personality. Moreover, they will appear as crucial in the arguments preparing the transitional steps to the third part of the book.

I have added my general comments on the Keynesian group as a whole in two further, separate pieces, interspliced at the middle (Interlude) and at the end (Postlude) of Book Two. In these pieces, I attempt to summarise my personal assessment both of the overall achievements and shared method of research and of the failures of this unique group of economists, of worldwide renown and reputation. In this way, I hope to give the reader enough material for judging for herself (or himself) what in the Cambridge School of economic thought *did not* work, and at the same time what *did* work and could now be rescued and resumed, in an attempt to make the Keynesian revolution proceed towards its accomplishment.

NB: The references for all the essays and comments will be given at the end of Book Two, except for the selected lists of works of each author, which are taken as an integral part of the corresponding essay and hence kept at its end. In the text of the essays, such references will be placed in square brackets.

Chapter III

Richard Ferdinand Kahn
(1905–1989)
Co-author of The General Theory?

Editorial note

This essay reproduces the memoir 'Richard Ferdinand Kahn: 1905–1989', commissioned to the author by the British Academy and published in 'Proceedings of the British Academy', vol. 76, 'Lectures and Memoirs', London, 1991, pp. 423–443.

1. Biographical essentials

Richard Kahn was born in London on 10 August 1905. He died, at the age of eighty-three, in the Evelyn Hospital, Cambridge, on 6 June 1989, after a few months' illness.

He had been a Fellow of King's College, Cambridge, since 1930 and a Professor of Economics at the University of Cambridge since 1951 (Emeritus since 1972). He was appointed CBE in 1946 and was made a life peer, as Baron Kahn of Hampstead, in 1965.

He was unmarried.

2. Kahn in the Cambridge Keynesian setting

The disappearance of Kahn marks the end of an historical phase, almost an era, in the history of Keynesian economic thought – an historical phase centred in Cambridge. Thanks to Keynes, in the 1930s, and to a formidable group of Keynes's

Plate 1 Richard Kahn, in 1972. Reproduced by permission of
the Ramsay and Muspratt collection.

pupils, in the immediate postwar period, Cambridge became,
for a few decades, a unique place for intellectual leadership
and imaginative, though unconventional, mode of thinking
in economic theory.

The Cambridge Keynesian School of Economics has left its
mark on the history of ideas, but, in the course of a few years,

its major representatives have all disappeared: Joan Robinson and Piero Sraffa both died in 1983, Nicholas Kaldor in 1986 (Roy Harrod, who had, however, remained in Oxford, had died in 1978). In 1989, it was the turn of Richard Kahn (see Pasinetti, 1989).

The chronological succession of events left it to Kahn to conclude the cycle, the man who might legitimately have claimed to have started it. For, Keynes himself was after all a traditional economist who, at the unusual age of fifty, became a convert to Keynesian economics. Kahn was a true Keynesian economist from the very beginning. Joan Robinson used to say: even before Keynes!

Kahn's association with Keynesian economics was complete. He was Keynes's favourite pupil and closest collaborator in the 1930s, at the time of elaboration of Keynes's celebrated work, *The General Theory of Employment, Interest and Money*.

At Keynes's death in 1946, he became at King's College his successor in all respects. He also succeeded him as First Bursar of the college. He was his literary executor and remained, throughout his life, the staunchest defender and the most faithful propounder of Keynes's original ideas. Yet Kahn never was a prominent protagonist. His influence was always exerted quietly and unobtrusively. This has created an air of mystery around the actual role played by this elusive figure, whose merits go well beyond those that can be attributed to him on the basis of his writings, and whose personality was known to few people beyond the small circle of his closest friends.

3.   Life and scientific contributions

Richard Ferdinand Kahn came from a Jewish family of strict religious observance, who lived in Hampstead (North-West London). His father, Augustus Kahn (1869–1944), was a first-generation Englishman (both his parents being German). He had graduated in mathematics at St John's College, Cambridge, and became a government inspector of schools. He actually went back to Germany to marry Regina Schoyer, Richard's mother. They had several children, four of whom survived infancy – three daughters and Richard, their eldest son.

The Kahn family was described as a 'comfortable, cultured family which had a commitment to communal service and combined punctilious and decorous orthodoxy with a thirst for education and culture . . . [following] . . . a form of Judaism associated with a very distinguished Jewish thinker, Rabbi Samson Raphael Hirsch, who, in the middle of the nineteenth century . . . [advocated] strict observance of the laws of the Torah, combined with openness to secular learning' (Tabor, 1989).

Richard remained strictly faithful to his religious upbringing well beyond his adolescence. It is said that, as Bursar of King's, he would not sign cheques on the Sabbath day. But later in life he abandoned orthodoxy. He was encouraged to eat meat on account of his health and became less and less active in religious practice. 'Only on rare occasions could one see him at Synagogue . . . observance, ritual and the religious tradition no longer touched him . . . [yet] . . . he retained his identity as a Jew with pride and took a positive – if sometimes somewhat critical – attitude to Israel . . . In his last years there was some turning back [to the Jewish religion]' (Tabor, 1989).

Richard was educated at St Paul's School in London, from 1918 to 1924. Then he won a scholarship to King's College, Cambridge, where he read mathematics, being placed in the first class of the Tripos Part I, and then physics, graduating in 1927. He was placed in the second class of the Natural Science Tripos, which was a disappointment to him. (But he was said to be a very clumsy experimenter and to get bored with carrying out experiments whose answer was already known.) His scholarship entitled him to a fourth year, but he was on the point of looking for a job, feeling that he should help the family. However, encouraged by Keynes and Shove, he stayed on to read economics. He attended lectures delivered, among others, by Pigou, Keynes, Shove, Dennis Robertson and (in the following year) Piero Sraffa. His determination was vindicated. After only one year, he was placed in the first class of the Economics Tripos Part II.

He himself recently described the beginning of his research in economics in the following way:

> Some months passed before I selected the subject of my dissertation. Keynes, who in addition to Gerald Shove, was my teacher when I was working for the Tripos, tried to secure for me access to the statistics of the Midland Bank, with a view to my making something of them. (. . .) I cannot conceive what use I could have made of the Midland Bank's statistics. But I was young and inexperienced, and unwilling to resist Keynes's influence.
>
> Keynes took me along to meet Reginald McKenna, the Chairman of the Midland Bank, who was easily persuaded by Keynes. I was then taken to his own room by the Head of the Intelligence Department of the Bank, A. W. Crick. He bluntly informed me that if anybody was going to make use of their statistics, it was he and his staff, and not I. Crick's attitude towards me is partly attributable to the fact that Keynes, as Editor of the *Economic Journal*, had rejected an article submitted by him in April 1928. I tremble to think how my career would have developed had he taken a conciliatory line. It was a miraculous escape from disaster. Keynes then left me to choose my own subject. Under the influence of Marshall's *Principles*, I chose the *Economics of the Short Period*. In making my choice, I was encouraged by Shove and Piero Sraffa. Keynes happily acquiesced. Neither he nor I had the slightest idea that my work on the short period was later on going to influence the development of Keynes's own thought. But there are no traces of Keynesian thought in the dissertation itself. [1989, pp. x–xi]

The Fellowship dissertation, with the title 'The Economics of the Short Period' [1929], was written in a remarkably short time. It was submitted to the King's Electors to Fellowships in December 1929 and secured Kahn a Fellowship at King's College (which he took up in March 1930 and retained for the whole of his life).

Kahn's Fellowship dissertation (which remained unpublished for fifty years) is one of the two substantial works (the other being Joan Robinson's *Economics of Imperfect Competition*, 1933) that developed in Cambridge on the trail of the devastating critique of Marshall's economics launched by Piero Sraffa in the late 1920s (Sraffa, 1925, 1926). Richard Kahn and Joan Robinson worked very much in collaboration, under the strong influence of Sraffa and Shove. For Kahn and Joan Robinson this was the beginning of an intense intellectual partnership that lasted for life.

The most interesting part of Kahn's 'Economics of the Short Period' is perhaps his analysis of the extent to which – in periods of depression – market imperfections affect the way in which output gets distributed among the various firms, the essential point being that market imperfections prevent the most efficient firms from reaching an optimum utilisation of their productive capacities and instead cause all firms (efficient and inefficient alike) to reach equilibrium at a point at which there is underutilisation of productive capacity and less than full employment. This sets obvious relations between the microeconomic behaviour of the single firm and the situations of underutilisation of productive capacity for the economic system as a whole.

Only a very short part of the dissertation reached publication in the 1930s (part of Chapter 7). Kahn re-elaborated it in the form of an elegant article [1937a] which since has become a standard reference in the economic literature on duopoly and oligopoly. But the whole of Kahn's dissertation deserves closer scrutiny. It has only recently become available, first in an Italian translation [1983] and then (in fact posthumously) in the English original [1989]. A careful study of it may well contribute to piecing together the great analytical puzzle of the relations between Sraffa's critique of Marshall's theory of the firm and Keynes's macroeconomic theory. There can be no doubt that, on a strictly intellectual level, these were Kahn's most productive years. It was in the summer of 1930, in the process of criticising a paper by Keynes and Henderson on public works, that Kahn discovered the principle of the multiplier.

The multiplier is a relation between the *increase* in exogenous aggregate expenditure and the *increase* in net national product thereby generated (and thus also in employment, if employment is proportional to net national product and the economy is in a situation of unemployment due to lack of effective aggregate demand). To put it in simple and compact terms, if c is the fraction of any increase in income that consumers tend to spend, it can be shown that any increase of £1 in the stream of exogenous expenditure (or else of such an amount that generates one extra job) will finally generate £1/(1 − c) of extra net national product, or else 1/(1 − c) extra jobs. This is Kahn's multiplier. The author originally presented it in an article with reference to employment [1931] and it immediately became relevant for the economic policy discussions of the time. The conventional view was that an increase in government expenditure would simply shift employment from the private to the public sector without affecting its total, as the amount of savings available was fixed. Kahn's analytical device showed not only that employment would increase but also by how much. The multiplier was then to be used by Keynes, more with reference to national income (and to the process of investments generating a corresponding amount of savings), as one of the major ingredients of his *General Theory*.

It was in 1930 that Kahn started chairing and conducting the so-called 'Cambridge Circus', a group (or rather a closed club) of young Cambridge economists (that included Joan and Austin Robinson, Piero Sraffa and James Meade, besides Kahn). It was originally set up to discuss Keynes's *Treatise on*

Money, but then went on regularly to discuss, criticise and propose changes to subsequent drafts of what was to become Keynes's *General Theory*.

But Kahn's contributions extended to microeconomic theory and to other debated subjects in the 1930s: the development of the concept of elasticity of substitution among factors of production, as an analytical tool in the traditional theory of income distribution [1933b], and the laying out of the foundations of welfare economics. Kahn's notes on 'ideal output' [1935a], and his article on 'tariffs and the terms of trade' [1947], were later to be basic to Jan Graaff's systematic (and rather pessimistic) theoretical work on welfare economics (Graaff, 1957).

Kahn was appointed a university lecturer in 1933 and became a member of King's economics teaching staff in 1936. There was later an interruption due to the war. But for this exception, he was responsible for the teaching of economics at King's College up to 1951 (first with Shove and Keynes and later, from 1949, with Kaldor).

He relinquished undergraduate teaching in 1951 – according to university regulations – on his appointment to an *ad hominem* university professorship, which he held until retirement age (1972).

Until a few years ago, little attention had been paid by his academic friends to his activity during the war. But in a more recently published long interview [see 1988], edited by Maria Cristina Marcuzzo, Kahn has emphasised at length, and in great detail, this little-known part of his life.

For seven troubled years, starting from 1939, he was completely absorbed, as a temporary civil servant, in government activity. In 1939, he served at the Board of Trade; his task was to devise ways of restricting the supply of goods to civilians to an essential level, so as to divert the supply of labour, raw materials, equipment, building and shipping space to the needs of the Armed Forces, and at the same time to ensure maximum efficiency in the limited production of civilian goods. In 1941, be moved to Cairo, as a member of the staff of the Middle East Supply Centre, again with tasks concerning war rationing and war production. In 1943 he was back in London, in the Raw Materials Department of the Ministry of Supply. He was then transferred in 1944 to the Ministry of Production as head of the General Division and, at the end of the war, when the Ministry of Production and the Board of Trade were merged, he became head of the General Division of the Board of Trade.

He did not return permanently to Cambridge until September 1946. Later on, his government activity continued only on a sporadic and temporary basis. In the 1960s he served for three years as a part-time member of the National Coal Board.

On an intellectual level, of great importance was his Memorandum of Evidence submitted to the government-appointed Committee on the Working of the Monetary System, known as the Radcliffe Committee. This Memorandum [1960a], jointly with his theoretical work on the extension of the concept of liquidity preference [1954a], was among the substantial pieces behind the formation of what has become known as 'The Radcliffe Committee view' on the working of the monetary system. When in the 1970s the more traditional 'monetarist' views once again became fashionable, Kahn was consistent in reacting vehemently against them and in rallying to the defence of the Keynesian approach [see 1976a, 1976b].

He also worked, now and then, for various international organisations. In 1955 he spent a year in Geneva as a member of the Research Division of the United Nations Economic Commission for Europe, contributing substantially to the *Economic Survey for Europe in 1955*.

In 1959 he was appointed a member of a Group of Experts of the Organisation for European Economic Cooperation (OEEC) to study the problem of rising prices. It was this Group of Experts that – in the early 1960s, when very few had yet realised the dangers of inflation – introduced the concept of 'wage-wage spiral-leap-frogging', connected with the consequences of excessive wage increases.

In the course of the years from 1965 to 1969, he served as a member of four Groups of Experts of UNCTAD, the United Nations Conference on Trade and Development. It was in this connection that the idea was developed of *linking* the expansion of the international liquidity, through the International Monetary Fund, to provisions in favour of the less developed countries.

With this distinguished record of service to national and international institutions, there was no surprise, in 1965, when in the first honours list of Harold Wilson's new Labour government, Richard Kahn appeared among the life peers.

Harold Wilson, himself a convinced Keynesian, was an admirer of Kahn's academic work. But Kahn was never part of the group of Labour Party counsellors; he always kept a detached attitude. In the House of Lords, he sat on the cross benches. In fact his attendance remained rather infrequent, the public limelight never being congenial to his inward-looking character. Only occasionally did he give speeches, all on economic matters.

Kahn's real place remained King's College and Cambridge University. The postwar period was the time of full maturity in his life. An extraordinary flurry of ideas characterised Cambridge economics in that period and made Cambridge one of the major world sources of original economic thought. Again Kahn was behind most of what was in the making. There was a time at which, as chairman of the Economics Faculty, Professorial Fellow and Fellowship Elector at King's, convener of the so-called Secret Seminar, he seemed to have the whole of the Cambridge economics thought process rotating around him. The teaching of economics in Cambridge was reshaped under his initiative. The 'Secret Seminar' (also known as the Tuesday Group, though it met on Mondays) was a postwar version of the early Cambridge *Circus*. It was held in Kahn's rooms in Webb's Court. There it was that the major contributions generated by the Cambridge Keynesian School of Economics took shape.

The secrecy of the initiative was a joke, but it was very characteristic of the atmosphere created by its convener and leader, Richard Kahn. Unsympathetic outsiders gave it all sorts of mysterious, even hidden meanings. But the essence of it was very simple: it was a way to keep the meetings closed to a small group. Kahn's character never brought him to extrovert expressions or to easy communication. He was a clumsy lecturer as soon as the size of the audience became moderately large. Very rarely did he go to conferences or to public meetings; never to large congresses. When decisive stands had to be taken, he let others come out on the battle forefront; he preferred to stay behind the scenes. But in private conversations or in small groups he was unequalled: persistent, punctilious, relentless, he gave his time – to colleagues, students and even visitors who submitted work to him – freely and with rare generosity.

One can find explicit signs of his contributions in at least three fields, where he broke new ground, beyond Keynes's *General Theory*. First, in the field of monetary theory, with his already mentioned article on liquidity preference [1954a] and the Radcliffe Committee Memorandum [1960a]. Second, on the inevitability of inflationary pressures in industrialised countries, once full employment is reached, unless some drastic changes are introduced into our institutions. And he specifically explored in considerable detail those institutional changes that he thought should be introduced into the process of wage negotiations [see 1976a, 1976b, 1977d]. Third, he played a major part in the shaping of the post-Keynesian theories of capital, growth and income distribution, as opposed to neoclassical theories [see 1954b, 1959a, 1959b], as well as in the development of a post-Keynesian approach to planning [1958].

On a personal level, he was 'a very private man' (Tabor 1989). Only 'the happy few' who belonged to the small group of his close friends had the privilege of appreciating the delicate sensitivity of a really exquisite personality that lay below the hard surface of the imposing mien of an apparently frightening authority. The warmth that was always in reserve broke loose now and then for the benefit of those who were among his guests, on the occasions of carefully prepared dinner parties, followed by attendance at theatrical or musical performances, many of them at the Arts Theatre (on whose board of trustees he succeeded Keynes). These were normal features of his way of life. He enjoyed playing the role of the impeccable host, who cared in the most minute detail for each of his guests, including short, handwritten (but almost illegible!) essential biographical information about the other guests.

He will also be remembered for his complete devotion to the cause of academic freedom. His unflinching efforts to help intellectuals in difficulty with political regimes were simply extraordinary. For many years (1954–76) he sat on the Executive Committee of the Society for the Protection of Science and Learning, an organisation whose aim was to help refugee scholars as they arrived in Great Britain.

His love for music and the arts was matched only by his love for the mountains. The Swiss, Austrian, Italian Alps, besides the home peaks in the Lake District, were for him places of regular visits and excursions. And of course, as a bachelor, he could enjoy college life fully, yet with no misogyny. The families of a few selected friends enjoyed his relaxed participation in their family life, of which he shared the profound humanity, involvement and responsibility. I myself, and my family, happened to have him as a guest in what must have been his last visit to the Italian pre-Alps (1982). We shall long remember his kindness, sensitivity and warmth, hidden behind his sometimes fastidious meticulousness. How amateurish we all felt on every excursion! And yet part of a memorable event. On any specific occasion, he turned out to be equipped with precisely what was needed, not only for himself but for all others: I mean not only maps, compass, spare watches, but things like small torches, lifeboat matches or even whistles for each single member of the expedition, so that no one might get lost in the event of fog. Needless to say, the children were delighted.

He kept his love for walking in Cambridge itself: his long Sunday walks remained a regular feature of his life up to his very last days.

In the last decade of his life Richard Kahn became more and more withdrawn. Though he continued his excursions and his visits to places of historic and artistic interest, very rarely did he accept invitations to lecture, at home or abroad. There were two exceptions: his *Raffaele Mattioli* lectures in Milan in 1978, from which came his book, *The Making of Keynes's General Theory*, and the presentation to him in Bologna in 1988 of the Italian version, in book form, of a long interview he had given, to which he gave a title that represents his own definition of himself: *Disciple of Keynes* [see 1988]. They now appear as the final expression of his consistent faithfulness to Keynes, and a symbol of his special relation with Italian economists.

But his aloofness, sometimes attributed to physical deafness, had deeper and more complex explanations. He did not approve of the turn that politics had taken in his country. He became dissatisfied with both major parties and in fact became a supporter of the Social Democratic Party. But, most of all, he was saddened by the turn that mainstream economics had taken. In his last few years he was a very deeply disappointed man. At times, he appeared grumpy. Yet he never made much apparent fuss about it, though never hiding his disapproval, if explicitly asked. He suffered in the depth of his conscience, but preferred the sombre dignity of silence to any form of what might have appeared old-age hysterical complaint. And he remained silent, in all respects, even after death. Surprisingly – for a bachelor and a punctilious scholar, who was also the scrupulous literary executor of John Maynard Keynes – he died, at eighty-three, leaving no will. The only after-death wish that he seems to have left is his instruction to be buried in the Jewish section of the Cambridge cemetery. The burial ceremony was conducted in Hebrew on 12 June 1989 by Professor David Tabor of Gonville and Caius College, who had succeeded him in 1946 as senior treasurer of The Cambridge University Jewish Society.

4.   Kahn and Keynes's *General Theory*

It is very unlikely, however, that Kahn's silence will be accepted by the historians of economic thought. There are at least two puzzling problems that his disappearance leaves wide open. The first concerns the role he played in the making of Keynes's *General Theory*. The second goes even deeper; it concerns the very nature of the Keynesian revolution.

We know that Keynes became deeply convinced in the 1930s of the revolutionary character of his new ideas.[1] At the same time he seemed to be strongly afraid of falling into mistakes. In the Preface to his masterpiece he explains:

> The writer of a book such as this, treading along unfamiliar paths, is extremely dependent on criticism and conversation if he is to avoid an undue proportion of mistakes. It is astonishing what foolish things one can temporarily believe if one thinks too long alone, particularly in economics . . . (Keynes, 1936a, p. vii)

This may contribute to explaining why Keynes took particular care to surround himself with a stable group of bright young intellectuals, with whom he could have delightful conversations and thorough discussions.

It may be recalled that Ludwig Wittgenstein, the brilliant Austrian philosopher, Piero Sraffa, the prominent Italian economist, Frank Ramsey, the talented mathematician and philosopher from King's College, who died so young, were

---

[1] The much-quoted reference on this is a letter Keynes wrote to G. B. Shaw on 1 January 1935 (see Caffè Lectures, above, p. 6).

all part of his entourage. But most of all he had around him a formidable group of young economists, among whom Richard Kahn undoubtedly gained a privileged position. Keynes's heaviest acknowledgements, in both his two major works, are to Kahn. In the Preface to the *Treatise on Money*, Keynes writes:

> In the gradual evolution of the book into its final form and in the avoidance of errors my greatest debt is to Mr R. F. Kahn of King's College, Cambridge, whose care and acuteness have left their trace on many pages . . . (Keynes, 1930a, p. vii)

and in the Preface to *The General Theory* Keynes again writes:

> In this book, even more perhaps than in writing my *Treatise on Money*, I have depended on the constant advice and constructive criticism of Mr R. F. Kahn. There is a great deal in this book which would not have taken the shape it has except at his suggestion. (Keynes, 1936a, p. viii)

Keynes's confidence in Kahn is further revealed by various documents recently published in his *Collected Writings*. For example, in a letter to Harold Macmillan, who in 1932 had asked his opinion of the typescript of Joan Robinson's *The Economics of Imperfect Competition*, Keynes writes:

> I have . . . confidence that [Joan Robinson's typescript] is reasonably free from minor slips and errors and fallacies because the authoress explains in the preface that it has been very elaborately and carefully criticised by R. F. Kahn; indeed I suspect that he has played a very substantial part in getting it to its present form. Now he is the most careful and accurate of all the younger economists, and mistakes do not easily get past him. I should say that he is a long way the ablest and most reliable critic of this type of work now to be found. Knowing the part that he has played in the preparation of the book, I have much greater confidence in its being free from . . . blunders . . . . (Keynes, 1983, p. 867)

For a check, here is what Joan Robinson herself writes, in her Foreword to the published book:

> Of not all the new ideas . . . can I definitely say 'this is my own invention'. In particular I have had the constant assistance of Mr R. F. Kahn. The whole technical apparatus was built up with his aid, and many of the major problems . . . were solved as much by him as by me. (Robinson, 1933, p. v)

It is no surprise, therefore, if Paul Samuelson once referred to Kahn as 'that elusive figure who hides in the prefaces of Cambridge books' (Samuelson, 1947, p. 159). This makes it even more appropriate to endeavour to go below the surface.

We know that it was Kahn who convened the Cambridge *Circus*; he picked up the problems from Keynes, brought them to the group and then took back the results of the discussions to Keynes. (In the colourful image of the wife of one of the young economists, Kahn played the role of the Angel-Messenger between 'God-Keynes' and the mortal discussants) (see Keynes, 1983, pp. 338–339).

In a recent reminiscence Kahn recounts that, for at least 'four years', starting from 1930, he spent 'part of most vacations staying with Keynes and Lydia [Keynes's wife] at Tilton [Keynes's country house] . . . The main object was to help Keynes with his work but also to enable me to carry on work of my own . . . During the morning we usually worked together in his study . . .' [1984, pp. 175, 177].

A very significant *coup d'oeil* on the effectiveness of Kahn's help transpires from what Keynes writes to Joan Robinson on 29 March 1934:

> I am going through a stiff week's supervision from RFK on my MS. He is a marvellous critic and suggester and improver – there never was anyone in the history of the world to whom it was so helpful to submit one's stuff. (Keynes, 1973a, p. 422)

Joseph Schumpeter – the most acute of all historians of economic thought – perceptively described Kahn (together with Shove) as belonging to a very peculiar category of scholars:

> ... scholars of a type that Cambridge produces much more readily than the other centres of scientific economics or rather of science in general. They throw their ideas into a common pool. By critical and positive suggestion they help other people's ideas into definite existence. And they exert anonymous influence – influence as leaders – far beyond anything that can be definitely credited to them from their publications. (Schumpeter, 1954, p. 1152)

But of course the most striking of all Schumpeter's assertions is that much-quoted conjecture of his:

> Next, we must record [in *The General Theory*] Keynes's acknowledgements of indebtedness, which in all cases can be independently established, to Mrs Joan Robinson, Mr R. G. Hawtrey, Mr R. F. Harrod, but especially to Mr R. F. Kahn, whose share in the historic achievement cannot have fallen very far short of co-authorship. (Schumpeter, 1954, p. 1172)

Co-authorship? Was it really something of the sort? Kahn himself, with his characteristically instinctive modesty about his achievements, always denied it. When asked specifically, he referred to Schumpeter's claim as 'clearly absurd. Perhaps it was inspired by unconscious hostility to Keynes' [1984, p. 178; see also p. 240].

On the other hand, the evidence mentioned above is quite compelling.

It may further be pointed out:

1. that the 'revolutionary' change in Keynes's thinking that brought him from his *Treatise on Money* (a work in the Marshallian tradition) to his *General Theory* (a 'revolutionary' work) took place after Keynes had submitted his theories to the regular and thorough discussions of the 'Cambridge Circus' organised and led by Kahn;

2. that it was Kahn, who, in conjunction with Austin and Joan Robinson, drew and signed the so-called 'manifesto' of April 1932, an open criticism of Keynes's monetary theory lectures at Cambridge, after which Keynes restructured radically his lectures, renamed them 'The monetary theory of production' and made that crucial shift from price to quantity adjustments, which laid the basis of *The General Theory* (see Keynes, 1979, pp. 42–45);

3. that it was Kahn who, in 1930, invented the multiplier, a major analytical ingredient of Keynes's revolutionary work.

Schumpeter's conjecture may well have gone too far. Yet it is quite clear that there was something decisively unusual in the participation of this 'elusive figure' in that 'historical achievement'. How far such participation did in fact go will probably remain for long the subject of speculation and debate.

5.   Kahn and the Keynesian revolution

Some further light on the question just raised may come from considering what happened *after* Keynes's death. Kahn continued in his usual way his discrete influence on what was being elaborated in Cambridge; suffice it to report what Joan Robinson acknowledges in the Preface to her *Accumulation of Capital*, the most ambitious of all her works: 'As so often, it was R. F. Kahn who saw the point that we were groping for and enabled us to get it into a comprehensible form' (Robinson, 1956, p. vi). And a few lines further on, with reference to a specific but basic tool of analysis (the production function): 'In this understanding I had invaluable help from R. F. Kahn, who, once more, found the essential clue to rescue the argument from the tangle into which I had ravelled it' (ibid., p. vii).

But Keynes was no longer in Cambridge. In his place there was a powerful group of intellectually formidable direct pupils of his. What appeared striking was that, to their proud awareness of the greatness of the Keynesian message and to their strong conviction of expressing the true continuation and the genuine interpretation of the Keynesian revolution, there corresponded an increasingly hostile reaction from the outside academic world, added to the opposition (which had never disappeared) of the more traditionally minded, moderate and conservative part of the Cambridge establishment.

The Keynesian theories and policies had been accepted in the United States during and immediately after the war. This meant worldwide relevance. The first two decades of the postwar period were characterised, in all industrialised countries, by unprecedented low levels of unemployment, and, in the whole world, by unprecedented economic expansion. This exceptionally long wave of prosperity was generally associated with the universally applied Keynesian policies. But later on, concurrently with the oil crisis of the 1970s, economic difficulties began to reappear; in particular, persistently increasing levels of prices. This encouraged the return of anti-Keynesian, and even pre-Keynesian, modes of thinking, both in academic and in political circles, especially in the United States and, as a reflex, in Great Britain. Mass unemployment reappeared in all industrialised countries, but preoccupations with unemployment fell into second place with respect to those concerning inflation (rather unexpectedly at first sight, but with some justification, given the changes that the Keynesian policies themselves had brought about).

For a few years, monetarism (as opposed to Keynesianism) became fashionable. But it did not last for long. Strict monetarist recipes quickly fell into disrepute. Yet they left their mark. Mainstream economics did *not* go back to Keynesian theories and policies in a full way; it stopped somewhat halfway.

It did so by drawing a sharp distinction, or rather by suddenly opening a break, between Keynes and his Cambridge school. The latter, with all its developments of Keynesian thought in various directions, was set aside and ignored. At the same time, Keynes's *General Theory* was increasingly linked back to Keynes's pre-*General Theory* works and subjected to a series of reinterpretations.

Very significantly, Don Patinkin, in his 1989 British Academy Keynes Lecture, chose to address himself to the 'different interpretations of the *General Theory'*. He has also – rather ingenuously, it would seem to me – shown surprise at finding that different interpretations of Keynes's major work did not begin to appear until a quarter of a century after its publication.

The interpretation that Patinkin himself favours is the one that has grown up slowly from inside traditional economics. Patinkin looks at Keynes's theory as a sort of Walrasian general equilibrium macroeconomic model. By contrast the Cambridge Keynesian school, and in particular Kahn, always took Marshall's neoclassical economic theory – which was the British version of that stream of economics which on the continent was associated with the names of Walras, Pareto and Menger – as precisely the theory from which the Keynesian revolution broke away.

For Kahn, the Keynesian revolution could not but mean what it literally says – a revolution, a sharp break-away from traditional neoclassical economic theory; i.e., to use a fashionable Kuhnian term (Kuhn, 1970), 'a change of paradigm'.

In these terms, mainstream economics is in (at least terminological) contradiction. To make all the reinterpretation that is necessary to reabsorb the Keynesian revolution into the traditional fold is in fact to reduce the Keynesian revolution to no revolution at all.

This is what Richard Kahn finally saw taking place in dominant economic theory; and it is precisely this that saddened him so deeply in the last few years of his life. He felt somewhat deprived of his Keynesian roots.

In addition, what to Kahn appeared a 'tragedy' was that in Cambridge – i.e. in Keynes's own place – very few economists indeed were left to carry the Keynesian banner. At least in one respect, the Keynesian group had differed from Keynes: they had left no successor in an influential position. In the last few years of his life, Nicholas Kaldor was explicit enough to openly recognise this as a failure. Richard Kahn perhaps felt it even more deeply than Kaldor, but kept it to himself.

Yet, quite apart from any personal tragedy, which may have been experienced by any remarkable person at an exceptional time, fascinating as it may be as a source of emotions, curiosity and reflections, there remains the more substantial and widely relevant intellectual problem of what it is that the Keynesian revolution really was (or failed to be).

Was it really that break-away, that discontinuity with Marshallian (and Walrasian) neoclassical economic theory, which Kahn and the Cambridge group very convincingly felt since the beginning, and which they were so excited to work for, in a major effort to reconstruct economic theory on sounder foundations? Or was it in the end (contrary to what they felt) perhaps a sharp or even a violent but *temporary* turmoil, to be reabsorbed into the traditional fold, as the contingent events behind it faded away?

No one can honestly claim to have been able to answer these questions in a conclusive way so far. Nor should we expect that a disappointed Richard Kahn, at the end of his life, would have been willing to answer them for us.

6.   Scientific writings of R. F. Kahn

1929, 'The Economics of the Short Period', fellowship dissertation, submitted to King's College, Cambridge, in December 1929; published, with the addition of thirteen-page Acknowledgements, by

Macmillan, London, 1989; also published in Italian by Boringhieri, Torino, 1983, with an introduction by Marco Dardi.

1931, 'The Relation of Home Investment to Unemployment', *Economic Journal*, vol. 41, pp. 173–198; reprinted in Kahn 1972.

1932a, 'The Financing of Public Works: A Note', *Economic Journal*, vol. 42, pp. 492–495.

1932b, 'Decreasing Costs: a Note on the Contributions of Mr Harrod and Mr Allen', *Economic Journal*, vol. 42, pp. 657–661.

1933a, 'Public Works and Inflation', *Journal of the American Statistical Association*, Supplement, Papers and Proceedings, pp. 168–173; reprinted in Kahn (1972).

1933b, 'The Elasticity of Substitution and Relative Share of a Factor', *Review of Economic Studies*, vol. 1, pp. 72–78.

1935a, 'Some Notes on Ideal Output', *Economic Journal*, vol. 45, pp. 1–35.

1935b, 'Two Applications of the Concept of Elasticity of Substitution', *Economic Journal*, vol. 45, pp. 242–245.

1936a, 'Dr Neisser on Secondary Employment: a Note', *Review of Economics and Statistics*, vol. 18, pp. 144–147.

1936b, 'Mr Paine and Rationalisation: a Note', *Economica*, vol. 3, 327–329.

1936c, *Interest and Prices. A study of the Causes Regulating the Value of Money*. English translation of K. Wicksell, *Geldzins und Güterpreise*. London: Macmillan.

1937a, 'The Problem of Duopoly', *Economic Journal*, vol. 47, pp. 1–20.

1937b, 'The League of Nations Enquiry into the Trade Cycle' (a review article of Gottfried von Haberler's

Prosperity and Depression: A Theoretical Analysis of Cyclical Movements), Economic Journal, vol. 47, pp. 670–679.

1947, 'Tariffs and the Terms of Trade', *Review of Economic Studies,* vol. 15, pp. 14–19.

1948, 'The 1948 Budget: An Economist's Criticism', *The Listener,* 6 May, pp. 738–739.

1949a, 'Professor Meade on Planning', *Economic Journal,* vol. 59, pp. 1–16.

1949b, 'Our Economic Complacency', *The Listener,* 3 February, pp. 166–167 and 181.

1949c, 'A Possible Intra-European Payments Scheme', *Economica,* vol. 16, pp. 293–304.

1950a, 'The Dollar Shortage and Devaluation', *Economia Internazionale,* vol. 5, pp. 89–113; reprinted in Kahn (1972).

1950b, 'The European Payments Union', *Economica,* vol. 17, pp. 306–316.

1951a, 'Home and Export Trade', *Economic Journal,* vol. 62, pp. 279–289.

1951b, 'The Balance of Payments and the Sterling Area', *District Bank Review,* vol. 100, pp. 3–17.

1952a, 'Oxford Studies in the Price Mechanism', *Economic Journal,* vol. 62, pp. 119–130.

1952b, 'Britain's Economic Position 1952', *The Listener,* 3 July, pp. 18–22.

1952c, 'Monetary Policy and the Balance of Payments', *Political Quarterly,* vol. 23 (July–September); reprinted in Kahn (1972).

1952d, 'International Regulation of Trade and Exchanges', *Banking and Foreign Trade* (5th International Banking Summer School, Oxford 1952). London, Institute of Bankers: Europa Publications.

1954a, 'Some Notes on Liquidity Preference', *Manchester School of Economic and Social Studies,* vol. 22, pp. 229–257; reprinted in Kahn (1972).

1954b (with D. G. Champernowne), 'The Value of Invested Capital; a Mathematical Addendum to Mrs. Robinson's article', *Review of Economic Studies*, vol. 21, pp. 107–111; reprinted in J. Robinson, *The Accumulation of Capital*, London: Macmillan, 1956.

1955, 'Short Term Business Indicators in Western Europe', *Economic Bulletin for Europe*, vol. 7, pp. 34–78.

1956a, 'Lord Keynes and Inflation', *The Listener*, 3 May, pp. 543–545.

1956b, 'Lord Keynes and the Balance of Payments', *The Listener*, 10 May, pp. 591–593; reprinted in Kahn (1972).

1956c, 'An Answer to the Capital Question', *Westminster Bank Review*, August, pp. 1–26.

1956d, 'Full Employment and British Economic Policy', *Nihon Keizai Shimbun;* reprinted in Kahn (1972).

1957a, 'Doubts about the Free Trade Area', *The Listener*, 28 February, pp. 331–333.

1957b, 'A Positive Contribution?', *Bulletin of the Oxford Institute of Statistics*, vol. 19, pp. 63–68.

1958, 'The Pace of Development', *The Challenge of Development*, The Eliezer Kaplan School of Economics, The Hebrew University; reprinted in Kahn (1972).

1959a, 'Exercises in the Analysis of Growth', *Oxford Economic Papers*, vol. 11, pp. 146–163; reprinted in Kahn (1972).

1959b, 'Sur l'analyse de la croissance', *L'accumulation du capital*, Colloques Economiques Franco-Britanniques sur l'Accumulation du Capital, Paris, pp. 51–69.

1960a, 'Memorandum of Evidence Submitted to the Radcliffe Committee (on 27 May 1958)', *Committee on the Working of the Monetary System, Principal*

Memoranda of Evidence, pp. 138–146, London: HMSO; reprinted in Kahn (1972).

1960b, 'Evidence Submitted to the Radcliffe Committee, Q. 10938–11024, (1958)', *Committee on the Working of the Monetary System, Minutes of Evidence*, pp. 739–746, London: HMSO.

1961, *The Problem of Rising Prices* (with contributions by W. Fellner, M. Gilbert, B. Hansen, R. Kahn, Friedrich Lutz, Pietar de Wolff), Paris: Organisation for Economic Cooperation and Development (OECD).

1964 (with R. Cohen, W. B. Reddaway, J. Robinson), 'Statements Submitted to the Committee on Resale Price Maintenance', *Bulletin of the Oxford Institute of Statistics*, vol. 26, pp. 113–121.

1965a, *International Monetary Issues and the Developing Countries* (report of the group of experts), New York: UNCTAD.

1965b, 'Un confronto fra la politica inglese e quella italiana', *Programmazione Economica: Confronti Italo-inglesi*, ed. G. Fuà, Urbino: Argalia Editore.

1966, *Payments Arrangements among the Developing Countries for Trade Expansion* (reports of a group of experts), New York: UNCTAD.

1969, *International Monetary Reform and Co-operation for Development* (reports of a group of experts), New York: UNCTAD.

1971, Notes on the Rate of Interest and the Growth of Firms (Kahn, 1972, pp. 208–232).

1972, *Selected Essays on Employment and Growth*, Cambridge: Cambridge University Press.

1973a, 'The International Monetary System', *American Economic Review*, vol. 63, Papers and Proceedings, pp. 181–188.

1973b, 'SDR and Aid', *Lloyds Bank Review*, vol. 110, pp. 1–18.

1974a, 'Plans for a Monetary System to Replace the Bretton Woods Agreement', *Problems of Balance of Payments and Trade*, N. S. Fatemi ed., New Jersey: Rutheford, pp. 199–226.

1974b, 'On Re-reading Keynes', *Proceedings of the British Academy*, vol. 60, pp. 361–392.

1974c (with M. V. Posner), 'Cambridge Economics and the Balance of Payments', *London and Cambridge Economic Bulletin*, vol. 85, pp. 19–30.

1974d (with M. V. Posner), 'The Effects of Public Expenditure on Inflation and the Balance of Payments', *Ninth Report from the Expenditure Committee: Public Expenditure, Inflation and the Balance of Payments*, London: HMSO.

1975, 'Oil and the Crisis', *IEA Occasional Papers*, vol. 43, pp. 34–38.

1976a, 'Thoughts on the Behaviour of Wages and Monetarism', *Lloyds Bank Review*, vol. 119 (January), pp. 1–11.

1976b, 'Inflation – A Keynesian View', *Scottish Journal of Political Economy*, vol. 23, pp. 11–16.

1976c, 'Political Attitudes Involved in Teaching Economics', *Oxford Review of Education*, vol. 2, pp. 91–95.

1976d, 'Unemployment as Seen by the Keynesians', *The Concept and Measurement of Involuntary Unemployment*, G. D. N. Worswick ed., London: Allen & Unwin, pp. 19–34.

1976e, 'Historical Origins of the International Monetary Fund', *Keynes and International Monetary Relations*, ed. A. P. Thirlwall, London: Macmillan, pp. 3–35.

1977a, 'Malinvaud on Keynes: Review Article', *Cambridge Journal of Economics*, vol. 1, pp. 375–388.

1977b, 'Mr. Eltis and the Keynesians', *Lloyds Bank Review*, vol. 124 (April), pp. 1–13.

1977c, 'A Comment', *Keynes Versus the 'Keynesians'*, T. W. Hutchison ed., London: Institute of Economic Affairs, pp. 48–57.

1977d (with M. V. Posner), 'Inflation, Unemployment and Growth', *National Westminster Bank Quarterly Review* (November), pp. 28–37.

1978, 'Some Aspects of the Development of Keynes's Thought', *Journal of Economic Literature*, vol. 16, pp. 544–559.

1984, *The Making of Keynes's General Theory* (The 'Raffaele Mattioli Lectures', delivered at Università Bocconi, Milan, 1978), Cambridge: Cambridge University Press.

1985, 'The Cambridge Circus', *Keynes and his Contemporaries*, G. C. Harcourt ed., London: Macmillan, pp. 42–51.

1987, 'Rostas L.' and 'Shove, G. F.', two entries in *The New Palgrave. A Dictionary of Economics*, J. Eatwell, M. Milgate and P. Newman eds., London: Macmillan, vol. 4, pp. 222–223 and 327–328.

1988, *Un discepolo di Keynes* (an interview), Maria Cristina Marcuzzo ed., Milan: Garzanti. English version: 'A Disciple of Keynes', *Department of Economics Discussion Paper*, no. 29, Modena: University of Modena.

Book reviews by R. F. Kahn

Gayer, A. D., *Public Works in Prosperity and Depression*, in *Economic Journal*, vol. 46 (September 1936), pp. 491–493.

Report of the Committee of Investigation for England on Complaints made by the Central Milk Distributive Committee and the Parliamentary Committee of the Co-operative Congress to the Operation of the

Milk Marketing Scheme, in *Economic Journal*, vol. 46 (September 1936), pp. 554–559.

Lundberg, E., *Studies in the Theory of Economic Expansion*, in *Economic Journal*, vol. 48 (June 1938), pp. 265–268.

Meade, J. E., *World Economic Survey. Seventh Year, 1937–8*, in *Economic Journal*, vol. 49 (March 1939), pp. 96–98.

Nourse, E. G. and Drury, H. B., *Industrial Price Policies and Economic Progress*, in *Economic Journal*, vol. 49 (June 1939), pp. 321–323.

Third Annual Report of the International Bank for Reconstruction and Development, in *Economic Journal*, vol. 59 (June 1949), pp. 445–447.

Final Report of the United Nations Economic Survey Mission for the Middle East, in *Economic Journal*, vol. 60 (September 1950), pp. 634–635.

Olhin, B., *The Problem of Employment Stabilisation*, in *American Economic Review*, vol. 42 (March 1952), pp. 180–182.

Hicks, J. R., *Economic Perspectives: Further Essays on Money and Growth*, in *Manchester School of Economic and Social Studies*, vol. 46 (March 1978), pp. 83–85.

Kahn's speeches at the House of Lords

1966, 'The Economic Situation', 28 July.

1966, 'The Prices and Incomes Policy', 3 August.

1967, 'European Economic Community', 8 May.

1968, 'The Economic Situation and Public Expenditure', 28 January.

1973, Economic and Industrial Affairs', 6 November.

1973, 'Counter-Inflation (Prices and Pay Code)', (2), 20 November.

1973, 'Economic Policy and Fuel Supplies', 18 December.

1974, 'Industrial and Economic Situation', 6 February.

1974, 'The Economic Position', 30 July.

1975, 'The Attack on Inflation', 30 July.

1977, 'The Economic Situation', 26 January.

Chapter IV

Joan Violet Robinson (1903–1983)
The woman who missed the Nobel Prize for Economics

Editorial note

This essay comes from 'Robinson, Joan Violet', an item of 'The New Palgrave Dictionary of Economics', edited by John Eatwell, Murray Milgate and Peter Newman, The Macmillan Press Ltd., London, vol. IV, 1987, pp. 212–217.

1. Foreword

Joan Robinson (née Maurice) was born at Camberley, Surrey, on 31 October 1903. She died in Cambridge on 5 August 1983.

She is the only woman (with the possible but controversial exception of Rosa Luxemburg) among the great economists. In 1975, which was proclaimed Woman's Year, most economists in the United States expected that she would naturally be chosen for the Nobel Memorial Prize in Economics for that year. She had received a triumphant acclaim, as a Special Ely Lecturer, at the American Economic Association annual meeting three years earlier, in spite of the harsh hostility that her theories had always met in the United States. The US magazine *Business Week*, after sounding out the American economics profession, felt so sure of the choice as to anticipate the event by publishing a long article, presenting her explicitly as being

Plate 2 Joan Robinson, in 1968. Reproduced by permission of
the Ramsay and Muspratt collection.

'on everyone's list for this year's Nobel Prize in Economics'.
But the Swedish Royal Academy missed that opportunity
(and, alas, never regained it). Ever since, in shoptalk among
economists, Joan Robinson has been the greatest Nobel Prize
winner that never was.

2.   Basic biography

Joan Robinson was the daughter of Major General Sir Frederick Maurice and of Helen Marsh (who was herself the daughter of a Professor of Surgery and Master of Downing College, Cambridge). Sir Frederick pursued a brilliant career in the British army, but in 1918 he found himself at the centre of a public debate and he gave up his army career on a point of principle. This was very much in the family tradition. Sir Frederick's grandfather – Joan Robinson's great-grandfather – was Frederick Denison Maurice, the Christian Socialist who lost his chair of theology at King's College, London, for his refusal to believe in eternal damnation.

Joan Robinson certainly had many of these traits: toughness and endurance of character, non-conformism and unorthodoxy of views, the absence of any reverential feeling or timidity, even in the face of the world's celebrities, a passionate longing for the new and the unknown.

She was educated at St Paul's Girls' School in London. (Curiously enough, Richard Kahn was educated in the boys' section of the same school.) In October 1922, she was admitted to the University of Cambridge, going up to Girton College, where she read economics at a time when the dominant figures in Cambridge were Marshall and Pigou. Marshall had retired (he died in 1924) but was extremely influential not only in Cambridge but in the whole of the British Isles. Pigou, his favourite pupil and chosen successor, was the Professor of Political Economy, at whose lectures Cambridge students absorbed the official *verbum* of Marshallian economics. Keynes was a sort of outsider, part-time in Cambridge and part-time in London, always involved with government policies, either at the Treasury or in public opposition. In those days he lectured on strictly orthodox monetary theory and policies. His lectures were not given regularly but were well attended.

The intellectual environment must have appeared solidly traditional. Joan graduated in 1925, as a good girl would: with second-class honours. The following year she married E. A. G. Robinson (later Professor Sir Austin Robinson), who was six years her senior and at the time a junior Fellow of Corpus Christi College. Together they left Cambridge and set off for India, where Austin Robinson served as tutor of the Maharajah of Gwalior. Joan was there as Austin's wife but did some teaching at the local school. When they returned, after their two-year Indian engagement, Austin Robinson took a permanent post as Lecturer in Economics at Cambridge, where they settled for life. They had two daughters.

It was on the return to Cambridge (summer 1928) that Joan Robinson began to do some college supervision of undergraduates, and then to do economics research in earnest. The Cambridge intellectual environment had changed dramatically. After Edgeworth's death (1926), Keynes had become the sole editor of the *Economic Journal* and was engaged on his *Treatise on Money* (Keynes, 1930a). Most of all, he had brought to Cambridge Piero Sraffa, the young Italian economist who had dared to launch a scathing attack on Marshallian economics (Sraffa, 1926). Moreover, some new stars were rising in the firmament of Keynes's entourage – Frank Ramsey, the brilliant mathematician; Ludwig Wittgenstein, the Austrian philosopher whom Keynes persuaded to come to Cambridge; and Richard Kahn, Keynes's favourite pupil. It was with Richard Kahn that Joan Robinson began an intense intellectual partnership that lasted for her whole life.

On a strictly academic level, Joan Robinson ascended the academic ladder slowly: junior assistant lecturer in 1931, full lecturer in 1937, reader in 1949. It was suggested in Cambridge that the fact that her husband was in the same faculty kept her back at all stages of her academic career. She became full professor only on Austin Robinson's retirement, in 1965.

Her association with the Cambridge colleges was more irregular. But she was, in succession, a Fellow of Girton College and of Newnham College. Yet whatever the formal position in the faculty or in the Cambridge colleges, she was for years one of the major attractions in Cambridge for many generations of undergraduates, not only in economics. In the postwar period, she was certainly the best-known member of the Cambridge Economics faculty abroad. An indefatigable traveller, she did not limit her foreign visits to universities; she also wanted to know local customs and local conditions of life, even far away from urban centres. Her strong constitution and temperamental toughness helped her enormously. A friend from Makerere University, who took her, when she was already in her seventies, on a month's travel in tribal Africa was amazed at how much she could endure in terms of living in most primitive conditions with raw food, lack of facilities and exposure to harsh tropical weather, day and night.

It would be impossible to list here all the places she visited or the talks, seminars and public lectures she gave all over the world. She rarely stayed in Cambridge during the summer or term vacations or during her sabbatical years, though punctually and punctiliously returning there on the eve of terms of her teaching. Asia was her favourite continent (especially India and China). But hundreds of students in North and South America, Australia, Africa and Europe also knew her at first hand.

In Cambridge she rarely missed her classes, lectures and seminars and she was a regular attendant of other people's seminars, especially visitors', never avoiding discussion and confrontation. Professor Pigou – a well-known misogynist – had included her in his category of 'honorary men'.

She was extremely popular with the students – a clear, brilliant, stimulating teacher. She was a person who inspired strong feelings – of love and hate. Her opponents were frightened by her and her friends really admired, almost worshipped, her. Her non-conformism in everyday life and even in her clothing (most of which she bought in India) was renowned.

She retired from her professorship in Cambridge on September 1971. On retirement she did not agree to continue lecturing in Cambridge. (Later on, in the late 1970s, she gave in partially, giving a course of lectures on 'the Cambridge tradition'.) But her writing and lecturing abroad, at the invitation of economics faculties and students all over the world, continued unabated.

When, in the late 1970s, King's College (Keynes's college) finally dropped the traditional anachronistic ban on women and became co-educational, Joan Robinson, upon enthusiastic and unanimous proposal by all economists of the college, became the first woman to be made an Honorary Fellow of King's College. (She had earlier become an Honorary Fellow of Girton College and of Newnham College.)

Towards the end of her life, she became very concerned and disappointed with the direction in which economic theory had turned and with the ease with which the younger economists could bend their elegant models to suit the new conservative moods and the selfish economic policies of politicians and governments. Her friends also noticed a sort of stiffening rigidity in her views that had not appeared before. This was unfortunate, as it contributed to increasing her opponents' hostility towards her and their accusations of intolerance.

She suffered a stroke in early February 1983, from which she never recovered. She lay for a few months in a Cambridge hospital and died peacefully six months later.

3. Distinctive traits of her intellectual personality

In order to understand better the nature of Joan Robinson's contributions to economic theory, it may be helpful to begin by considering explicitly a few characteristic traits of her intellectual personality.

Joan Robinson had a remarkable analytical ability. Since she did not normally use mathematics, this remarkable intellectual ability was of a nature that defies conventional description. In her early works she made use of geometrical representations, backed up by calculus (normally provided by Richard Kahn). In her mature works, her way of reasoning took up a more personal feature. Her style is difficult to imitate (as when she invites the readers to follow her in the construction of economic exercises) but very effective. The results are always impressive. Those who used to argue with her knew that she could grasp and keep in the back of her mind (to be brought out at the appropriate moment) a whole series of chain effects and interdependencies, which her interlocutors could hardly imagine.

She was not the type of person who could go on thinking in isolation. The way she could best express herself was by having somebody in constant confrontation. She could put her views best either in opposition or in support of somebody else's position. This made her extraordinarily open to concepts and contributions coming from the people she encountered. The accurate historian of economic ideas will probably find in her works traces of almost every person she met. It is therefore important, in considering Joan Robinson's contributions, to keep in mind at least the most important economists who influenced her. These include her teachers (Marshall through Pigou, Keynes, Shove), her contemporaries (Sraffa, Kaldor and Kalecki, whom she particularly admired and through whom she went back to Marx, but especially Richard Kahn, who read, criticised and improved every single one of her works) and also a whole series of other (younger) people – pupils and students.

This raises the question of her originality. The prefaces to her books are packed with acknowledgements, sometimes heavy acknowledgements – consider, for example, the following excerpt from the *Economics of Imperfect Competition*:

. . . this book contains some matter which I believe to be new. Of not all the new ideas, however, can I definitely say that 'this is my own invention'. I particularly have had the constant assistance of Mr R. F. Kahn . . . many of the major problems . . . were solved as much by him as by me. [1933, p. v]

But one must remember what has been said above. In fact, Joan Robinson was a highly original thinker, but of a particular type. Besides the contributions to economic theory that are distinctly hers, she had her own highly original way, even in small details, of presenting other authors' views, which she always did through a distinctly personal re-elaboration. Sometimes the re-elaboration is so personal as to sound parochial. But this trait is not exclusive to Joan Robinson. Cambridge parochialism is shared by almost all purely Cambridge-bred economists since Marshall (Keynes included). It sometimes creates unnecessary difficulties of communication with economists outside Cambridge (i.e. with the overwhelming majority!) or introduces a few odd notes into an otherwise impeccable performance.

One can clearly detect an evolution in Joan Robinson's approach to economics that with age strengthened her innovative tendencies. It looks as if she was very cautious in her early years, preoccupied at first with building up solid analytical foundations. But as soon as she felt sure of her analytical equipment, she began to venture more and more into the exciting field of innovation. In her mature works her typical style became established. A sort of mixture of educational, temperamental and intellectual factors made her one of the leading unorthodox economists of the twentieth century. Always impatient with dogmas, constantly fighting for new unorthodox ideas, relentlessly attacking established beliefs, she acquired a sort of vocation to economic heresies [see 1971]. Her attitude reminds one of a dictum by Pietro Pomponazzi, the Italian Renaissance philosopher: 'It pays to be a heretic if one wishes to find the truth.'

Strongly related to this attitude is the social message that comes from her writings. Her 'box of tools' and her logical chain of arguments were not proposed for their own sake; they were always aimed at practical action, with a view to the world's most pressing problems – unemployment before the war, underdevelopment and the struggle of ex-colonial nations after the war (very noticeable is her special concern for Asia and her enthusiasm, at points rather naïve and misplaced, for Communist China). Consistently, she has been among the strongest assertors – second perhaps only to Gunnar Myrdal – of the non-neutrality of economic science and of the necessity of stating explicitly one's convictions and beliefs.

And yet, in spite of her bold attacks and her satirical mood, her literary style is surprisingly feminine – rich with fable-like parables, with down-to-earth examples from everyday life ('the price of a cup of tea . . .') and with similes from scenes and examples taken from nature (the *Accumulation of Capital* begins with the parable of the economic life of the robin). Her sparkling prose and her entertaining asides make Joan Robinson a most brilliant writer among economists and certainly one of the most enjoyable and delightful to read.

4.   Her scientific achievements

Joan Robinson wrote numerous books and an enormous number of articles, most of which have been collected in her *Collected Economic Papers* [1951–79].

They fall neatly into three broad groups, corresponding to the three basic phases of her intellectual development. A first group belongs to the phase of her by now classic *Economics of Imperfect Competition* [1933]. A second group belongs to the phase of explanation, propagation and defence of Keynes's *General Theory*. Finally, a third group of writings grew around the major work of her maturity, *The Accumulation of Capital* [1956]. Other books and articles have originated from miscellaneous or wider interests or from the desire to provide students with economics exercises or with a non-orthodox economics textbook [Robinson and Eatwell, 1973c]. Altogether, they make an impressive list. Even neglecting her articles (most of which are reprinted in the books), her bibliography contains no less than twenty-four books.

The most widely known of Joan Robinson's works is still the first, *The Economics of Imperfect Competition* [1933]. It was the book of her youth, which placed her immediately in the forefront of the development of economic theory. It is a work conceived in Cambridge, at the end of a decade characterised by intense controversy on cost curves and the laws of returns (see Sraffa 1926 and the symposium on the 'laws of returns' by Robertson, Sraffa and Shove, 1930). With this controversy in the background, Joan Robinson's book emerges in 1933 as a masterpiece in the traditional sense of the word. The restrictive conditions of perfect competition on which Marshall's theory was constructed are abandoned, and perfect competition is shown to be a very special case of what in general is a monopolistic situation. A whole new analysis of market behaviour is carried out on new, more general assumptions; yet the whole method of analysis, the whole approach – though refined and perfected – is still the traditional Marshallian one. Sraffa's criticism of the master is accepted, but is incorporated into the traditional fold by a generalisation of Marshall's own theoretical framework. The outcome is extremely elegant and impressive. The whole matter of market competition is clarified. Marshall's ambiguities are eliminated, the various market conditions are rigorously defined, a whole technical apparatus (a 'box of analytical tools') is developed to deal with the market situation in the general case (from demand and supply curves to marginal cost and marginal revenue curves). In a sense, therefore, rather than a radical critique, *The Economics of Imperfect Competition* might well be regarded as the completion and coronation of Marshallian analysis. This may help to explain why Joan Robinson herself came to like that book less and less, as her thought later developed along different lines. In 1969 she came to the point of writing a harsh eight-page criticism of it. Very courageously she published it, on the occasion of a reprint of the book, as a Preface to the second edition!

The book had appeared almost simultaneously with the *Theory of Monopolistic Competition* by Edward Chamberlin (1933) and the two books are normally bracketed together as indicating a decisive break-away of economic theory from the assumptions of perfect competition. Chamberlin always complained about this association. For although the two books represent the simultaneous discovery of basically the same thing, made quite independently by two different authors, they are in fact substantively different.

It may also be added that, looked at in retrospect, these two books do not appear so conclusive a contribution to the theory of the firm as they appeared in the 1930s. The behaviour of firms in oligopolistic markets and the policies of the large corporations have turned out to require more complicated analysis. At the same time, the assumption of perfect competition, far from being completely dead, has recently come back in different guises in the works of many theoretical economists. Yet there is no doubt that the two books remain there to represent a definite turning point in the development of the theory of the firm – so much so as to be referred to as representing the 'monopolistic competition revolution' (Samuelson, 1967). Very characteristically, Edward Chamberlin, after writing his *Theory of Monopolistic Competition*, spent the whole of his life in refining, completing and adding appendices to his masterpiece (which reached no less than eight editions). For Joan Robinson, the *Economics of Imperfect Competition* was only the first step on a very long way to a series of works in quite different and varied fields of economic theory.

It should be added that the *Economics of Imperfect Competition* was not Joan Robinson's only contribution to microeconomic theory in the 1930s. Her name appears again and again on the pages of the *avant-garde* economic journals of the time. From among her papers, an explicit mention must be made at least of her remarkably lucid article on 'rising supply price' and of her contribution to clarifying the meaning of Euler's theorem as applied to marginal productivities, in the traditional theory of production [see her *Collected Economic Papers*, vol. I, 1951].

But something of extraordinary importance was happening in Cambridge in the 1930s. Keynes was in the process of producing his revolutionary work (Keynes, 1936a). Joan Robinson abandoned the theory of the firm and threw herself selflessly and entirely into the new paths opened up by him. This was a really brave decision, if one thinks that her first book had gained her a great reputation in the economic profession. Very rarely do we find someone who, after striking success and becoming a leading figure in a certain field, pulls out of it and puts him or herself into the shadow of someone else, be this someone else even of the stature of Keynes. Joan Robinson did precisely that. She was one of the members – actually an important member, as is revealed by the recent publication of her correspondence with Keynes (see Keynes 1973a, 1979) – of that group of young economists known as the Cambridge Circus (and including Kahn, Sraffa, Harrod, Meade, besides Austin and Joan Robinson) who regularly met for discussion and played a crucial role in the evolving drafts of Keynes's *General Theory*.

It must be said that the new Keynes's ways were more congenial to her temperament. They were a break with tradition and this suited her non-conformist attitude; they dealt with the deep social problems of unemployment and this appealed to her social conscience. It is in this vein that she published her *Essays in the Theory of Employment* [1937a] and her *Introduction to the Theory of Employment* [1937b]. These twin books were simply meant to be a help to the readers of Keynes's *General Theory*. In fact, they turned out to be much more than that. In particular, Joan Robinson contributes to the clarification of a major piece of Keynesian theory – the process through which investments determine savings – which had remained rather obscure from *The General Theory*. For her, this appeared important because it broke a crucial link in traditional theory, which presented the rate of interest as a compensation for the 'sacrifice' of supplying capital (i.e. for saving). Joan Robinson stressed the role of investment as an independent variable, while total saving is shown as being determined passively by investment through the operation of the multiplier, the conclusion being that the rate of interest cannot be remunerating anybody's 'sacrifice'. Even more so in depression times, when thrift – a 'private virtue' – becomes a 'public vice'. Other concepts, introduced by Joan Robinson at the time, that were to remain permanently in the following economic literature on the theory of employment are those concerning what she called 'beggar-my-neighbour' policies, 'disguised unemployment' and the generalisation of the Marshall/Lerner conditions on international trade, in terms of 'the four elasticities'.

Towards the end of the 1930s, Joan Robinson met Kalecki and discovered that quite independently of, and in fact earlier than, Keynes, he had come to the same conclusions. Kalecki had started from a Marxist background, against which Keynes was prejudiced. This led her to rereading Marx and to rethinking her own position *vis-à-vis* Marxian theory [1942].

Joan Robinson's flirtation with Marx is very curious. It has all the charm of a meeting and all the clamour of a clash. She is no doubt attracted by Marx's general conception of society. She finds in Marx much which she approves of. But she finds his scientific nucleus embedded in, and in need of being liberated from, ideology. To obtain this, she says, one must work hard. Her writings on Marx are specifically aimed at 'separating the wheat of science from the chaff of ideology'. Needless to say, this has caused her a lot of trouble with the Marxists. It should be kept in mind that in continental Europe, discussions on Marx have a long and complex tradition of philological heaviness and ideological passion. Joan Robinson's discussion is short and simple. She is always looking at Marx as 'a serious economist'. Accordingly, she always tries to go straight to what she thinks is his economic analysis. Her insistence on the necessity of rescuing Marx, as a scholar and a first-rate analytical mind, has recently been vindicated, especially after the publication of Sraffa's book (1960; see also, for example, Samuelson 1971).

But the postwar period was opening up new vistas. With Keynes's *General Theory* in the background, Joan Robinson saw a formidable task ahead, consisting of nothing less than a reconstruction of economic theory. This led, after a decade of intense work, to the publication of her second major contribution to economic theory, *The Accumulation of Capital* [1956], the work of her maturity and the one that expresses Joan Robinson's genius at her best. Here she has chosen to move on new and controversial ground. While in her first book the direction – once established – was clear and she had to fill in the details, here the direction itself is not entirely clear and has to be continually adjusted. The details acquire less importance and may well be abandoned altogether and replaced with others at a second attempt. As a consequence, a lot of rewriting had to be done.

The Rate of Interest and Other Essays [1952], with its central essay devoted to a 'Generalisation of the *General Theory*', turned out to be a sort of preparation. *The Accumulation of Capital* represents the central nucleus of what she perceived as a new framework for economic theory. Then *Exercises in Economic Analysis* [1960b], *Essays in the Theory of Economic Growth* [1962a] and a series of other articles fill in the gaps, clarify obscurities and take the arguments further.

The 'Generalisation of the *General Theory*' represents Joan Robinson's response to an interchange with Harrod, following Harrod's *Towards a Dynamic Economics* (1948) and also his earlier review of her *Essays in the Theory of Employment*

[1937a]. Joan Robinson breaks away from the limitations of the short run, but has not yet defined clearly her direction. Yet once the process of 'generalisation', i.e. 'dynamisation', of *The General Theory* is started, the author is compelled to recast the Keynesian arguments in terms of the more fundamental categories of capital accumulation, labour supply, technical progress and natural resources. Through this recasting, it became inevitable that she should go to the earlier methodological approach (common to Ricardo and Marx) of stating the problems in terms of social aggregates. The evidence of her intense searching may be found at the end of the book in a chapter of acknowledgements and disclaimers where she describes in succession the way she has been influenced by, or has reacted to, Marx, Marshall, Rosa Luxemburg, Kalecki and Harrod.

The years of transition from *The Rate of Interest and Other Essays* [1952] to *The Accumulation of Capital* [1956] had been marked by a series of intense discussions in Cambridge, especially with Kahn, Sraffa, Kaldor and Champernowne. In the end, Joan Robinson emerged centring her attention on the problem of capital accumulation as the basic process in the development of a capitalist economy. She began with a scathing attack on the traditional concept of 'production function' (in a well-known article, now in her *Collected Economic Papers*, vol. II, 1960a, which elicited a chain of angry responses: see, for example, Solow, 1955–56, and Swan, 1956). Then she patiently proceeded to a reconstruction. A crucial step was her own way of rediscovering the Swedish economist Knut Wicksell.

The Accumulation of Capital [1956] bears the same title as Rosa Luxemburg's book, to whose translation into English Joan Robinson wrote an introduction (Luxemburg, 1951). This was a great tribute to another woman economist. But we should not be misled. Joan Robinson's book belongs to an entirely different age and takes an entirely different approach. Set into a Keynesian framework extended to the long run, it takes its origin from a welding together of Harrod's economic dynamics and of Wicksell's capital theory. The main question Joan Robinson poses to herself is by now a typically classical one: what are the conditions for the achievement of a cumulative long-term steady growth of income and capital (what she characteristically christened a 'golden age'); and what is the outcome of this process, in terms of growth of gross and net output and of the distribution of income between wages and profits, given a certain evolution through time of the labour force and the technology? To answer these questions Joan Robinson builds up a two-sector dynamic model with a finite number of techniques and goes on to show the interactions of the relations between wages and profits, the stock of capital and the techniques of production, entrepreneurial expectations and the degree of competition in the economy, bringing in the effects of higher degrees of mechanisation and both 'neutral' and 'biased' technical progress. The basic model and the basic answers are all worked out very quickly in the book. The rest is then devoted to relaxing the simplifying assumptions. The whole analysis is carried out *without* the use of mathematics. This is remarkable. Joan Robinson squeezes out of the model, one by one, all the answers that are needed. The non-use of mathematics has certain obvious disadvantages. Though the analysis need not necessarily be any less rigorous, in many passages it is not so easy to follow. It has, however, some advantages, which Joan Robinson is very ready and able to exploit. She succeeds, for example, in freeing herself from the symmetry that a mathematically formulated model normally imposes. In Joan Robinson's model, certain results are always more likely to happen than their symmetrical counterpart. Symmetry and formal elegance play no part; only relevance does, or at least it does in the way perceived by the author.

The overall result is, again, impressive. The oversimplified dynamic model of Harrod is enormously enriched by the introduction of the choice among a finite number of alternative techniques. At the same time the Wicksellian analysis of accumulation at a given technology is completed by the new analysis of a constant flow of inventions of various types. And this marriage of Harrod's model to Wicksellian analysis is made to fructify in a number of directions. So many and so rich are in fact these directions that Joan Robinson herself did not pursue all of them, as became evident from the abundant literature that followed.

To this literature, Joan Robinson contributed a whole series of essays and books [see 1960b, 1962a and her *Collected Economic Papers*, II, III, IV, V, i.e. 1960a, 1965, 1973a, 1979a), which represent clarifications and further elaborations. They also represent her way of recasting and adjusting her arguments in response to opposition from her critics and to comments, remarks and stimuli of any sort from her friends, as well as her way of coming to grips with results – not always or not entirely compatible with hers – from the works of other scholars, colleagues and pupils, who were broadly working on similar problems and with the same aims.

Meanwhile, proceeding on parallel lines, many other separate strands of thinking were emerging from her remarkable intellectual activity. At least a few must briefly be mentioned.

First, a whole series of concepts and ideas was coming to fruition, which – though not belonging to her major fields of interest – came to complete her overall coverage of economic theory: writings on the theory of international trade (including her professorial inaugural lecture at Cambridge, *The New Mercantilism*, 1966a), on Marxian economics (at various stages in her career) and on the theory of economic development and planning, reproducing her lectures delivered during her world travels or coming from calm reflection once she had returned home (see her *Collected Economic Papers* [1951–1979a] and also 1970b and 1979b.

Second, her deeply felt concern with economics students and economics teaching in general gave origin to books, such

as 1966b, 1971 and especially 1973c, with Eatwell, which
contributed to giving substance to, and disseminating all
over the world, her strongly felt convictions that an overall
approach to economic reality, alternative to that of traditional
economics, does exist and is viable.

Third, the ideas, reflections, rationalisations, accumulated
in the course of her life took the form of books such as
Economic Philosophy [1962b] and *Freedom and Necessity*
[1970a], which were concerned with wider issues than economics itself, attempting to give an overall conception of the
world and a whole philosophy of life. These writings contribute, not marginally, to place Joan Robinson among the
influential thinkers of this century. At the same time, they
may well be enjoyed, by the general reader, even more than
her masterpieces. From a purely literary point of view, they
make delightful reading.

It should be added that there are, moreover, many themes
which, while not being exclusively connected with any specific work of Joan Robinson's, recur time and again in her
writings, so as to have become characteristically associated
with her approach. Here are a few:

a) the concept of 'entrepreneurs' animal spirits' – an
    expression picked up from Keynes and developed as an
    important element contributing to explain investment
    in capitalist economies;

b) the conviction that Marshall's notions of prices and rate
    of profit, with reference to industry, are much more akin
    to Ricardo's notions than to Walras's;

c) a sharp distinction between 'logical' time and 'histori-
    cal' time, both of which have a place in economic anal-
    ysis but with different roles. On this point Joan Robin-
    son's characterisation of the evolution of an economy
    in historical time, as concerning decisions to be taken
    between 'an irrevocable past and an uncertain future',
    is well known;

d)   an equally sharp distinction between comparisons of
      equilibrium-growth positions and *movements* from one
      equilibrium-growth position to another, in dynamic
      analysis;

e)   a tendency, especially in the later part of her life, to
      shift nearer to the position of Kalecki, as opposed to
      that of Keynes, in interpreting the overall working of
      the institutions of capitalist economies, especially with
      reference to what she found as a more satisfactory inte-
      gration, in Kalecki, of the concept of effective demand
      with the process of price formation.

Finally, one must mention specifically an issue which may
well continue to give rise to controversial evaluations. This
concerns the role that may be assigned to Joan Robinson in
the well-known controversy on capital theory that flared up
between the two Cambridges in the 1960s (see Pasinetti *et al.*,
1966). One view on this issue is that Joan Robinson had the
merit of anticipating the controversy by means of her (already
mentioned) attacks on the neoclassical production function
in the mid-1950s (see Harcourt, 1972). Another view is that
Joan Robinson, herself a victim of her emotional temperament, started her attacks on the traditional concepts too early
and misplaced the whole criticism, by neglecting the really
basic point (the phenomenon of reswitching of techniques;
see Sraffa, 1960) that in the end delivered the fatal blow to the
neoclassical notion of production function. What one can say
for certain is that a hint at the reswitching phenomenon does
appear in *The Accumulation of Capital* (on p. 109), but is rel-
egated to the role of a curiosum (the so-called *Ruth Cohen
curiosum*), in an entirely secondary section. Perhaps the
phenomenon had been pointed out to her, but she grossly
underestimated its importance. What is curious is that she
continued to underestimate it, even after it was brought to the
foreground (see her 'Unimportance of Re-switching' in *Collected Economic Papers*, V [1979a]. See also Pasinetti, 1996).

But at this point the works of Joan Robinson merge into those of that remarkable group of Cambridge economists – notably, Piero Sraffa, Nicholas Kaldor and Richard Kahn, among others, besides Joan Robinson herself (on this, see the Preface to Pasinetti, 1981) – who happened to be concentrated in Cambridge in the postwar period and who took up, continued and expanded the challenge that Keynes had launched on orthodox economic theory. This remarkable group of economists started a stream of economic thought which is obviously far from complete. Its basic features, however, are clear enough; they embody a determined effort to shift the whole focus of economic theorising away from the problems of optimum allocation of given resources, where it had remained for almost a century, and move it towards the fundamental factors responsible for the dynamics of industrial societies. This shift of focus inevitably brings into the foreground the once-central themes of capital accumulation, population growth, production expansion and income distribution, while at the same time opening up the investigations towards technical progress and structural change.

It is perhaps too early to try to evaluate the relative role played by Joan Robinson as a member of this remarkable group of economists. The single components of the group have made contributions which are sometimes complementary, at other times overlapping, and at yet other times even partly in contradiction. To mention only one major problem, Piero Sraffa's book appeared too late for Joan Robinson to be able to incorporate it into her theoretical framework, and the brave efforts she later made to this effect are not always convincing. They actually reveal here and there a sort of ambivalent attitude. At the same time, her *Accumulation of Capital* ventures into fields of economic dynamics which Sraffa does not touch at all. Quite obviously, the common fundamental thrust behind post-Keynesian analysis does not presuppose complete identity of views or complete harmony of approach.

Future developments will clarify issues and will reveal which of the lines of approach proposed are the most useful, fruitful or fecund. There can be little doubt, however, that if this theoretical movement is going to prove successful, quite a lot of rewriting will have to be done in economic theory. If, and when, this rewriting were to occur, Joan Robinson's contributions are going to come back into a major place.

5.   Selected works of Joan Robinson

1933, *The Economics of Imperfect Competition*, London: Macmillan, 2nd edition, 1969.

1937a, *Essays in the Theory of Employment*, London: Macmillan.

1937b, *Introduction to the Theory of Employment*, London: Macmillan.

1942, *An Essay on Marxian Economics*, London: Macmillan.

1951, *Collected Economic Papers*, vol. I, Oxford: Basil Blackwell (vol. II, 1960a; vol. III, 1965; vol. IV, 1973a; vol. V, 1979a).

1952, *The Rate of Interest and Other Essays*, London: Macmillan.

1956, *The Accumulation of Capital*, London: Macmillan.

1960a, *Collected Economic Papers*, vol. II, Oxford: Basil Blackwell.

1960b, *Exercises in Economic Analysis*, London: Macmillan.

1962a, *Essays in the Theory of Economic Growth*, London: Macmillan.

1962b, *Economic Philosophy*, London: C. A. Watts.

1965, *Collected Economic Papers*, vol. III, Oxford: Basil Blackwell.

1966a, *The New Mercantilism – an Inaugural Lecture*, Cambridge: Cambridge University Press.

1966b, *Economics – an Awkward Corner*, London: Allen & Unwin.

1970a, *Freedom and Necessity*, London: Allen & Unwin.

1970b, *The Cultural Revolution in China*, London: Penguin Books.

1971, *Economic Heresies: Some Old-fashioned Questions in Economic Theory*, London: Macmillan.

1973a, *Collected Economic Papers*, vol. IV, Oxford: Basil Blackwell.

1973b (ed.), *After Keynes*, papers presented to Section F (economics) of the 1972 annual meeting of the British Association for Advancement of Science, Oxford: Basil Blackwell.

1973c (with John Eatwell), *An Introduction to Modern Economics*, New York: McGraw-Hill.

1978, *Contributions to Modern Economics*, Oxford: Basil Blackwell.

1979a, *Collected Economic Papers*, vol. V, Oxford: Basil Blackwell.

1979b, *Aspects of Development and Underdevelopment*, Cambridge: Cambridge University Press.

1980, *Further Contributions to Modern Economics*, Oxford: Basil Blackwell.

Chapter V

Nicholas Kaldor (1908–1986)
Growth, income distribution, technical progress

Editorial note

This paper is a synthesis of two pieces: 'Kaldor, Nicholas', in vol. 18, Biographical Supplement, 'International Encyclopedia of the Social Sciences', New York: The Free Press and London: Collier Macmillan Publishers, 1979, pp. 366–369; and 'Nicholas Kaldor', an introduction to: Nicholas Kaldor, Economia senza equilibrio (Italian version of Kaldor's Yale Lectures), Bologna: Il Mulino, 1985 (pp. 9–21). A few rearrangements and completions have been added.

1. The man

Nicholas Kaldor was one of the most provocative and original economic thinkers of the twentieth century. He belonged to that remarkable group of Central European intellectuals who, for various reasons, emigrated from their countries of origin during the inter-war period and came to enrich and strengthen the intellectual standing of Anglo-Saxon universities. Kaldor settled in England, first at the London School of Economics and then at the University of Cambridge.

His relations with United States universities may appear a curious one. He visited the United States on many occasions. He was a Rockefeller Travelling Fellow in 1935–36, and then a Visiting Research Professor at Berkeley (University of California) in 1960–61. He also gave innumerable lectures on various other occasions and in various places. Yet in the United States, Kaldor has never been a popular figure. He had of course many friends, but he hardly had real admirers, in either academic or government circles. During the whole of his career, Kaldor was a prominent adviser, on matters of taxation, fiscal and monetary policy and economic development, to a surprisingly high number of governments (India, Ceylon, Turkey, Iran, Ghana, British Guyana, Mexico, Venezuela), to many central banks, to the Economic Commission for Europe, and to the Economic Commission for Latin America. In Great Britain he held the position of *Special Adviser* to the Chancellor of the Exchequer of the Labour Governments in 1964–68 and in 1974–76. But in the United States, he was never asked for advice by any official institution, whether progressive or conservative, at any time. The only involvement he had with a US government agency was in 1945, immediately after World War Two, but in Europe, when he worked as Chief of the Economic Planning Staff for the US Strategic Bombing Survey of Europe.

All this has its logic. Most American economists are prepared to accept almost infinite variations on the theme of Walrasian general equilibrium analysis and of models of optimum allocation of *given* resources. They may also be prepared to tolerate, by contrast, analyses on the theme of Marxian theories of value and exploitation. Nicholas Kaldor has been a staunch opponent of both. He was indeed a radical thinker, but within the framework of established market institutions. And this is what has always appeared so irritating to many of his colleagues, especially American. He was a passionate advocate of reforms, but not a revolutionary. His overall view of the working of a market economy was basically an optimistic one – not however in the traditional sense of believing that the market, and even less a policy of *laissez-faire*, will automatically bring about the best of all situations. He was however extraordinarily open to paying

Plate 3 Nicholas Kaldor, in 1975. Reproduced by permission of
Professor Frances Stewart.

attention to criticisms and was ready to change his mind, if
it was convincingly shown to him that he was wrong.

As a research student, I happened to arrive in Cambridge
in October 1956, the year of publication of Kaldor's theory
of income distribution and of Joan Robinson's *Accumulation of Capital.* The sense of achievement that one could
feel in the on-going debates is difficult to describe, and the
intellectual stimulation for the students was really exceptional. I also had the experience, after interludes at Harvard and at Oxford, of becoming a Fellow of King's College
in 1961, the year that followed the publication of Sraffa's
book. I dared, while being the youngest member, to present
the results of my work on income distribution (Pasinetti,
1962) to a session of the so-called 'Secret Seminar' in King's

College (a post-war version of Keynes's more famous *Circus*) – a unique experience for me. I presented my results as a *criticism* of Kaldor's theory. The members of the audience were stunned, or suspicious, or disbelieving, with one exception: Nicky Kaldor. He was extraordinarily quick in grasping the gist of the idea and in seeing that the concession of his having fallen into a 'logical slip' led to a generalisation of the post-Keynesian (in fact of Kaldor's) theory of income distribution and moreover to a new, long-run, Keynesian theory of the rate of profits. Nicky Kaldor was always extremely generous to those who succeeded in convincing him to change his mind.

2. Basic biography

Nicholas Kaldor was born in Budapest, the son of a barrister, on 12 May 1908. His parents, Dr Julius and Joan Kaldor, must have been expecting the child with some trepidation. They had only one daughter; two elder sons had died in infancy. When Nicholas arrived, there can be no doubt of the happiness he brought to his parents and of the attention and affection he received in return: all this in a rather well-off Jewish family, in one of the major capitals of Central European culture.

The deep mark of this privileged childhood remained in Kaldor's attitude and demeanour for the whole of his life. It may help, to a certain extent, to explain his exuberant, egocentric, undisciplined character.

In Budapest, from 1918 to 1924, he attended a famous 'Model Gymnasium' – a school for the *élite*. Incidentally this was the same school which John von Neumann had attended a few years earlier. But Kaldor did not meet him until later, in the 1930s, in Budapest, when both, as *emigrés*, were coming back to visit their respective families. They became friendly, and Kaldor came to know von Neumann's paper on a growing economic system. It was in fact Kaldor who, immediately after the war, as editor of the *Review of Economic Studies*, had von Neumann's article translated into English and published in the *Review*.

In 1925–26, Kaldor attended lectures at the University of Berlin but soon moved to London, where, in 1927–30, he was an undergraduate at the London School of Economics. He graduated with First Class Honours in 1930. He has always mentioned, as teachers who influenced him deeply, Lionel Robbins, Friedrich von Hayek and most of all Allyn Young, an American professor who had come to LSE from Harvard University. Among his contemporaries at LSE he was friendly with John Hicks, Erwin Rothbarth and Tibor Scitovsky. He was appointed an assistant lecturer at LSE in 1932. In subsequent years, he became a lecturer and then a reader in economics.

In 1934 Nicholas Kaldor married Clarissa Goldschmidt, a charming girl (and a charming woman, for the whole of her life up to her death in 1994) who had brilliantly graduated in history at Sommerville College, Oxford. She gave up a career of her own to give him four daughters and a remarkably happy family life.

During the war, the whole of LSE (and the Kaldors) moved to Cambridge. But after the war, while the LSE staff and students returned to London, Kaldor went to Geneva for two years as a director of research at the Economic Commission for Europe. On his return to academic life, in 1949, he joined the Economics Faculty of Cambridge University. He was appointed a Fellow of King's College (Keynes's own college) and then a reader in economics at the University of Cambridge and subsequently a professor in 1966. In 1974, in recognition of his services to the British government, he was elevated to the House of Lords as a life peer and took the name Baron Kaldor of Newnham in the City of Cambridge. He retired from teaching in 1975, but he continued his academic (and political) activity without interruption for many years until the end of his life.

Kaldor also continued to play his renowned role of host for visitors and friends in his large house at 2, Adams Road, Cambridge. Weekends were always eventful at the Kaldors, especially during those parts of the year (late spring and early autumn) when the Cambridge weather becomes shining and provides insistent invitation to go out in the marvellously green and colourful gardens. At tea time at the Kaldors, one could meet Joan Robinson, Kahn, Sraffa, who were separately dropping in at the end of their Sunday outings, mixing with the family. One could meet the latest arrivals among the King's brightest economics students; one could unexpectedly find remarkable visitors: friends from Scotland or Hungary, but also eminent figures, in the economic, political or literary circles, from the most remote parts of our little world.

Typically, Nicholas Kaldor was working on a lecture, which was meant to be given a few days later abroad, when he was taken, fatally ill, to a Cambridge hospital. He died on Tuesday 30 September 1986.

3.   Kaldor's major contributions to economics

A distinct mark of Kaldor's contributions to economic theory and practice is to be found in the striking originality of his approach and in the persistent evolution of his way of thinking.

His early contributions – while he was at the London School of Economics – were within the strict orthodoxy of marginal economic theory. They concerned the problems under discussion at the time – notably the theories of imperfect and monopolistic competition, and welfare economics. They immediately revealed his originality. It was Kaldor [1934] who gave the name 'cobweb theorem' to the, by now well-known, theorem concerning the conditions of market stability in terms of relative elasticities of demand and supply. Later [1939a], he proposed a 'compensation of the loser's test' in the hypothetical event of personal income redistribution. It has since become known as 'Kaldor's compensation test' in the literature on welfare economics. He is also the author of a well-known survey of capital theory published in *Econometrica* [1937].

But for Kaldor, as for so many economists of his generation, the crucial turning point came with the publication in 1936 of Keynes's *General Theory*. Kaldor was twenty-eight – and yet an already established economist in the tradition which Keynes put under strong attack. He was deeply struck. One noticed in him, at first, a change of interests, mainly from micro- to macroeconomic problems, and then a complete and radical change of his whole way of thinking about economic theory and about the practical role of an economist. Around 1939 he wrote a series of articles on macroeconomic problems, the most remarkable of which is 'A Model of the Trade Cycle' [1940], which relies on non-linear investment and savings functions to produce 'limit cycles'. Another important article of his, in this period, is on financial instability [1939b].

Later, the break with tradition became wider, and then final. It coincided with his moving from London to the University of Cambridge.

At Cambridge, Kaldor did most of his mature work and finally emerged as one of the major authors – with Richard Kahn, Joan Robinson and Piero Sraffa – of what is here called the Cambridge School of Keynesian Economic Theory. Kaldor's original contributions to this theory are numerous. They are contained in a long series of polemical papers, among which there are three different versions of a model of economic growth [1957, 1961, 1962]. His major original contribution, however, is given in a few pages at the end of an article [1956], where he proposes a 'Keynesian' theory of income distribution. The theory is in fact distinctly Kaldor's, and so it has (rightly) been called since.

Kaldor's theory of income distribution is based on the idea that profit recipients have a much higher propensity to save than wage earners. Therefore, in an economic system in which entrepreneurs carry out those investments that correspond to full employment, there exists a distribution of income between profits and wages which, owing to the differentiated propensities to save, will generate precisely that share of profits in national income that is necessary to sustain the pre-determined investments. In this way, Kaldor uses Keynes's concepts of saving propensities and inserts them into a macroeconomic theoretical conception of income distribution, which is reminiscent of Ricardo's. But Kaldor reverses Ricardo's causation chain. In Ricardo, wages were the exogenous magnitude (determined by the sheer necessity of workers' subsistence) and profits emerged as a residual, or rather as a 'surplus'. In Kaldor, profits take on the character of an exogenous magnitude (determined by the necessity of full employment investments), while wages become the residual. The consequences are far-reaching, both on a theoretical level (for a critique of the marginal theory of income distribution) and also on a practical level (for taxation policy). It can be no surprise that Kaldor's income distribution theory was immediately the target of strong and even bitter attacks, with a long series of discussions. There is by now an enormous literature on the subject.

On lines parallel to those on income distribution, Kaldor developed his ideas of an 'expenditure tax', proposed in a book [1955], which has by now become a classic. Kaldor's contention is that the present taxation system, basically based on personal incomes, is inequitable in many respects. People who inherit private fortunes have an enormous spending and economic power, without contributing in any due proportion to the community's needs and welfare. On the other hand, thrifty people are taxed twice – once on the income they save and a second time on the income they derive from accumulated savings. Kaldor proposes a radical change of the taxation basis, so that people may be taxed no longer on their incomes but on their actual expenditures.

In the latter part of his academic career, Kaldor became more and more interested in empirical work. An example is given by his inaugural lecture as a professor [1966] on the 'causes of the Slow Rate of Economic Growth of the United Kingdom'. Another interesting example is a paper written in co-authorship with Professors Hart and Tinbergen, for UNCTAD, the United Nations Conference on Trade and Development, Geneva [1963]. The authors proposed a scheme for an international currency based on stocks of many physical commodities. They provided computations on the basis of the thirty most traded commodities in the international market, trying to show the actual workability and the advantages of such a commodity-based monetary system. The authors themselves judged the scheme 'too radical' to hope it would be accepted under present conditions. It was meant to be advantageous to less developed countries and to be aiming at breaking their dependence on the institutions of the more advanced, industrialised countries. Its implementation looks even more remote today than at the time it was proposed. Yet, with the always impending threat of crises in international economic relations, and inflation never entirely conquered, it is not excluded that the proposed scheme might still find some reconsideration, by those lower-income countries that are rich in natural resources.

Kaldor devoted many efforts to building a theoretical construction based on the idea that the 'Keynesian' features of an economy may apply to its industrial sector, while, side by side to it, the primary sector, providing food and raw materials, may be operating with 'non-Keynesian' features. He thought that this antithetic sectoral analysis could also be applied to the relations between developed and less developed countries. If the 'industrial' sector (or country) operates with 'increasing returns to scale' (an idea going back to Allyn Young, whose lifelong influence is explicitly brought out, especially in Kaldor, 1975), and the primary sector (or country) operates at decreasing returns to scale (à la Ricardo, only mitigated now and then by 'land-saving' innovations), then a whole series of important consequences follow, though they may not be susceptible to being easily and neatly formalised. Kaldor has written a series of articles along these lines, which have been resumed and synthesised in his *Raffaele Mattioli Lectures* (to which reference will be made below).

The reader may be surprised that I have constantly been referring to papers and articles in order to present Kaldor's contributions to economics, but this was the way in which he worked. Kaldor was not the type of scholar who could sit down and write systematic treatises. He did not have the patience or perseverance to pursue such a task or – as he characteristically put it – he had been too intent on listening to criticisms in order to improve (and modify) his views. But this process was neverending with him. It was clearly more congenial to his temperament to put his ideas into short papers and then go on to other problems, often changing his mind when going back to the old ones. In this way, he was able to cover an amazingly wide field.

Kaldor's ideas are scattered in an incredibly large number of articles, papers, memoranda and reports, the only exception being the already-mentioned short book on an expenditure tax (on which he was helped by Ann Jackson) and the two sets of *Lectures* to which mention will be made in a moment. Fortunately, in the latter part of his life, Kaldor let himself be convinced – his pride perhaps overcoming his reluctance and apparent laziness – to collect most of his writings into a series of eight volumes (1960–80), which divide neatly into three volumes of theoretical writings, three volumes of applied economics-and-taxation writings, and two volumes of reports and memoranda concerning the United Kingdom and to foreign governments, respectively. To read these books is an extremely rewarding experience for any economist, provided one does not let oneself get irritated by the darts he continually fires at traditional economic thinking. Unorthodox remarks, unexpected clever insights, original ideas are disseminated everywhere, even in the most 'applied' writings. The introductions to the eight volumes – which Kaldor *had* to write – are illuminating and precious to anybody interested in following the evolution of his economic thought. The whole set will remain a rich source of ideas for years to come.

We will never be able to have his own comments and report on the results of his scientific activity – an activity which was singularly rich, especially in connection with the numerous invitations, from universities all over the world, to pay visits and to give lectures – in the last seven years of his life. But most of these papers and lectures have been gathered, and edited, by Ferdinando Targetti and Anthony P. Thirlwall in what effectively is the ninth volume of his 'Collected Economic Essays', published posthumously, in 1989. From his cosmopolitan activity, two books have moreover emerged: one containing his *Okun Memorial Lectures* (delivered at Yale University in 1983) and the other containing his *Raffaele Mattioli Lectures* (delivered in Milan in 1985), then revised and rewritten at length, at last published posthumously in 1996 by Cambridge University Press with the editorship of Ferdinando Targetti and Anthony Thirlwall.

The *Okun Memorial Lectures* were published quickly as a short book, where Kaldor presents, with real efficacy, a theme which has been recurring very often in his long-standing critique of traditional economic theory. The basic thesis is that the theory of general economic equilibrium (an economic theory which remains nowadays as the backbone of dominant economic theory, and which he himself shared and taught and to which he made original contributions, in his LSE period) refers to a purely *hypothetical* world and is founded on hypotheses which have no relevance to the understanding of the *real* world. He claims that such a theory relies on highly unrealistic assumptions, the number of which must grow continuously, in order to dodge the increasing objections. A recurring image he has used is that of an ever-widening scaffolding (of assumptions) with which to sustain a building that could never stand by itself. And yet, Kaldor claims, many economists are going on to draw out implications as if the scaffolding had been removed. Keynesian theory, as he intended it, was doing exactly the opposite: to theorise only with reference to facts, real or – with a colourful expression he coined on purpose – 'stylised', yet facts.

The *Raffaele Mattioli Lectures* have represented a much more engaging task. Since they were delivered partly from a very provisional typescript and partly in an extemporaneous way, they then absorbed him in a long work of revision that was not really congenial to him, but that he carried out for years, without ever being completely satisfied with it. They were devoted to the *Causes of Growth and Stagnation in the World Economy* and were aimed, in a sort of model for the whole world, at synthesising the ideas that are scattered in many of the papers of the last part of his life. The purpose is to make growth or stagnation emerge as the consequences of the trade relations between regions where production is inevitably facing decreasing returns to scale (mainly in countries relying on primary activities, such as agricultural and mining) and regions where, on the other hand, production is carried out with the benefit of increasing returns to scale (mainly countries relying on manufacture and advanced technology activities). The more recent literature on 'new' growth models has unjustly paid little attention to these contributions of Kaldor's, which yet are surprisingly rich in concepts, intuitions and constructive suggestions. We owe thanks to the determination of Targetti and Thirlwall (the editors) if we are now able to see the (posthumous) publication of this work.

These two sets of *Lectures* also contribute to give an idea of the concreteness of Kaldor's preoccupations. Economic theory has never been for him a purely intellectual pastime but – as after all it was for Keynes, his ideal Master – has always been finalised to the understanding, and solution, of real economic problems. It may be interesting to recall that he used to tell his friends that he was fifteen when he decided to become an economist. He claimed he did so out of curiosity about the mechanism that was causing the German hyperinflation of the post World War One, as he personally experienced it directly, 'bargain-hunting for goods at yesterday's price', while on a family vacation in the Bavarian Alps. Ever since, his interest for the economic facts of the real world has remained the constant stimulus to his economic investigations. But most of all, this has been accompanied by the positive intention of influencing them, as is witnessed by his extraordinarily intense activity – already mentioned – as an economic adviser to an incredibly high number of governments, central banks and international agencies.

4.   Political activity

Kaldor certainly did not consider his elevation to the House of Lords as a purely honorary incumbency. He was one of the most severe and persistent opponents of the economic policies of the Conservative British governments of the 1980s, and particularly of the policies pursued by Mrs Thatcher.

Kaldor's attendance at the House of Lords intensified in time. During the last years of his life one can say that no major debate on economic policy went on in the House of Lords without some speech or intervention or interruption by him. His contributions to the House of Lords form in fact a charming series of speeches. They show Kaldor at his best, as a debater and polemist, besides being an acute observer of the British and international political and economic situation. The main targets of his attacks were monetarism ('a terrible curse, a visitation of evil spirits') and more particularly Thatcherism ('a menace to the United Kingdom'). When these speeches are collected and published, they will provide delightful reading to economists and to the informed general public alike. It must be added that, precisely for the controversial stands which he took up, Kaldor has always generated hard feelings, especially on the part of property-owning people, not only in Great Britain but in all those countries whose governments he had advised. In the last years of his life, the opposition to him grew precisely on account of his very harsh attacks on the government monetary policies. Curiously enough, he never showed preoccupations. He never minded; showing a sort of toughness and nonchalance that was astonishing and further contributed to irritating his opponents. But all those who knew him well could not but feel affection for him.

5.   Kaldor and Keynes

A few concluding remarks on this notable representative of the Cambridge School of post-Keynesian economics may be appropriate at this point. Perhaps it is not far from the truth to affirm that, among the major exponents of that school, Kaldor, though not originally a pupil of Keynes, was the person who more than anybody else was near the Master, in the global conception of the market economies and in the role which an economist can perform. It was not only his continual commuting between the spheres of high economic theory and the actual preoccupations of practical applications that revealed the closest affinities between the two men. At a deeper and more fundamental level, these affinities concerned their basic vision of the world. Like Keynes, Kaldor was convinced that a revolution is necessary in *economic theory* – not in the basic (market) institutional set-up of our societies. He was a great believer in the powerful forces of the market mechanism. But he was at the same time aware of the weaknesses of the market and of the social injustices it is bound to bring about, in terms of an unequal distribution of income and wealth, of too-high levels of unemployment and of disorder and injustices in international relations. For this reason, he was a passionate supporter of reforms. But he was also of the opinion that the defects of the market economies can be corrected by enlightened actions of governments and by international cooperation.

Kaldor belonged to that generation of British socialists, à la Gaitskell, profoundly imbued with the Fabian tradition, which are idealist at heart. He was a great asserter of the power of reason and intellect, a strong believer in the possibilities that intelligent people can develop and apply analytical and practical instruments, which may contribute to shape the society in which they live, in the way they want. He also had, similarly to Keynes, an unsurpassable tendency to over-estimate the possibilities of intellect to overcome and limit diffused stupidity. He was indeed a great believer in the role of intellectuals and scornful of what he thought to be a widespread mediocrity of the ruling classes. He was not – contrary to what has been stated with reference to some superficial evaluation of his behaviour – unconcerned with the lot of the underdog. His social commitment is witnessed by the great pains he took to devise, for Britain and for less developed countries alike, ways and expediencies to make the rich pay taxes and induce relief for the poor, by making them obtain more, either for their goods or for their work.

A 'revolution' was indeed intended from the depth of his heart. This too was, after all, in line with Keynes's conception. What was intended was a profound change in the way of thinking, a revolution in the way of understanding and applying economic theories – indeed *all* economic theories inherited from the past; theories which are conditioning us, even when they are no longer relevant, from the remotest and most hidden corners of our minds.

In this, he may not have been sufficiently understood.

6.   Selected works of Nicholas Kaldor

1934, 'A Classificatory Note on the Determinateness of Equilibrium', *Review of Economic Studies*, vol. 1, pp. 122–136; reprinted in Kaldor, 1960–1979, vol. 1, pp. 13–33.

1937, 'The Recent Controversy on the Theory of Capital', *Econometrica*, pp. 201–233; reprinted in Kaldor, 1960–1979, vol. 1, pp. 153–205.

1939a, 'Welfare Propositions of Economics and Interpersonal Comparisons of Utility', *Economic Journal*, vol. 49, pp. 549–554; reprinted in Kaldor, 1960–1979, vol. 1, pp. 143–146, with the title 'Welfare Propositions in Economics'.

1939b, 'Speculation and Economic Stability', *Review of Economic Studies*, vol. 6, October, pp. 1–27; reprinted in Kaldor, 1960–1979, vol. 2, pp. 17–58.

1940, 'A Model of the Trade Cycle', *Economic Journal*, vol. 50, pp. 78–92; reprinted in Kaldor, 1960–1979, vol. 2, pp. 177–192.

1955, *An Expenditure Tax*, London: Allen & Unwin.

1956, 'Alternative Theories of Distribution', *Review of Economic Studies*, vol. 22, pp. 83–100; reprinted in Kaldor, 1960–1979, vol. 1, pp. 209–236.

1957, 'A Model of Economic Growth', *Economic Journal*, vol. 67, pp. 591–624; reprinted in Kaldor, 1960–1979, vol. 2, pp. 259–300.

1960–1979, 'Collected Economic Essays', 8 volumes, London: Duckworth. Volume 1: *Essays on Value and Distribution*, 1960. Volume 2: *Essays on Economic Stability and Growth*, 1960. Volume 3: *Essays on Economic Policy, I*, 1964. Volume 4: *Essays on Economic Policy, II*, 1964. Volume 5: *Further Essays on Economic Theory*, 1978. Volume 6: *Further Essays on Applied Economics*, 1978. Volume 7: *Reports on Taxation, I: Papers Relating to the United Kingdom*, 1979. Volume 8: *Reports on Taxation, II: Reports to Foreign Governments*, 1979.

1961, 'Capital Accumulation and Economic Growth', pp. 177–222 in: Hague, Douglas C. and Lutz,

Friedrich, eds., *The Theory of Capital*, London: Macmillan; reprinted in Kaldor, 1960–1979, vol. 5, pp. 1–53.

1962 (with J. A. Mirrlees), 'A New Model of Economic Growth', *Review of Economic Studies*, vol. 29, pp. 174–192; reprinted in Kaldor, 1960–1979, vol. 5, pp. 54–80.

1963 (with A. G. Hart and J. Tinbergen), 'The Case for an International Commodity Reserve Currency', submitted to the UN Conference on Trade and Development (UNCTAD), Geneva, March–June 1964; reprinted in Kaldor, 1960–1979, vol. 4, pp. 131–177.

1966, *Causes of the Slow Rate of Economic Growth of the United Kingdom*, Cambridge: Cambridge University Press; reprinted in Kaldor, 1960–1979, vol. 5, pp. 100–138.

1975, 'What is Wrong with Economic Theory', *Quarterly Journal of Economics*, vol. 89, pp. 347–357; reprinted in Kaldor, 1960–1979, vol. 5, pp. 202–213.

1989 (edited by F. Targetti and A. P. Thirlwall), 'Collected Economic Essays', vol. 9, *Further Essays on Economic Theory and Policy*, London: Duckworth.

1985, *Economics without Equilibrium*, The Okun Memorial Lectures at Yale University 1983, Armonk, New York: M. E. Sharpe, Inc.

1996, *Causes of Growth and Stagnation in the World Economy*; the 'Raffaele Mattioli' Lectures, delivered in Milan, 1985, revised and posthumously published with the editorship of Ferdinando Targetti and Anthony Thirlwall, Cambridge: Cambridge University Press.

Postscript

Two major biographies of Nicholas Kaldor have appeared since his death:

- Thirlwall, Anthony P., 1987, *Nicholas Kaldor*, Brighton: Wheatsheaf Books.

- Targetti, Ferdinando, 1992, *Nicholas Kaldor – The Economics and Politics of Capitalism as a Dynamic System*, Oxford: Clarendon Press.

Chapter VI

Piero Sraffa (1898–1983)
The critical mind

Editorial note

The trilogy of essays reproduced below was originally written for different purposes and at different times.

The first essay was written while Piero Sraffa was still alive, as an entry – a brief bio-bibliographical sketch (SRAFFA PIERO) – for vol. 18 ('Biographical Supplement') of The International Encyclopedia of the Social Sciences, *New York: The Free Press, a division of Macmillan Publ. Co., 1979, pp. 736–739. It is here republished with subdivisions in sections, subtitles and a few additions.*

The two other essays happened to be presented at the same place (Fondazione Luigi Einaudi Torino), fifteen years apart, on two different celebrations. The first originated as a memorial speech, delivered on 16 December 1983, three months after Sraffa's death. It was published in Economia Politica, *vol. II, 1985, pp. 315–332, as 'In memoria di Piero Sraffa, economista italiano a Cambridge', and was later translated into English for the* Italian Economic Papers, *vol. 3, Bologna: Il Mulino and Oxford University Press, 1998, pp. 365–383. It is here reproduced with the omission of a few opening sentences, referring to contingent circumstances, and with some additions, corrections and a subdivision in sections. The title of the essay is meant to be reminiscent of the way Sraffa defined himself ('An Italian in England') in a letter to the* Manchester Guardian *(24 October 1927), in which he openly denounced the methods of the Fascist regime in dealing with political prisoners, in particular with Antonio Gramsci. The other essay was written in September 1998, at a meeting held to commemorate the centenary of Piero Sraffa's birth. It has been published in Cozzi, T. and Marchionatti, R. (eds.) (2000) Piero Sraffa: a Centenary Estimate, London: Routledge, pp. 139–156. It is reproduced here with a few adaptations and additions.*

Chapter VI.1

A brief bio-bibliographical sketch

1. Biography

Piero Sraffa died in Cambridge, England, on 3 September 1983 at the age of eighty-five. He had left Italy and had come to Cambridge, as a protégé of John Maynard Keynes, in 1927. A friend of Antonio Gramsci, the founder of the Italian Communist party, of Raffaele Mattioli, the prominent Italian banker, and of Ludwig Wittgenstein, the founder of linguistic philosophy. Sraffa spent almost the whole of his active life as an unmarried don in the quiet atmosphere of the Cambridge colleges, which suited marvellously his withdrawn and reserved personality. He was rarely seen at academic congresses or conferences around the world. Yet his writings have been twice in his life at the centre of major breakthroughs in economic theory. He is most probably bound to remain one of the most disconcerting and controversial theoretical economists of the twentieth century.

Piero Sraffa was born in Turin, northern Italy, on 5 August 1898, the only child of Angelo Sraffa and Irma Tivoli. The family was of Jewish origin, on both parents' sides. The father, Angelo Sraffa, from Pisa, was a well-known Italian university professor, who started his teaching at the University of Macerata and then moved on, in succession, to the universities of Messina, Parma and Turin. He finally became Rector of the Luigi Bocconi University of Milan (from 1916 to 1926).

Plate 4 Piero Sraffa, in 1976. Reproduced by permission of
Professor Alessandro Roncaglia.

The mother, Irma Tivoli, from Turin, came from a family of a
rather matriarchal character and had a strong impact on her
son's education.

As a child, Piero Sraffa obviously followed the where-
abouts of his family. He started his primary education in
Parma and continued it in Milan, where he then attended the
well-known Giuseppe Parini Gymnasium. When he moved to
Turin, he attended the Massimo D'Azeglio Lycée, where one
of his teachers was Umberto Cosmo, a literary professor and
a complex personality of socialist tendencies, who also was
in charge of a course of university lectures on Italian literature, which happened to be attended by Antonio Gramsci. It

was through Umberto Cosmo that Piero Sraffa first met Antonio Gramsci. The two were not contemporary, Gramsci being seven years his senior.

At Turin University, Sraffa wrote his dissertation on 'Monetary inflation in Italy during and after the War' [1920], supervised by Luigi Einaudi, the Italian economist and public finance expert, later – after World War Two – to become the second President of the Italian Republic.

In January 1921, after graduation, Sraffa followed, as a research student, some courses of lectures at the London School of Economics, where he seems to have been particularly impressed by Edwin Cannan, who was at that time lecturing on Classical theories of production and income distribution. It was in the summer of that year, during a brief and occasional visit to Cambridge, that Sraffa met Keynes. Sraffa seems to have made on him a strong impression. So much so that Keynes decided to commission him to write an article on the Italian financial markets and banking crisis. Sraffa was flattered and accepted with enthusiasm. The article was published in two versions: in *The Economic Journal* [1922a] and in a section on the 'Reconstruction of Europe' – edited by Keynes – in the weekly *Manchester Guardian Commercial* [1922b]. This event turned out to be of crucial importance in Sraffa's life. Especially the second version of that article (the one published in the *Manchester Guardian Commercial*) marked the beginning of a series of difficulties with the Fascist regime. Mussolini, who had just seized power, was enraged by that article and tried to exert pressure on Piero Sraffa to withdraw what he had written. He did so by a sort of blackmail involving Piero Sraffa's father, then the Rector of the Bocconi University of Milan. For Sraffa this incident was the beginning of a series of troubles with the Fascist regime and at the same time of increasing contacts with Keynes.

A few years later (1923) Sraffa began to lecture on political economy and finance at the University of Perugia. He then won a chair of Political Economy at the University of Cagliari

(Sardinia) in 1926. But the Fascist regime was increasing in strength and when, in 1927, Keynes was able to offer him a lectureship at the University of Cambridge, Sraffa accepted. He emigrated to England, where he stayed for the rest of his life.

Piero Sraffa remained nevertheless an 'Italian in England', always keeping his Italian citizenship. Had he taken up British citizenship, he would have lost the Italian one, according to the Italian law of the time. Sraffa never did that, even at the cost of facing difficulties during World War Two, when he was compelled to leave Cambridge for a certain time and to go – with other Italian intellectuals who refused to go back to Italy – to an internment camp in the Isle of Man, in the Irish Sea.

The position of Piero Sraffa in the Italian University was a most unusual one. He took up his chair at the University of Cagliari in March 1926 and went there for a while. But then – after taking up his lectureship at Cambridge – he resigned his Cagliari professorship. After the end of World War Two, however, Sraffa was reinstated as a Full Professor ('Professore Ordinario') on account of the fact that, owing to his resignation in the early 1930s, he was one of the very few Italian university professors who had not sworn allegiance to the Fascist regime. However, Sraffa did not return to any Italian university (in spite of much insistence on the part of many of his friends). He did resume regular visits to Italy, to see friends (in particular Raffaele Mattioli), to visit antiquarian booksellers and to spend holidays in tourist resorts (especially Rapallo). He reasserted explicitly, in writing, his intention to maintain his resignation from his chair. But the Minister of Education invented an expedient in order to be able not to accept formally his resignations. (The expedient consisted in 'commanding' him to the University of Cambridge to carry out the task of editing Ricardo's *Works*). Sraffa therefore remained an Italian Full Professor till retirement ('in soprannumero', i.e. in a position created specifically for him and not available for anybody else) at the University of Cagliari. But he never cashed his stipends or pensions. On his retirement, he sent a letter of donation of what was due to him to the Library of the Economics Institute of the University of Cagliari.

2.   Returns to scale, costs and value

When Piero Sraffa settled in Cambridge, he was twenty-nine. Yet he had already established himself as a theoretical economist of international reputation.

In an article written in Italian [1925], he had carried out a meticulous criticism, centred on the question of returns to scale, of Alfred Marshall's theory of the firm, arguing that the only logically consistent assumption to make in that theory was that of constant returns to scale. Almost simultaneously, in a remarkably concise article, Sraffa [1926] exposed the glaring weaknesses of the perfect competition model that traditional economics until then had generally used. By stressing the importance of monopolistic market situations and the consistency of increasing returns to scale with limited production, when the single firm demand curve is negatively sloped, he had laid the foundations of an entire branch of new theories of value and pricing. That branch developed a few years later, especially through the works of Richard Kahn (1929) and of Joan Robinson (1933) in England, and Edward Chamberlin (1933) in the United States, though the latter had started from quite an independent line of thought.

In Cambridge, Sraffa was soon a major protagonist, with Gerald Shove and Dennis Robertson, in a famous symposium on increasing returns [1930a]. Shortly afterwards, he launched a devastating critique [1932] of the traditional theory of money and capital, as proposed by Friedrich A. von Hayek (1931).

But Sraffa was also able to devote time to more leisurely activities. He loved collecting first editions of rare books, especially of eighteenth-century economists and philosophers. He did this, sometimes in competition with, and sometimes jointly with, two of his dearest friends: Raffaele Mattioli and John Maynard Keynes. It was in this way for example that, in collaboration with Keynes, he enjoyed retracing, editing and publishing [1938], after correctly attributing it to David Hume, an anonymous pamphlet called *An Abstract of a Treatise on Human Nature* that was previously (but incorrectly) attributed to Adam Smith.[1] Yet this was no more than a hobby.

3.   The edition of Ricardo's *Works*

A much bigger task was ahead. Cambridge University made it possible for Sraffa to realise a great ambition of his: the collection and editing of the *Works and Correspondence of David Ricardo* [1951–1973], the classical economist whom Sraffa admired most. This was a lifelong undertaking. It went through many, even dramatic, phases.[2] Sraffa began this great work in the early 1930s and carried it through World War Two. The accuracy and completeness of the collation of the texts, the richness and accuracy of the editorial notes and, most important, the analyses contained in the long 'Introduction' to volume I and in the (shorter) introductions to the following volumes have made this work an almost unique masterpiece in the publications of economic classics of political economy. It is bound to remain for a long time a sort of ideal, almost unequalled model, of editorial work.

What is even more important, this edition of Ricardo's *Works*, besides providing a first-rate critical apparatus, has proposed a new interpretation of the theoretical foundations of classical political economy. The classical 'standpoint', as Sraffa calls it, is presented not merely as a set of conceptions having relevance within the history of economic thought but

---

[1] See footnote 13 of the following essay.

[2] See Sraffa's Introduction to the first volume of Ricardo's *Works* [Sraffa, 1951].

also as a theoretical apparatus, very much relevant and with great analytical possibilities for the problems of our days. Sraffa's edition of Ricardo has led to a truly new rediscovery of classical political economics. At the same time Sraffa has set so high a standard of excellence in editorial scholarship as to make it unlikely that it may be equalled for a long time to come.

4. *Production of Commodities*

Few people expected anything more from Sraffa, after the publication of Ricardo's *Works*. But in 1960, at the age of sixty-two, Sraffa published an admirably concise ninety-nine-page book, on which he had been working for more than thirty years. The title was baffling – *Production of Commodities by Means of Commodities: Prelude to a Critique of Economic Theory*. The content of the book was even more so. In it, Sraffa abandoned the 'marginal method' of analysis, which had characterised established economic theory for more than a century, and went back to the "standpoint, which is that of old classical economists from Adam Smith to Ricardo, [which] has been submerged and forgotten since the advent of the 'marginal' method" [1960, p. v].

The problem that Sraffa explored in this investigation concerns the properties of an economic system in which there is no change in the scale of production or in the proportions among the 'factors' of production. Like François Quesnay in his *Tableau Economique* (1758), Sraffa considers the net national product as a 'surplus' over and above what is required to replace the means of production, and he regards production as a 'circular process' in which the same commodities appear both as means of production and as final products. This approach may look very similar to Leontief's input-output analysis. But Sraffa goes deeper. He resumes a more classical line of thought, on the theories of value and income distribution, starting with Ricardo (1821) and continuing through Karl Marx (1867, 1885, 1894), Ladislaus von Bortkiewicz (1907) and Vladimir Karpovich Dmitriev (1904). The classical theories had been abandoned at a certain stage because a few basic concepts on which they were built seemed to contain deficiencies, ambiguities and even contradictions. Sraffa's contribution consists precisely in dispelling those deficiencies, ambiguities and contradictions. Three examples may suffice to illustrate the point:

1. All classical economists, from Adam Smith onwards, had made a sharp distinction between necessary (or wage) goods and luxury goods. The distinction was important because it led to radically different conclusions for the two kinds of goods; but it had later been abandoned because it seemed arbitrary. Sraffa shifts the ground for the distinction back to technology, drawing the line between commodities that are technologically required for the production of all commodities – 'basic commodities' – and commodities that are not so required – 'non-basic' commodities. In these terms, a mathematical notation can be used and concepts become unambiguous.

2. Ricardo had considered the distribution of income as 'the principal problem of political economy', but he had encountered insuperable difficulties when he tried to investigate income distribution independently of prices. He realised that he could overcome these difficulties only if he could find an 'invariable standard of value', defined as a commodity whose value does not change when income distribution changes and when improvement in techniques takes place. But he never succeeded in finding such a commodity. Sraffa demonstrates that, at least with reference to the first (the income distribution) problem, an 'invariable standard' can indeed be analytically constructed in the form of a composite commodity – the 'standard commodity' –

that characterises any given technique.[3] Interestingly enough, this 'standard commodity' coincides with the composition of production in von Neumann's growth model (1937).

3. Finally, economists for years debated whether Marx's problem of the 'transformation of values into prices of production' did or did not make any sense. Sraffa's analysis solves all the analytical difficulties. A relationship between the quantities of embodied labour (i.e. Marxian 'values') and prices of production is indeed shown to exist, but is much more complex than Marx imagined. It is, in any case, such as to give no analytical ground for the claim that Marxian 'values' have any logical priority over competitive prices, in the same way as there would be no analytical ground for claiming that competitive prices have any logical priority over Marxian 'values'.

A puzzling, and perhaps unsatisfactory, feature of Sraffa's book is that the author explicitly presents his propositions as preparatory to a critique of 'economic theory', presumably to be intended as the marginal theory of value and income distribution. Yet he does not himself carry out such a critique. This has led many economists, especially in the United States, to regard Sraffa's analysis as a merely abstract exercise in pure theory. Later developments, however, point to different directions. In the late 1960s, a debate on capital theory, originating from a few propositions of Sraffa's (see Pasinetti *et al.*, 1966), led to the discarding of concepts – specifically the neoclassical aggregate production function – that had for almost a century formed the basis of the marginal theory of capital and income distribution. Another debate among Marxists, also

---

[3] There is in fact the possibility of constructing a 'dynamic' standard commodity also with reference to the second of Ricardo's problems (i.e. invariability with respect to improvements of technology – see below, pp. 290–291). No possibility has been so far discovered to cover simultaneously both Ricardo's problems.

originating from Sraffa's book, has led many of them to the conclusion that Marx's pure labour theory of value must be abandoned (see Morishima, 1973; Steedman, 1977).

It is curious that Sraffa's analysis should emerge as the basis for a critique and discarding of well-established concepts both in marginal economic theory and in Marxian economic theory. Yet it is clearly in relation to developments of this sort that the significance of Sraffa's book will eventually have to be assessed.

In 1961 the Swedish Royal Academy of Sciences awarded Piero Sraffa the Södestrom medal, which at the time was considered as a sort of substitute for a Nobel Prize for Economics. But since 1969, when a Memorial Nobel Prize for Economics was actually established, many economists (including some of those who were actually awarded the Nobel Prize) had openly and repeatedly expressed surprise at the failure of any announcement of Piero Sraffa's name as a Nobel Laureate. The future will tell whether these economists or the Royal Swedish Academy of Science were right.

5. The principal works of Piero Sraffa

1920, *L'inflazione monetaria in Italia durante e dopo la guerra*, a dissertation thesis, presented at the University of Turin, November 1920, recently translated as 'Monetary inflation in Italy during and after the war', *Cambridge Journal of Economics*, 1993, pp. 7–26.

1922a, 'The Bank Crisis in Italy', *The Economic Journal*, vol. XXXII, pp. 178–197.

1922b, 'Italian Banking Today', *Manchester Guardian Commercial: Reconstruction in Europe*, section XI, December, 7, pp. 675–676.

1924, 'Obituary – Maffeo Pantaleoni', *The Economic Journal*, vol. XXXIV, pp. 648–653.

1925, 'Sulle relazioni fra costo e quantità prodotta', *Annali di Economia*, vol. II, pp. 277–328 [English translation: 'On the Relations between Cost and Quantity Produced', in *Italian Economic Papers*, vol. 3, edited by Luigi Pasinetti on behalf of Società Italiana degli Economisti, Bologna: il Mulino and Oxford: Oxford University Press, 1998, pp. 322–363].

1926, 'The Laws of Returns under Competitive Conditions', *The Economic Journal*, vol. XXXVI, pp. 535–550.

1930a, 'A critique' (pp. 89–92) and 'A rejoinder' (p. 93), in 'Increasing Returns and the Representative Firm: A Symposium', *The Economic Journal*, vol. XL.

1930b, 'An Alleged Correction of Ricardo', *The Quarterly Journal of Economics*, vol. XLIV, pp. 539–544.

1932, 'Dr Hayek on Money and Capital' and 'A rejoinder', *The Economic Journal*, vol. XLII, pp. 42–53 and pp. 249–251.

1938 (jointly with J. M. Keynes), 'Introduction' to David Hume, *An Abstract of a Treatise on Human Nature* [1740], Cambridge: Cambridge University Press, pp. V–XXXII.

1951–1973 (with the collaboration of Maurice Dobb), *The Works and Correspondence of David Ricardo*, vols I–IV, 1951; V–IX, 1952; X, 1955; XI, 1973; a publication of the Royal Economic Society, Cambridge: Cambridge University Press.

1960, *Production of Commodities by Means of Commodities – Prelude to a Critique of Economic Theory*, Cambridge: Cambridge University Press (Italian version: 'Produzione di merci a mezzo di merci – Premessa a una critica della teoria economica', Torino: Einaudi, 1960).

1962, 'Production of Commodities – A Comment', *The Economic Journal*, vol. LXXII, pp. 477–479. (This is a comment on a book review by Roy F. Harrod.)

Chapter VI.2

An Italian economist at Cambridge

1. Preamble

Those who were close to Piero Sraffa during the last few years of his life were prepared for the news of his death, which occurred, in a Cambridge nursing home, in the early morning of Saturday 3 September 1983. For two years he had been forced to bed, though with some short periods of respite in an armchair, being able to do practically nothing without somebody else's help. He must have suffered deeply: shy, discreet, as he was, afraid of hurting anybody's feelings, always trying not to bother anyone; jealous of his identity, autonomy and freedom in the widest sense of the word, including that of not obeying anyone's prescriptions, including those of his doctors. The visits to the nursing home, and the conversations at his bedside – fragmentary and repetitive – had become painful. On a rational level, his death should bring a sense of relief to those who knew him. At an emotional level, the heart is full of anguish at the thought that such an extraordinary man is no longer with us.

In the present speech, delivered at a meeting held in his memory, I shall try to concentrate my remarks on the relationships, which can be detected, or recalled, or figured out, concerning Sraffa and the Cambridge intellectual environment, where he spent most of his life. Obviously, to be dealt with satisfactorily, the subject would need further time and reflections. My present talk is a collection of emotive reactions, quick reflections, reminiscences, which, disorderly, come to my mind at this moment.

2.   1926: a new rising star

Let me begin with a quotation:

> The times are decidedly hostile to economic science; not because economists' advice is not listened to. On the contrary, the scientist thinks, studies, draws conclusions and is satisfied with pushing ahead the frontiers of the discipline. The times are hostile because the best economists are quickly passing away one after another. In less than one year, Pareto, Barone, Marshall, Pantaleoni have all died.

The last line provides a clue to the date. These are the initial propositions of an article written by Marco Fanno, and devoted to Marshall, in issue number 1, volume II of *Annali di Economia*, November 1925 – a surprising issue indeed, containing a series of articles by Augusto Graziani on Adam Smith, Achille Loria on Ricardo, Giuseppe Prato on Malthus, Luigi Amoroso on Jevons, Gino Arias on John Stuart Mill. Last comes the article by Marco Fanno from which the quotation is taken. But the editors of the journal must have thought that there still was some space available if, at the end of the issue – as if it were a way of filling up some remaining pages – they added two articles which had nothing to do with the previous ones: an article by Attilio Cabiati on monetary return to gold and an article by a young economist, Piero Sraffa, unknown at that time to the readers of the journal, on 'the relations between cost and quantity produced'.[1]

The quotation appears appropriate to the present meeting, which seems to be one of those occasions when a sort of nemesis is wandering. I am thinking of the recent deaths

---

[1] This is Sraffa [1925].

of Joan Robinson and Maurice Dobb, which have preceded that of Piero Sraffa. Moreover, I am thinking of the somewhat precarious health of other leading figures of contemporary Cambridge post-Keynesian economic thought, who have been associated with Piero Sraffa for a long time, both in professional activity and in personal friendships.[2]

But the same quotation may be taken as a good omen by many young economists here gathered. Just at a time when Marco Fanno was feeling such an empty void in the discipline, a young economist – to whom scarce attention was paid at that time: Piero Sraffa, the person who is being commemorated at the present meeting – was rising as a new star in the discipline's firmament.

This also seems to me a good starting point for my talk. At that time, Piero Sraffa was competing in a national competition for a chair. At the date of publication of that issue of *Annali di Economia* (November 1925), a *concours* was open for a professorship of political economy at the University of Cagliari. In those days, in Italy, national competitions for professorships concerned only one post at a time; but the committee that was appointed by the Ministry of Education was invited to give evaluations of *all* candidates and to form a 'terna', i.e. a set of three winning candidates, who had to be ranked in order of merit. On that occasion, the committee was composed of Augusto Graziani (chairman), Costantino Bresciani-Turroni, Attilio Cabiati, Lorenzo Mossa (Secretary) and Umberto Ricci (*Rapporteur*). Eleven candidates had applied. Among them we find names, such as Roberto Michels, Giuseppe Ugo Papi, Carlo Rosselli, that were to become well known later on but were excluded from the winning 'terna'. The winners were Carlo Grilli (ranked as first), a civil servant at the Ministry of Public Works, Piero Sraffa (second) and Angelo Fraccareta (third). Needless to say,

---

[2] The references were clearly to Nicholas Kaldor and to Richard Kahn, who were to die in 1986 and in 1989, respectively.

it is the second name that gave relevance to that *concours*. It may be interesting to reproduce the brief evaluation which the committee gave of his works:

> *Sraffa Piero* – Lecturer in Political Economy at the University of Perugia in the academic year 1923–4 and at present also lecturer in Public Finance. He gained his *libera docenza* in Political Economy in 1925. The scientific production of this candidate is not abundant: it consists of an essay on 'Relazioni fra costo e quantità prodotta', an essay on 'Inflazione monetaria in Italia durante e dopo la guerra', an article published in the *Economic Journal*, concerning the crisis of the banking system in Italy (it deals with the bankruptcy of *Banca di Sconto*), an obituary note on Pantaleoni, and another note 'Sulla situazione delle banche italiane', published in the Commercial Supplement to the *Manchester Guardian*.[3] The Committee praises above all the first of the writings mentioned above, in which the author deals with one of the most difficult subjects in pure Economics. However, the Committee criticizes the conclusion to which the author arrives. The Committee has also noticed that the author's preoccupation to be dense and concise has sometimes led him to a laborious expository style and to a conciseness which is bordering obscurity. But there is no doubt that the author establishes himself as a vigorous logician and an acute critic. Moreover he shows a complete mastership of the literature on the subject. The essay on the crisis of the banking system and also the very short but dense note in the *Manchester Guardian* prove the author's ability to observe and acutely interpret actual economic events. The Committee is therefore unanimous in acknowledging the candidate's 'maturity' and ability to teach at university level. (Ministero della Pubblica Istruzione, 1926. *My translation*)

This 'evaluation', which is exemplary from many points of view, was written in January 1926 and Sraffa took up his job in Cagliari on March of that year. We do not find, of course, in the 'evaluation' what was to become the most famous of his

---

articles (Sraffa 1926 in the *Economic Journal*), which was still to be written and to be published in the summer of that same year. And, of course, we do not find his later writings – the Prefaces and Introductions to the *Works and Correspondence of David Ricardo* and his book *Production of Commodities by Means of Commodities* [1960]. Yet it is quite clear that, by that time, the personality of Piero Sraffa as an economist had already taken shape.

3.   Piero Sraffa's education as an economist

One may well ask how, and where, Sraffa received his education as an economist. To those who were asking him questions on this topic, Sraffa always used to answer in a dismissive way, especially with reference to the time spent at the university. He never gave any impression of valuing in any way his university years. His interests in social and economic matters arose no doubt much before – at the 'Liceo', if not even at the 'Ginnasio'. Sraffa had kept dear memories of his teachers at the secondary education level; he used to talk of them at length and with affection, even, at many years' distance, in his old age, sometimes enjoying telling jokes about them, in a surprisingly hilarious mood. I shall simply recall that Umberto Cosmo was among his teachers at the 'Liceo'.

On the contrary, the university period, which overlapped for a great deal with his military service, did not leave noticeable or pleasant memories in him. His privileged position, as a son of a prominent university professor, had taught him all the tricks on how to pass exams almost without doing any work. He used to tell stories, with great elation, on this topic. He used to boast that, with the exception of the cases of a few exams, where he knew the professors were very severe, he really never did any serious work at the university. He used to say that it was enough for him to get a leave of absence from the Army (that could be obtained on account of exams at the university) and then go to the examination room, wearing his uniform of an Army junior officer. The professor would first of all congratulate him and, after a few praising comments such as 'you are indeed a brave young man, carrying on your studies while serving the country, and coming back from the front line to submit yourself to an examination', would add something like: 'Well, tell me: is there any specific topic in which you have particularly been keenly interested?' At this point, Sraffa added, the trick was to have a ready-made, well-prepared answer – a brief topic, well presented, and the exam was over.[4] One would obtain the best marks and could go home to enjoy the rest of one's leave from military service.

This is roughly the way Sraffa talked of his university times. Yet, in his faculty, there were famous professors, such as Einaudi and Jannaccone. But no doubt there were exaggerations in what Sraffa was saying about his university professors. His deep-rooted aversion towards the Italian academic world had an obvious psychological component due to his being the son of a well-known university professor.

In any case, on the occasions when I had the opportunity of talking to him about his youth, I obtained the clear impression that, on the one side, his interests in social and economic matters dated back long *before* his university years and, on the other side, that the shaping of his major ideas in the field of economic *theory* took place *after*. However, Sraffa used to talk with satisfaction of his dissertation thesis – on monetary inflation in Italy after the war [1920] – at least for one reason; namely that it was the source of discussions with Luigi Einaudi. Sraffa claimed, in conversations, that, after his university thesis, Einaudi changed his mind and softened his earlier rigid opposition to any modification of the lira exchange rate. It should in fact be possible to check whether one can find any hint at something like any change of mind in Einaudi's

---

[4] It may be useful to note that, for his degree, all exams were oral. No written text was required.

views, by looking through his articles in the daily *Corriere della Sera* of those years.

As to the following period, my impression is that, for the young Sraffa, of basic importance must have been the time he spent at the London School of Economics (Spring 1921). At LSE Sraffa attended, no doubt with great interest, Edwin Cannan's lectures. The notable book, in which Cannan presents his 'review of economic theory', was published much later (1929), but it originated from the lectures he had given in those years.[5] I would not hesitate in stating (from what I was able to gather from the many conversations I had with Piero Sraffa) that those lectures must have exerted on him a profound influence, so as to shape much of his economic thinking.

4. First contacts with Keynes

The year 1921 was also the time when Sraffa came first in contact with Keynes. More precisely, their first meeting took place in the summer of 1921, when Piero Sraffa went to see Keynes, bearing with him a by now well-known letter of introduction written to Keynes by Mary Berenson.[6] The letter was sent to Piero Sraffa, thanks to his father's initiative, via Gaetano Salvemini, a family friend and a good acquaintance of the Berensons. On one occasion Sraffa told me, maybe out of coyness, that he did not even know who had written that letter. Anyway, in 1921 Sraffa went to see Keynes, with that letter, for a meeting that turned out to be crucial for the whole

---

[5] This origin is confirmed by Cannan himself who, in the Preface, says he aims at supplying a supplement to his previous book, *A History of the Theories of Production and Distribution from 1776 to 1848* (London, 1903). He expresses the 'hope . . . [to be] able to supplement that book by one in which the period dealt with in it might be put in its proper relation both with what preceded and with what followed it' (Cannan 1929, p. v).

[6] Mary was the wife of Professor Bernhard Berenson, the well-known art critic. An American of Russian origin, he lived, for many years, at Villa 'I Tatti' in Florence, where Keynes paid visits to him, in company with his artist friends of the 'Bloomsbury Group'.

of his future career. At that time, Keynes was editing a series
of articles for a monthly supplement (called 'Reconstruction
in Europe') to the weekly *Manchester Guardian Commercial*.
Keynes – confirming, as we may note, his remarkable intuition and ability to take advantage of any event – thought
immediately to put young Sraffa to the test. He asked him to
write an article, for the monthly supplement to the *Manchester Guardian Commercial*, on Italy's financial crises. The
young man felt flattered. He went back to Italy and started
working on it, very hard. He wrote the article (in Italian) in
a very short time, had it translated into English by a London
friend, and sent it to Keynes, who realised immediately that
the article was so well argued and documented as to be
suitable for a scientific journal, not for a newspaper. Hence,
Keynes proposed to Sraffa to have that article published in
the *Economic Journal* and at the same time asked him to
write *another* piece, much simpler and more popular, for the
monthly *Manchester Guardian* supplement. Of the two articles, both published in 1922, it is the latter – the popular one –
(in the *Manchester Guardian Commercial*, monthly supplement 'Reconstruction in Europe', 7 December 1922) that
caused a stir – simply because Mussolini (a true newspaper
devourer) read it and got furious. He thought young Sraffa
was guilty of denigrating his fatherland. The circumstances
are by now well known and I shall not go into details.[7]

The prospects for Sraffa's career changed radically. In a
way, Keynes felt himself responsible for having led Sraffa into
trouble and invited him to come back to Cambridge, England,

[7] What happened is that Mussolini asked directly Piero Sraffa's father (a
well-known national figure) to induce his son to withdraw the accusations of corruption and interference he had levelled at the Italian politi-
cal/financial system. Not unexpectedly, Piero Sraffa did not comply. The
article was followed (in the *Manchester Guardian Commercial*, monthly
supplement 'Reconstruction in Europe', 29 March 1923) by an exchange of
letters between the director of Banca Commerciale Italiana, Dr Giuseppe
Toepliz (on pressure from Mussolini), and the editor of the newspaper
series, J. M. Keynes (who obviously wrote the reply in consultations with
Piero Sraffa).

at least for some time. But Sraffa was unable to enter England. He actually tried to, but was blocked by the Dover immigration office and was invited to turn back. He was no longer able to enter England until two years later (summer 1924). Keynes had to wait for a change of government before being able to have Sraffa's name removed from the British list of *persona non grata*, where Sraffa's name was inserted in 1922 after the publication of his *Manchester Guardian* article, most probably under pressure on the British (Conservative) government from the Foreign Ministry of Mussolini's government.

5. The beginning of a university career

It was during those years (in Italy) that Sraffa translated into Italian Keynes's *Tract on Monetary Reform*. Sraffa remained in Italy, though on a few occasions, when fearing some trouble from the Fascists, he temporarily expatriated (in Switzerland and France). He obtained a position as a lecturer at the University of Perugia. (It is very likely that, on this occasion too, his being the son of a university professor was of help.) In Perugia, while preparing and delivering his lectures, his ideas started clashing with mainstream economics. It is significant that the clash was with Marshallian economics, not with the economic theory proposed by the Italian economists, even though these were quite prominent at those times, and right at the frontier of general equilibrium (Paretian) economic theory. It seems reasonable to infer that this must have been a consequence of the study period he had spent in England, especially of his attendance at Cannan's lectures at LSE.

It was in Perugia that Sraffa conceived and wrote his contribution on the relations between cost and quantity produced,[8] from which then originated his 1926 *Economic Journal* article, which marked the starting point of the 'imperfect competition revolution' (anti-Marshallian, at least in his intention).

---

[8] See Sraffa [1925].

It would take too long, given space constraints, to try to go here into details on the personal relationships that Sraffa developed in those years. I am going therefore to take a short-cut and consider these personal relationships from a particular point of view, that seems singularly appropriate for the present occasion: the point of view of Sraffa's friendships.

6.   Sraffa's personal relationships

Those who met Piero Sraffa know how he reacted to people visiting him. The immediate impression was that of an extremely kind, polite, open-minded person. I believe he very rarely refused an appointment to any student, or to any visiting professor or even to any journalist. He was always available; yet, at the same time, he was detached, discreet, shy, not to say introvert. His character had no doubt been deeply marked, by being their only child, by the two remarkable personalities of his father and his mother, both of whom came from families of Jewish origin.

His father was a well-known university professor, with many influential contacts and acquaintances. He was Rector of the Bocconi University of Milan from 1916 to 1926, founder of the Faculty of Law of the Milan State University, founder of the most important Italian journal of commercial law. His mother, who moved to Cambridge to live with her son after her husband's death (1937), was also a crucial figure in Piero Sraffa's life. She must have had a very strong influence on him if in one of the letters I received from Sraffa, many years after her death, he was still speaking of his 'beloved mother'. There is strong evidence of a very intense relationship; and it is not really necessary to resort to Freud to understand that, if Sraffa remained a bachelor, that is not surprising.

It was clearly lucky for him to come to live in a milieu like that of the Cambridge colleges, where all the minute daily matters are regularly taken care of as a matter of course; where – especially in his youth – he could stay far away from his father's cumbersome fame (that probably annoyed him, particularly in the 1920s); where he could devote himself entirely to his studies, escaping even the task of giving lectures: a combination of truly exceptional and lucky events. We may thus understand why Sraffa never moved away from Cambridge. In the postwar period, many Italian friends tried to exert pressure on him for a return to Italy. But, in Cambridge, he had settled down for good.

7. Friendships: Mattioli, Gramsci, Wittgenstein

Let me now resume the topic of Sraffa's friendships. No doubt, Piero Sraffa met innumerable persons throughout his life: it was easy to get in touch with him; there was no difficulty in going to talk to him. But true friendship was an entirely different matter. I believe his true friends have been very few indeed. But with the few people that became his friends, relations were extraordinarily intense. A distinction must obviously be made on generational grounds. I shall talk here of those friendships that took shape with people of his own generation, with the persons with whom a reciprocal, give-and-take, two-way relation could take shape.[9] I think that his friendships of this kind can be counted on the fingers of one hand.

There was first of all his friendship with Raffaele Mattioli, which represents Sraffa's longest association. The two had come to know each other just after graduation. Although in different universities, they had prepared their theses on similar topics. Mattioli graduated in Genoa, supervised by Attilio Cabiati, who also held a lectureship at the Bocconi University of Milan, where Mattioli became his teaching assistant and where Sraffa's very alert father must have spotted his talent

---

[9] A separate chapter should be opened concerning his friendships with younger persons and students, with whom a relation of the mentor/pupil type developed. But it is obviously too early to give any assessment of these friendships.

and created an occasion for the first contact with his son. This friendship lasted until Mattioli's death, in 1973, when – while already fatally ill – he received, just in time, a copy, especially bound for him, of the last (the eleventh) volume of Ricardo's works.[10] The friendship of Sraffa and Mattioli is a subject that would deserve a special investigation of its own. There was then his friendship with Antonio Gramsci. Since Sraffa's death, the Italian press, especially the one associated with the Communist party, has concentrated attention mainly on this friendship, which, as was to be expected, has been investigated at length from Gramsci's side and from that of the Italian Communist party. This is understandable. The Italian communists have many reasons to be grateful to Piero Sraffa. Gramsci and Sraffa were not exactly contemporary: Sraffa went up to the University of Turin when Gramsci had already gone down. But both of them fell under the fascination of the same teacher, Umberto Cosmo, who was the source, for both of them, of excitement, fervour and sensitivity to problems of social injustice. (As a matter of fact, Sraffa had Cosmo as a high school – 'Liceo' – teacher, while Gramsci came to know him at the university, where Cosmo was in charge of a course of 'free lectures' on Italian literature.) When, in the 1920s, Gramsci was put in jail by Mussolini, Sraffa tried the impossible in order to alleviate him from the physical strain, keep alive his intellectual activity, ensure that his letters could reach their destination, and their text be preserved. Moreover, by taking advantage of the expertise, advice and acquaintances of an uncle of his, Judge Mariano D'Amelio, chairman of the 'Corte di Cassazione', Sraffa

[10] Raffaele Mattioli (1895–1973) was officially a banker. He was associated with Banca Commerciale Italiana from 1926 to 1972. In the early 1930s he was the youngest member of the Central Directorate. He became then managing director and finally president of the bank. In the postwar period, he built up a great reputation not only as a banker but also as a patron of literature and arts. Sraffa used to go and see him on every occasion he visited Milan. Mattioli was also crucial in convincing, and practically helping, Piero Sraffa to immediately publish an Italian version of his 1960 book.

undertook a long legal battle – very subtle and persistent, that got to a point very close indeed to success[11] – to obtain Gramsci's release from prison. It must be added, for a complete assessment of Sraffa's personality, that he never was a member of the Communist party, or for that matter of any political party, though he never hesitated to express his views and ideas, and to give his political evaluations, on current events. To me (at least during the many years I had contacts with him), Piero Sraffa has always appeared, deep down, a man of culture; never a partisan or an active member of any political party. For this reason, it would be interesting to investigate his friendship with Gramsci also from Sraffa's point of view.

There was, moreover, the friendship with Ludwig Wittgenstein. It was rather natural that they should get together. For different reasons, their conditions had much in common. It is well known by now that Keynes played a crucial role in the journey of the *Tractatus* (Wittgenstein 1922) from the knapsack of soldier Wittgenstein, while he was a prisoner of war in Italy, to Cambridge.[12] It is also well known that Keynes was so concerned with his work becoming available in Cambridge as to send Frank Ramsey on purpose to Italy, to exert persuasion on Wittgenstein.

Ludwig Wittgenstein moved definitely to Cambridge in 1929, shortly after Sraffa's arrival. It is understandable that the two should meet and develop a liking for each other, the two being both strangers to the place, brought, one could even say 'captured', to Cambridge by that sort of 'fox of culture' that Keynes was; who after discovering exceptional talents

---

[11] A question that will remain a subject of speculation is that of whether, for the sad breakdown of Sraffa's patient and painstaking legal action to obtain Gramsci's release from prison, a decisive factor was played by the leak of news that took place in 1933 from the group of Italian communists exiled in Paris. This news, the source of which was Sraffa, was meant to remain secret, but was suddenly leaked to the press and reported in newspapers' headlines. In reserved conversations, Sraffa was still talking of those events with deep sadness and emotion in the very last years of his life.

[12] This was the first relevant work by Ludwig Wittgenstein (1922).

in them, did everything he could to convince them to move to Cambridge; in this, taking advantage even of the misfortunes or personal vicissitudes they had undergone in their respective home countries.

8. Sraffa and Keynes

Last, I shall come to consider Sraffa's friendship with Keynes, to which I shall devote some space, as it concerns a relationship between two of the most original economists of the twentieth century.

As far as Sraffa is concerned, this friendship was surely the most important of his life. From their first meeting, until Keynes' death (1946), their relationship was uninterrupted. I have earlier recalled the circumstances that brought Sraffa to his first meeting with Keynes (in 1921). But it is clear that, on strictly scientific matters, their relationship started in earnest in the years 1927/28, when Sraffa moved to Cambridge as a lecturer. By that time, Sraffa had already conceived almost everything of theoretical importance that he published in the field of economic theory. And we now know from the Preface to *Production of Commodities* that 'the draft of the opening propositions' of that book had been shown to Keynes in 1928.

Let me briefly recall the sequence of events. Sraffa becomes full professor at Cagliari on 1 March 1926, a few months after the publication of his article in the *Annali di Economia*. This article is brought to Keynes's attention by Maurice Dobb, who had heard about it during a visit to Italy and, not knowing Italian, had asked friends, and most probably Sraffa himself, to report and explain to him the results of that article. Keynes asks Edgeworth, who knows Italian, to have a look at Sraffa's article (at that time, Edgeworth was the editor of the *Economic Journal*; Keynes was the assistant editor). Edgeworth realises immediately the importance of the article and allows Keynes to ask Sraffa to write an English version of it, for the *Economic Journal*. As is well known, Sraffa accepts, but writes a *different* – much shorter, and soon to become more famous than the original – article, in which the results of the previous article are only briefly recalled and summarised at the beginning. In the Cambridge scientific economic community, Sraffa's *Economic Journal* article has an explosive effect: it becomes the starting point of the 'imperfect competition revolution', against dominant Marshallian economic theory. Keynes, by that time definitively convinced of Sraffa's genius, offers him a lectureship in Cambridge. Keynes had earlier stimulated some of Sraffa's writings, which – among other things – had helped Keynes through some of his problems. By this time, Keynes decides to make Sraffa a permanent member of his intellectual Cambridge entourage.

On Sraffa's arrival in Cambridge, Keynes gives him to read the manuscript of his *Treatise on Money*, on which Keynes had been working for many years – at that time not yet ready for publication. (The *Treatise* was to be published in Keynes, 1930a.) It is certain that Sraffa read, and commented extensively on, the manuscript and the proofs of the *Treatise*. It may seem odd that Sraffa's name does not appear in Keynes's Preface. But we know by now that the published version of the *Treatise*'s Preface differs from the proofs (which have been partly published by Moggridge in his edition of Keynes's writings) by the suppression, from the acknowledgements, of Sraffa's name. Keynes's sentence, which appears in the proofs, is the following: 'I owe the discovery of innumerable mistakes and muddles to Mr F. P. Ramsey, Mr P. Sraffa and Mr R. F. Kahn' (Keynes, 1973a, vol. XIII, Part I, p. 83).

But, in the final version, Ramsey's and Sraffa's names are suppressed. For those people who have been acquainted with Sraffa, it is natural to think that – at least in the case of Sraffa – this must almost certainly have occurred at his request.[13]

---

[13] I remember myself a similar circumstance, concerning Joan Robinson's (1956) *The Accumulation of Capital*. The complimentary copy of this book was sent to Piero Sraffa with a letter (which I have had the opportunity of seeing) in which Joan Robinson expressed deep regret for not being allowed (by Sraffa) to include his name in the acknowledgements.

This may make one think that something similar might have occurred for *The General Theory* (Keynes, 1936a), for which however Moggridge does not provide earlier versions of the Preface. Keynes's unpublished papers are enormous and something might still be found. In any case, it is quite evident that Keynes, having discovered in Sraffa a first-rate critical mind, passes on to him his writings, urging him to read and scrutinise them for possible errors. Sraffa did undoubtedly read the *Treatise* accurately. It is possible that he scrutinised *The General Theory* with less accuracy or with less enthusiasm, although he must have had several discussions on it with Keynes. I may also recall the forming in 1930–31 of the by-now famous Cambridge *Circus*. Sraffa is one of its members. The impression one gets is that Sraffa follows with some detachment the evolution of *The General Theory*. On this aspect, not everything is yet entirely known. The relevant published material so far is in volumes XIII–XIV [and XXIX] of Keynes's *Writings*, edited by Moggridge. It would be of interest to carry out further research, not only on Keynes's unpublished papers but most of all on Sraffa's papers. One relevant aspect worth pointing out is that the way in which Moggridge has gathered information on the *Circus* (Keynes 1973a, vol. XIII, pp. 337–343) cannot be taken as entirely satisfactory. He reconstructs the story on the basis of personal interviews with the surviving people who were involved in the *Circus*. It is inevitable that, in so doing, one obtains a story that mainly depends upon the versions given by those people who have been most willing to talk, and Sraffa, surely, has not been one of them.

In any case, what I intend to stress is that it is difficult to try to find ways in which Keynes might have influenced Sraffa's theoretical thinking. Although Sraffa was fifteen years his junior, he had already conceived, or even published, his major contributions *before* his scientific discussions with Keynes got under way. Yet, on a personal level, the relationship between Keynes and Sraffa belongs to one of those very

complex friendships that ramify in most unexpected mean-
ders.[14] Keynes's concern for Sraffa goes to the extent of taking
care of the minute matters of everyday life, to suit his attitudes
and idiosyncrasies. Sraffa enjoys all the advantages of living
in a Cambridge college, without suffering from its associated
duties. For example, Sraffa is not a Fellow of King's College,
but he is a member of the High Table; he enjoys all the college
facilities, without being involved in his colleagues' administrative work, such as normal attendance at the college congre-
gations or even undergraduate supervisions. Moreover, after
just a few years of lecturing (by the way, there exists a clear
and complete manuscript of Sraffa's lecture notes), Sraffa is
exempted from lecturing, thanks to a device thought out with
Keynes's help. Sraffa gives up his position as lecturer and
becomes assistant director of research. From a formal point
of view, this sounds like a downgrading. In point of fact, it is
only so because of his not lecturing any more. Sraffa takes part
in all faculty activities. Anybody who has been a member of
the Cambridge faculty board knows very well how important
it is to have a right to vote for electing its members. Sraffa does
have the right to vote, like any other colleague who is delivering lectures, but he has no lecturing duty. Furthermore,
and most of all, precisely in that period, Keynes convinces
Dr T. E. Gregory of the London School of Economics, who
had been earlier appointed by the Royal Economic Society to

---

[14] A delightful expression of their personal relationship is the only work
they have published jointly. This is not a work in economics, but a work
in literary criticism and philology; the fruit of their common bibliophile
passion. After having found, in 1933, at an antiquarian bookshop, a copy
of an anonymous pamphlet, dated 1740 (*An Abstract of a book entitled
A Treatise of Human Nature etc*) and after having pinched it from each
other, with reciprocal consternations and satisfactions, the two of them
took great pleasure (with a patient work of internal criticism, based on
textual analysis and external checks) to demonstrate that the pamphlet
(earlier, erroneously, attributed to Adam Smith) could in fact have been
written by nobody else but David Hume himself. The latter, saddened by
the lack of understanding that surrounded his major work, had decided
at a certain point to write an anonymous review of it – in fact a puff:
precisely this pamphlet [Sraffa, 1938].

edit the complete works of David Ricardo, to withdraw. The same appointment – with Dr Gregory's assent – is transferred to Piero Sraffa.

To conclude, Keynes undoubtedly shows great concern for Sraffa, yet I find it difficult to think of problems on which one might trace a direct influence of Keynes on the development of Sraffa's economic thought.

But at the same time I find it equally difficult to find examples to the contrary. Keynes was carrying out his own 'revolution'. He was passing from the *Treatise* (a traditional work) to *The General Theory* (a 'revolutionary' work). If we consider the most important among Keynes's contributions – the principle of effective demand, the macroeconomic analysis of consumption, the crucial role of investments and of expectations, the relationship between investment and savings, the liquidity preference function, etc. – nothing of this suggests that Sraffa may have had any significant role in their development. The only parts of *The General Theory* that may be directly linked up with Sraffa's ideas are Chapter 16 ('Sundry Observations on the Nature of Capital') and the hints at the 'own rates of interest', explicitly attributed to Sraffa by Keynes. Yet these are secondary aspects, within the theoretical context provided by *The General Theory* or with reference to its immediate policy implications.

It seems reasonable to conclude that it is difficult to find clear evidence supporting the view of a relevant influence, on scientific grounds, of Keynes on Sraffa; and at the same time that it is equally difficult to find clear evidence of a substantial influence of Sraffa on Keynes.

One could say nevertheless, for sure, that there is, for both Keynes and Sraffa, the common conviction that traditional economic theory is inadequate and that a radical reconstruction is necessary. On this point, it might also be said that this conviction had always been present in Sraffa, while in Keynes it became evident only with the passage from the *Treatise* to *The General Theory*. This passage coincided with the 'Keynesian revolution' and took place at the time of Sraffa's arrival in Cambridge. But arguments of this type would raise more complex problems, especially with reference to all other Cambridge witnesses of that 'revolution'. I shall therefore leave the subject at this stage. I feel that adding anything more would be pure speculation, unless one takes the courageous step of proposing a logical framework in which to insert the separate contributions of both.[15]

9.   A superb critic

Something more may be added, however, on the role of Sraffa within the Cambridge intellectual milieu. It seems to me that the difficulties one meets when one tries to analyse the relationship between Sraffa and Keynes – two personalities intellectually too strong to make any concession to each other – are similar to those that have induced Perry Anderson to write that oft-quoted passage concerning the relationship between Gramsci and Sraffa:

> . . . ironically and mysteriously, one of his [i.e. of Gramsci's] closest and most life-long friends was Piero Sraffa . . . There is a certain symbolism in this strange relationship between the greatest Marxist political thinker in the West and the most original economic theorist of the post-war epoch, with its combination of personal intimacy and intellectual separation. There appears to have been no remote connection between the universes of their respective works. Sraffa's eventual critique of neo-classical economics was to be more rigorous and damaging than anything achieved within the field of Marxism itself. Yet this signal achievement was accomplished by a return, beyond Marx, to Ricardo, and the system which emerged from it was scarcely less inclement for the theory of value in *Capital*. (Anderson, 1976, p. 75n)

My conviction is however that this is not a case of lack of communication; it is rather a case of strong intellectual

---

[15] This problem will be faced in Book Three below.

independence. In my own experience, I found this typical of Sraffa's relationships with all the intellectually relevant people he met. Similar intellectual counterpositions, sometimes carried to extremes for dialectical reasons, characterised also the relationships of Sraffa with his friends in Cambridge and elsewhere. It is a kind of behaviour that might be judged negatively by those who would like to discover easy connections. But for those people who accepted discussion with him, it had the positive role of stimulating reciprocal, sometimes merciless, criticism.

It is a fact that, in discussions, when the ice was broken and Sraffa felt free to discuss, he was thoroughly destructive. It was very difficult to submit to his scrutiny any idea without seeing it overturned, broken to pieces, destroyed, sometimes in a disconcerting way, on first impact and apparently without reason.

I may recall a sentence, attributed to Wittgenstein, according to whom 'his discussions with Sraffa made him feel like a tree from which all branches had been cut' (von Wright, 1958, p. 16). Those who had the experience of submitting to and discussing with him any theoretical construction know only too well the meaning of Wittgenstein's sentence.

The role of inexorable critic played by Sraffa became even legendary in Cambridge. I myself remember that, when I returned to my college after submitting to his attention an early draft of my mathematical formulation of the Ricardian system, a friend immediately asked me: 'Have you now thrown it into the paper basket?' At my answer, 'I have, but only the first section; the major part of the work seems to stand', the surprised reply was, 'Well, if it has gone through Sraffa's scrutiny, it will hold for good.'

10.   Sraffa and Keynes's pupils

Of a more complex nature are Sraffa's relationships with Keynes's Cambridge pupils, as these relationships have been undergoing a life-long evolution. At the beginning, Sraffa's influence has obviously been preponderant. (He was in his thirties, while Kahn and Joan Robinson were in their twenties.) From Richard Kahn's (1984) 'Mattioli Lecture' one can get an idea of how intense the discussions around Sraffa's 1926 *Economic Journal* article must have been. They were the starting point of the works of Richard Kahn (1929) and of Joan Robinson (1933).[16] It seems nowadays surprising that Keynes should have taken so little account of such developments in writing *The General Theory*. Had he been more sensitive to such theoretical developments, centred on the works of Sraffa, Kahn and Joan Robinson, and on the 'Symposium on Increasing Returns' – that he enjoyed publishing as a journal editor (Robertson *et al.*, 1930, pp. 80–116), but in which he did not participate – it is possible that certain recent criticisms of *The General Theory*, on account of its lack of 'micro-foundations', could have been avoided or could even have been prevented from arising.

Later on, in the post-World War Two period, one can find that sort of intellectual independence that was mentioned above with reference to Keynes also emerging in Sraffa's relationships with the other Cambridge Keynesians (specifically with Joan Robinson, Richard Kahn and Nicholas Kaldor). Sraffa was clearly aware of the flow of new ideas (which he did not always share) and of the discussions, which were taking place in Cambridge, on problems concerning economic growth and technical progress. He must have participated (perhaps reluctantly) in discussions on the inadequacies of the traditional production function, especially with reference

---

[16] Richard F. Kahn's dissertation, *The Economics of the Short Period*, was presented in 1929 to the Electors to Fellowships Committee of King's College, Cambridge. This dissertation has been published recently, with an unchanged title, by Macmillan (see Kahn, 1989). Curiously enough, it was earlier translated and published in Italian, as *Economia del breve periodo*, edited with an Introduction by Marco Dardi (Kahn, 1929, transl. 1983); Dardi's Introduction has been translated into English in Pasinetti (1994).

to its insertion into a context in which there is technical progress. But nothing on these topics can be found in *Production of Commodities*. One might at least have expected some hints at the von Neumann growth model, but even on this one can find nothing. In the post-war period, Sraffa does not use his theoretical scheme to go in the directions along which the whole Keynesian group is moving. Actually, in his theoretical scheme, he punctiliously avoids dealing with any change in the level of the quantities produced, which he takes as given (as they may be observed at a given point of time).[17] He openly disregards precisely those phenomena on which the other Cambridge Keynesians have been concentrating attention, although these were the phenomena – concerning major movements of the economic systems over time – which were being rediscovered, and resumed, directly from classical economic theory. The impression I have had, from several conversations with Sraffa, is that he reacted, if at all, to the discussions of the Keynesian group by going back to a kind of pure circular model, removing on purpose, from the final version of his book, all those elaborations – that might perhaps have been present in earlier versions (and on this point it would be interesting to look into his unpublished papers) – that could lead the reader to find connections with the problems of economic growth, which were precisely at the centre of interest of the post-Keynesian group.[18]

At the same time, and similarly, in the 1960s, one could notice many difficulties in the opposite direction, namely on the side of the members of the Keynesian group, in assimilating the ideas contained in Sraffa's book. While one can say without any hesitation that the early works of Sraffa had an enormous influence on Keynes's pupils and, more

---

[17] This is a change, with respect to his earlier works, and particularly with respect to his 1925 article. See also Essay VI.3 below.
[18] Here is another example of the perverse effects of that attitude of extreme intellectual independence already hinted at (in section 9) above.

generally, on the economists who were working in Cambridge at the time, the same cannot be said of the work published in his maturity. Even Maurice Dobb, who wrote an enthusiastic review of *Production of Commodities* and who had been collaborating with Sraffa on the publication of the 'Works and Correspondence of David Ricardo', reveals misunderstandings of Sraffa's book. Joan Robinson tried very hard to assimilate the most important propositions of *Production of Commodities*, but I believe she has not been quite successful. Kaldor seems to have remained almost entirely extraneous to it. The same thing may be said of Richard Kahn.

In this respect, too, there seems to be something lying in the middle, even if not exactly half way, between strong intellectual independence and personal difficulties of communication, within a context of intricate and complex intellectual relationships, which were at the same time imbued with strong personal emotions.

11. The Cambridge Keynesian group

I shall here recall that, in the postwar period, this group of economists were pushing in the direction of an evolution of economic thought of an extraordinary character.

Those who were in Cambridge in the 1950s and 1960s and followed the economics debates that were taking place there know how unique that period was. I may say myself that I had the impression of living through an experience characterised by a degree of intellectual creativity, probably without comparison, originated within a group of people who were tied together by very close friendships, which were mixed with jealousy and even distrust; sometimes with reciprocal incomprehension. Those who were close to them in Cambridge in those years felt a sort of fascination and an intellectual stimulus from this group of economists that – albeit in their diversity – shared a series of profound affinities.

There is a background assonance among their ideas, besides the intense personal friendship in their relationships, that gave rise to a mixture of human feelings, on the whole rather difficult to express.

The interesting aspect for me was that one sensed rather neatly a background complementarity that involved them, but at the same time did not extend to the other economists who were teaching in Cambridge at the time. Yet among these other economists, there were notable personalities, who later on were even awarded Nobel Prizes in Economics. But they embodied another vision of economics and of economic reality, in a sense more 'normal', nearer the mainstream, and no doubt less exciting.

Those who took an active part in those private discussions (and here the witnesses are few), who met for the so-called 'secret' seminars that were taking place, know that the difference, or at least the impression of the difference, in intellectual stature between the Keynesian group and all the others was impressive.

It becomes now quite natural to ask oneself about the significance of the contributions of that Cambridge group, considered as a whole, and on this the ideas are not at all, or are not as yet, clear. Was it, after all, an illusion? Or was there, in the end, something that went wrong? Or was there something missing? Some people suggest that, in the end, what failed to materialise was an overall synthesis. It is a fact that the members of that extraordinary and unique vintage of economists stand out – if considered one by one – on a background which still is not clearly defined, where it still is difficult to fit in clearly the contributions of each one of them and even more difficult to put them into relationship with those of the others. And – I daresay – the members of the group did almost nothing to help us in the task of elaborating the required connections and syntheses.

Perhaps the worst injustice we might do to them would be precisely that of following them too closely, individually, in the peculiarities of their conceptions, in the idiosyncrasies of their behaviour, in the emotivity of their reactions. This attitude would render barren their seminal ideas with reference to the problems coming from the real world, which moves ahead continuously, along paths that they could not foresee.

It seems to me that one should avert precisely this kind of attitude, in order to avoid rigidity and mental narrowness where, on the contrary, flexibility and openness of mind are needed; in order to avoid surrendering to nostalgia, where what is needed is a fresh spring of intellectual adventure; in order to avoid reductionism, where extensions and generalisations become imperative.

Chapter VI.3

Continuity and change in Piero Sraffa's thought

1. Premise

The present essay originates from curiosity spurred by a letter written in September 1974 by Piero Sraffa to John Eatwell and Alessandro Roncaglia, who had been working for months on an English translation of Piero Sraffa's 1925 *Annali* article. They had had endless sessions with him, discussing minute details of the translation. When everything was finished and the article was ready for publication, Sraffa had second thoughts and withdrew, at least temporarily, his permission to publish.

The letter (here reproduced as document 1 in the Appendix) implies that, with respect to the time he had written the *Annali* article, his opinion had undergone some changes. Presumably, he did not like to bring the issue into the open in any discussion which might arise from publication of his article in English. He preferred – as he wrote – to postpone publication until after his death.[1]

But what kind of changes of opinion may have taken place? This is what triggered off my curiosity.

---

[1] Only recently has the English translation of Sraffa's article finally appeared in print (in Pasinetti, 1998). The translation is precisely the one carried out by Eatwell and Roncaglia and discussed by them with Sraffa in 1973–74.

2.   Evolution in Piero Sraffa's thought

The *Annali* article was published, in Italian, in 1925. It contains the background analytical scheme which is behind Sraffa's more famous 1926 E. J. article (as he explicitly says in his opening sentences).[2] It may be interesting to underline that Sraffa had never refused permission to publish translations of his articles. The *Annali* article itself had already been translated from Italian into French, German, Spanish, Japanese and Polish and had also been reprinted in Italian. Was an English translation so special? And, more importantly, what was it that made Sraffa so sensitive?

To begin with, it seems necessary to establish some sense of proportion. In the history of economic thought, changes of opinion have not been uncommon. There have been famous, and in fact radical, changes of opinion. Think of the case of Keynes, who changed his mind, in the early 1930s, by repudiating his *Treatise on Money* and moving towards his 'revolutionary' *General Theory* (Keynes, 1930a, 1936a). Think of Kaldor, who around 1940 repudiated his marginal theory writings and went through a 'conversion' to Keynesian economics.

Nothing of this sort can evidently have been the case for Sraffa.

Yet something must have taken place. Some hints may be found in the Preface to Sraffa's *Production of Commodities* (1960), where he refers to the question of returns to scale. Sraffa had claimed in 1925 that the only logically consistent hypothesis to make, in a theory of production, is that of constant returns to scale. But in his 1960 book he claims that his analysis does not imply any assumption on returns to scale. It would be difficult to class this as a radical change, especially if we consider that Sraffa himself, for the benefit of the reader, suggests that:

[2] Sraffa, 1926, pp. 277–328.

If such a supposition [i.e. that of constant returns] is found help-ful, there is no harm in the reader's adopting it as a temporary working hypothesis. In fact, however, no such assumption is made. (Sraffa, 1960, p. v)

Was the change all here? Or was there something else?

Some change should not be surprising after all: from 1925 to 1960 there elapsed thirty-five years! It is quite normal that the thoughts of any active intellectual always undergo some change or, as one might say, some evolution, as time goes on, owing to cumulation of intervening discussions and reflec-tions. This must certainly have happened in the case of such a scholar as Sraffa. Hence, to envisage a sort of evolution in his thought appears quite reasonable – an evolution that may have been quicker in certain periods than in others, some-times so rapid as to induce even to thinking of a sort of turning point. But nothing, one can imagine, could be like a break of the sort experienced by Keynes or by Kaldor, to take the cases earlier mentioned here, or even, to recall yet another famous case, of the kind that characterised the change that intervened from the *Tractatus* to the *Investigations* of Ludwig Wittgen-stein (1922, 1945); a change attributed, incidentally, to Sraffa himself.

Thus, if we accept that some sort of 'evolution' must have taken place in Sraffa's thought, what remains to be investi-gated is how far, or to what extent, it took place. This is the intriguing question.

3.   A personal immersion into Sraffa's papers

For a fortnight I have locked myself up in the Trinity College Wren Library at Cambridge and I have tried avidly to read notes and scripts, and files and files of papers, which seemed to be relevant to the question stated above.[3]

---

[3] This happened in the first half of September 1998.

To me, the consultation of Sraffa's papers and manuscripts, as at one time did the conversations with him, instantly brings into relief a personality of disconcerting complexity. In my search, I obviously began with the year 1925 and I tried to concentrate on anything that might have appeared relevant in order to detect Sraffa's long journey to his final book (*Production of Commodities*, 1960). Of course, the time devoted to this search has been too short, even by taking advantage of my previous consultations of Sraffa's papers (all since 1994, when Sraffa's archives were opened). Therefore much of what I am going to say may still be provisional.

The catalogue of Sraffa's papers at the Trinity College Wren Library is not perfect, yet is clear enough to give a helpful guide. Leaving aside the 'Personal papers' (classed as section A), those concerning his 'academic career' (section B), his 'Diaries' (section E), the 'Memoirs of colleagues' and 'Publications of others' (sections F and G), the 'Bibliographical material' (sections H and I) and finally the 'Miscellaneous material' (section J), it was natural for me to concentrate partly on the 'Correspondence' (section C) and partly on the 'Notes, lectures, publications' (section D).

The correspondence is inevitably fragmentary and a bit disorderly, but is a mine of information, direct and indirect, and a potent stimulus for conjectures. The publications are well known. The unpublished lectures are many and varied. The most important of them are the sixteen lectures on *The Advanced Theory of Value*, delivered for the first time in 1928 (Michaelmas Term) and then repeated, with amendments and additions (all clearly handwritten), in the three subsequent years.

For the purpose that I had in mind it is, however, the 'Notes' that revealed themselves to be relevant and interesting. I found them fascinating but disconcerting: an enormous number of various sheets, of any dimensions, backs of other documents, small books, block notes, small and large, fragments of printed papers (newspapers or else), on which one finds notes, and notes, and corrections of notes, sometimes very brief, some other times of the full length of proper articles, on the most disparate and unexpected subjects. The language used is Italian, at the beginning, slipping then gradually into English, in time, and in fact always being a mixture of the two, in different (and obviously changing) proportions. There are quotations and here also French and German appear (copied in his clear handwriting). There are comments and there is a number, which seems never to end, of criticisms, counter-criticisms, reflections and second thoughts. Not all but most of these notes are *dated* by Piero Sraffa himself, with indication of day, month and year. (Many of those that are not dated are datable from the context.) A query immediately arises: for whom are these dates? Most probably for himself: in order to remember the circumstances behind the notes when coming back to the problems concerned, especially after long interruptions. But really only for himself? The conjecture is difficult to repress – thinking of Sraffa as a historian, a careful philologist, a powerful and highly critical intellectual – that they could also have been put there for the benefit of those who might be interested in reading them in the future. If this were so, his purposes would appear to be, or to have become, really far-reaching.

4.   A few hints at the Sraffa archives subdivisions

It is important to recall that the classification of Sraffa's notes was made, by a professional catalogue expert, *after* Sraffa's death. It is by all means natural to take Sraffa's publications as the points of reference and of attraction of his notes. This has full justification when the notes are near, in time, to the corresponding actual publications. But when, between the notes and publication, there elapses a long period of time, such justification becomes weaker. In this perspective (if we exclude the early publications on monetary subjects), the notes in preparation of the articles of 1925 and 1926 and the notes in preparation of the (unpublished) 1928 lectures can be singled out with sufficient clarity. Then, from 1928 onwards, all theory notes that do not refer to Ricardo's *Works and Correspondence* are classified as being 'in preparation of *Production of Commodities*'. This may not be entirely justified.

The period of time from 1928 to 1960 – more than thirty years! – is a very long period indeed in any scholar's life. A distinction of these notes from the previous ones is however clear enough. On the cover of more than one file Sraffa himself writes 'notes after 1927'. And the catalogue makes a distinction between pre- and post-1928 notes. It seems clear that a distinction is drawn by Sraffa himself between the earlier notes, that were specifically aimed at imminent publications, and a more substantial, far-reaching set of notes, aimed at a more considerable kind of work. Sraffa seems to have something definite, perhaps great, in mind. In normal circumstances, one might have expected from him the writing of a book. And in fact there is a note in his files that is headed 'Impostazione del libro' – an explicit statement of his intentions on how to write 'the book' (see document 2 in the Appendix). But if this was so, the period of preparation of such a book kept on becoming longer and longer, while being characterised by various events, abrupt halts, new engagements, with long interruptions. It is reasonable to expect that, on this tortuous way, his original intentions may have been affected, and may have changed, to a certain extent.

Let me review, schematically, what is revealed by the grouping of the theory notes (i.e. those that do *not* refer to the edition of Ricardo's *Works*):

– there is first of all the period 1928–31, which obviously must have been a crucial period in framing Sraffa's aims and intentions;
– then there is a gap that extends up to the beginning of the 1940s. This is the period in which Sraffa devotes himself, fully as it appears, to the edition of Ricardo's *Works*;

- the notes are resumed in 1941, all of a sudden and very intensively, then at a slower pace as the years proceed, up to 1945;
- there comes another interruption from 1946 to 1955. This is the period in which Sraffa is engaged in taking Ricardo's *Works* to actual publication. He is also victim of a terrible mountaineering accident in a sadly famous holiday in Norway;
- finally, there is the period from 1955 to 1960, where one finds Sraffa's final efforts to gather at least part of his notes into a book, finished to all purposes in 1958, but published, amongst endless hesitations, at the end of May (Italian version, a week later, early June) 1960.

Overall, I found therefore three relevant, but separate, periods for my purposes, with three corresponding groups of notes: 1928–31, 1941–45, 1955–59.

These three groups of notes are quite distinct in terms of the subjects investigated. In the archives, they are *all* classified as 'notes in preparation of *Production of Commodities*', simply because no publication took place, except at the end, in 1960. However, this way of considering Sraffa's notes, reflections and self-criticisms risks being misleading in many respects. Sraffa *did not know* in 1928 that, in 1960, he was going to publish a small book called *Production of Commodities by Means of Commodities*. He intended indeed to write a book, as pointed out above, but his intentions about the kind of publication(s) that would come may have been quite different at the beginning, and they may have changed or 'evolved' quite a lot from the early 1930s to the final year (1960).

5.   Three streams of thought

On reading Sraffa's notes, one remains disconcerted and bewildered – I was for days and days. But when I went back and reflected, and looked over my notes and tried to synthesise in my mind the hundreds of bits of thoughts, criticisms, reformulations, counter-thoughts, etc., forcing myself to take a detached and far-away overview, as from a bird's eye view on a high flight, I got the impression of at least three well-distinguished, though intermingling, strands, from beginning to end, in Sraffa's remarkable set of notes. These three strands concern the development of three corresponding streams of thought.

First stream of thought. One thing that appears quite clearly from the notes since 1928, starting immediately after the publication of the 1925 and 1926 articles and parallel to the revision of the 1928–31 lecture notes, is that Sraffa is convinced, since the beginning, that an aberrant distortion has taken place in economic theory in the second part of the nineteenth century. From 1870 onwards, dominant (marginalist) economics has caused a change in the content of the whole subject, with respect to what it used to be previously. More precisely, Sraffa finds that, since 1870, economic theorists use indeed the same vocabulary, the same language and terms of reference as before, but the underlying concepts have undergone a 'terrific' change. Sraffa shows astonishment: did not Smith and Ricardo on the one side and the marginalists and Marshall on the other speak the same English language? Why does one not realise that the actual content, the concepts behind the same words, have been twisted to mean entirely different things? There is an 'abysmal gulf' (S. P., D 3/12/4, f.14) between the marginal economists' writings since 1870 and those of the economists of the beginning of the nineteenth century (see Appendix, document 3).[4] The basic problem is not, or not only, a question of a different theory. We are not simply facing a question of 'marginal theory' versus 'classical theory', as one may be inclined to think. For Sraffa, marginal theory is an aberration. There exists, for him, a sensible

---

[4] I shall use the symbols S. P. to refer to excerpts from Sraffa's papers, followed by the section (a capital letter) and the reference numbers.

economic theory and an aberrant economic theory. The change of the name itself – from classical 'political economy' to Marshall's 'economics' – is there to 'mark the cleavage' and 'Marshall's attempt to bridge over the cleavage and establish a continuity in the tradition is futile and misguided' (S. P. D/12/4). In Sraffa's convictions, one must discard the aberrations and go back to an economic theory that is sensible, true and reasonable: the economic theory that existed before the 1870s.

This first stream of thought in Sraffa's notes would appear therefore to belong to the history of economic thought.

Second stream of thought. From what is said above, Sraffa appears to be convinced that it is a question of absolute priority and necessity to develop a ruthless critique of the aberrations brought into existence by marginal economic theory. The bulk of his notes and reflections and comments is in this direction. They form an impressive set of critical arguments and in this Sraffa really reveals himself as an exceptional critical mind. The notes in the Archives provide a determined, reiterated, punctilious set of criticisms of the economic theory that has come into being since 1870. Within this critical stream of thought, one can find many substreams. Since the field is immense and the notes are numerous, I may mention at least four themes that repeatedly recur as the specific targets of his poisonous arrows: i) the marginal theory of production and distribution, ii) the theory of value (which the marginalists call price theory), iii) the theory of marginal utility, iv) the theory of interest, when interest is presented as a reward for abstinence (his remarks on this subject are particularly caustic).

This second stream of thought in Sraffa's notes is thus aimed at a critique of dominant economic theory. It is by far the most extensive and prevailing stream of thought in Sraffa's notes, especially in the early periods.

Third stream of thought. A third strand of arguments unfolds as a logical consequence of the previous two. For

Sraffa, it is absolutely necessary to return to the point where sensible economic theory stood, i.e. to the point where its development was interrupted and distorted. It is necessary to return to the 'political economy' of the Physiocrats, Smith, Ricardo, Marx. One must resume genuine economic theory at the point where it was discontinued. And one must proceed in two directions: i) to cleanse it of all difficulties and incongruities that the classical economists (and Marx) had not been able to overcome, and ii) to go on and develop the relevant economic theory as this should have evolved, from 'Petty, Cantillon, the Physiocrats, Smith, Ricardo, Marx'. This natural and consistent flow of ideas had suddenly been interrupted and buried under the all-invading, submerging, overwhelming tidal wave of marginal economics. It should be rescued.

This third stream of thought appears therefore, at last, as a constructive stream of thought.

6.   An impossibly grand research programme

The three streams of thought sketched out above make up such a huge research programme as to frighten anybody who might think of carrying it out in isolation. Yet Piero Sraffa, at the beginning, seems to have aimed at doing precisely that.

One can see such a programme as showing up at the time of his coming to Cambridge, and more clearly at the stage of the revision of his (yet unpublished) *Lectures on Advanced Theory of Value*, i.e. in the years 1928–31. But it must not have taken long for him to realise the sheer impossibility of bringing such an atrociously grand research programme into actual shape. The contrast between aims and realistic possibilities begins to emerge strikingly from his notes, while he is preparing the amendments to his *Lectures on Advanced Theory of Value*. These *Lectures* had all been handwritten in 1927. They were delivered in the three subsequent years, with changes and amendments, which one can find added, in his clear writing, on the manuscript, with a clearly perceptible increasing dissatisfaction.

The sheer fact of being compelled to lecture stimulates Sraffa's mind to the limit of endurance. One can see from his critical notes that he goes in depth, he goes into analysis, he goes in extension. Never does one find him going towards a synthesis. Thus he writes notes, which are essentially critical and provisional. Apparently these notes are for himself, but perhaps he may have begun quite early to look ahead and hope that someone in the future might pick them up. (One could understand in this way also his care in marking them with a date.) Criticisms add themselves to criticisms and to the critique of criticisms.

It is a fact that, at a certain point, even delivering his *already written-up* lectures becomes for him an excruciating experience. It must indeed have become a hard task for him to guard himself from frustration.

We can infer that Keynes's intuition was sharp enough to realise that Sraffa was in a serious predicament, without perhaps understanding clearly the basic source and wide extent of his drama. In any case, Keynes is sufficiently impressed to become convinced that in some way somebody or something should come to the rescue. Thus Keynes manages to convince Professor T. E. Gregory of LSE to withdraw from his already signed-up agreement with the Royal Economic Society to collect and edit the works and correspondence of David Ricardo. The contract is transferred from Gregory to Sraffa. A real blessing. God knows what Sraffa would have done otherwise.

At that point, Piero Sraffa is relieved. He resigns his Cambridge lectureship so as to stop the nightmare of delivering lectures and he immerses himself, for the following thirty years, into his newly acquired task – a task which to external observers appears, from that point on, as his major concern. Behind the scenes, his principal grandiose research programme is temporarily put aside. Not entirely, though. If nothing else, he catches the opportunity to clarify to himself, and to clear up, the incongruities in classical economic thought. This merges well with item i) of what I have called above his 'constructive' strand of thought.

Sraffa becomes so aware of the relevance of Ricardo's works to his research programme that when, in 1941, the bulk of Ricardo's writings have gone to the printer (to remain there for years, owing to his difficulties in writing the introductions and then owing to the discovery of new documents, as will be said in a moment), he goes back to his programme and begins to shape up a new phase which, from the notes, now appears as leading him to concentrate on the correct formulation, in terms of equations, of at least some of his 'classical' propositions. This is quite evident in his 1941 notes, where one can see his earlier thoughts being resumed at the point where they had been left. In fact he had already tried to formulate his theory in terms of 'equations' as early as in 1928. He had even shown such equations to Keynes. This event is mentioned at many points in the drafts and then, though in a slightly more diluted form, in the published Preface to his book. But in the late 1920s he had barely been able to satisfactorily go beyond the 'equations without a surplus'. In 1941–44 he really makes a breakthrough. With the advice, not always followed and actually sometimes disputed, of Abram Besicovitch, he succeeds in formulating correctly the equations with a surplus and with labour explicitly introduced,[5] while discovering the notions of a maximum rate of profit independent of prices, of basics and non-basics, and of the 'Standard system'. These results really represent a remarkable achievement. Obtained in isolation and silence, they will be included in the first part of his book, twenty years later. But at the time they absorb all his efforts. There is very little else he can

---

[5] Giancarlo de Vivo (2004) confirms this, in his detailed analysis of Sraffa's 'path' to the final formulation of the equations of his book.

do on the rest of his original research programme. He goes back, now and then, to his previous notes and adds some comments or self-criticism or further reflections. Not much more than that. As a consequence, the horizon of his research programme gets drastically restricted. As he proceeds, he is excited by the remarkable properties he is discovering in the mathematical formulation of his equations. But this absorbs time. He is compelled to postpone or cut down the other aspects.

Precisely at this point, another interruption comes in his way. Unexpected events, during the war, lead Sraffa to take advantage of an exciting discovery of a different sort. In July 1943, by chance, a locked metal box containing a considerable number of earlier missing Ricardo papers, actually the whole series of his letters to James Mill and other manuscripts, is unexpectedly found at Raheny, Co. Dublin. As soon as Sraffa is informed and becomes aware of the discovery, he gets so excited as to decide – in spite of all the difficulties connected with the war, but at the same time by taking advantage of Keynes's connections – to leave immediately for Dublin. On his return, he has no hesitation in deciding that he must rethink the whole layout of the plan of publication of Ricardo's *Works*, even though the volumes are already in print! Increasingly, especially from 1944, his concern is shifted away from his theory notes. Very rapidly, his energies are fully diverted to the task (including the excruciating experience of writing the Introductions, with the help of Maurice Dobb) required to restructure and then to carry Ricardo's volumes I to X to actual publication (1953–1957). He could hardly have done otherwise, under the mounting pressure of the Royal Economic Society for the long-overdue publication of a work that had been in print for more than ten years. To this purpose, his energies are absorbed almost fully from 1945 up to 1955 (with the added misfortune of time forcedly lost as a consequence of the already-mentioned mountaineering accident in Norway).

When, in the end, all Ricardo's works are published (with the only exception of the indexes, which were to remain in the pipeline of publication until 1973), Sraffa finally does go back and resume his theoretical work, as it was left in the 1940s. From 1955 to 1960, when nobody would have expected it, he succeeds in setting together enough propositions to be able to complete and, at long last, publish a book. We all know it well: a ninety-nine-page book, amazingly dense in concepts, terse and essential, extraordinarily compact and disconcertingly cryptic – *Production of Commodities by Means of Commodities*. Sraffa abstains from making any claim. He presents it as no more than 'a prelude to a critique of economic theory'.

7. What fraction of the original programme?

What fraction of the original programme and, most of all, which aspects of such a programme have eventually come to fruition? This becomes an irrepressible question at this point. The richness of the existing manuscripts can give us at least some idea of the wide gap that has grown in time between the original intentions and what Piero Sraffa finally becomes convinced to publish.

First of all, one must record with sadness that Sraffa abandons the aim of publishing anything on the history of economic thought. This is by itself an extraordinary decision, if we consider his original intentions. An idea of the width of the original purpose may be seen from a very clear and telling scheme (see document 4 in the Appendix) of how he sees the development of economic thought from Petty to Marshall. In the same folder, one finds a page – headed 'Principio' – giving his intended plan of exposition (document 5 in the Appendix).

The ten-year interruption that follows, due to his ground work for the edition of Ricardo's *Works and Correspondence*, induces him – as one may clearly perceive from the postwar

notes – to a severe reassessment. His original grand programme – left aside for ten years – undergoes a radical, down-
to-earth reconsideration, presumably in view of a more realistic awareness of what can be done, given the effort and
time absorbed by the setting together of a satisfactory formulation of his equations. In a note, which in the *Sraffa Papers*
is among the post-1945 notes, we find a scheme headed
'? Preface', where Sraffa gives an explicit account of the cuts
he has decided to make with respect to the originally
intended scheme (see document 6 in the Appendix). But the
restructuring does not stop at this stage and goes on and on,
as one may realise by comparing what is said in document 6
itself with what one finds in the final publication.[6] Quite surprisingly, in the end, nothing explicit remains on the history
of economic thought. Only indirectly do we find brief (though
important) fragments pertaining to the history of economic
thought in the eleven-volume edition of Ricardo's *Works*. In
Production of Commodities, all that one can find is a two-
and-a-half-page appendix called 'Appendix D – References
to the Literature'. And that is really all. It seems incredible, if
we think that these two and a half pages are what is actually
published on the history of economic thought by a person
who is considered as one of the greatest scholars in the field.

The same process of a progressive restriction of horizon
also comes to affect the major stream of Sraffa's work: the
one referring to the critique of current economic theory. It is
indeed astonishing to realise that, in the end, no explicit critique of marginal economic theory remains (with the exception of very short bits here and there, such as the one on the
average period of production), though the concern with this

---

[6] There is a witty letter from Raffaele Mattioli to Piero Sraffa, dated
15 March 1955, revealing that they had talked about the intended resumption of Sraffa's project and the drastic cuts that needed to be made. Mattioli writes (my translation from Italian): '. . . I hope you have succeeded
in the past thirty days to reduce to half a kilogram the twenty kilos of
paperasse . . . and I wish you to write the first rough draft of the 'modest
little book'. Keep me informed . . .' (S. P. D3/11/83, f.6)

critique is the major objective that Sraffa has had in mind since the beginning. A hint is given in the opening sentences of the Preface to his book. He states: 'It is . . . a peculiar feature of the set of propositions now published that, although they do not enter into any discussion of the marginal theory of value and distribution, they have nevertheless been designed to serve as the basis for a critique of that theory. If the foundation holds, the critique may be attempted later, either by the writer or by someone younger and better equipped for the task' [1960, p. vi]. Consistently, he subtitles the book: 'A prelude to a critique of economic theory' – an implicit confession of his awareness of remaining very far away from what his manuscripts reveal to be his original targets. At the same time, his last sentence just cited reveals the beginning of his opening up to the hope that some people of the younger generation may follow his lead and carry on his (originally conceived) task.

One must conclude that, *as far as actual publication is concerned*, what have been called above the first and the second streams of thought in Sraffa's original programme – really two major strands of thought in his notes – have, in the end, been abandoned.

It sounds paradoxical – if one thinks of Sraffa's well-known powerful, critical mind – that he should decide in the end to leave critique aside altogether and go straight on – and in an amazingly concise way – to what has been singled out above as the third stream in his thought: the constructive stream of thought. But even this part of his analysis is by no means an all-comprehensive type of investigation. Very significantly and quite explicitly, he narrows it down to what, in presenting his book, he defines as 'pure economic theory'. And it sounds almost unbelievable that, after scolding Marx, in his earlier notes (see Appendix, document 2), for not having presented, first, a historical explanation, thus being the cause of his not being understood, he should do exactly the same. Albeit much worse: not only by dropping his historical conception of the evolution of economic thought but also by leaving any critique of current economic theory aside altogether; and on top of that by using an extraordinarily compact method of exposition, compressing his arguments to the limit of incomprehension. No wonder the result has been found puzzling, cryptic and, by some people, even obscure. The state of Sraffian understanding has somewhat improved since. Many economists of the younger generation have not disappointed his hopes. His constructive contributions to the analysis of the relations between value and income distribution, in a most general production economic system, have by now been perceived. His analytical results concerning the Standard system and the relations between prices and income distribution have been widely illustrated. Many of the proofs concerning the remarkable properties of his system of equations (such as uniqueness, non-negativity of solutions, joint production with fixed capital and land as special cases, etc.) have been reformulated with the help of powerful mathematical tools (such as Perron-Frobenius theorems for non-negative matrices). Again paradoxically, this improvement in understanding his achievements is largely due to an explicit use of mathematical tools for which Sraffa had so much reluctance.[7] Indeed, precisely due to the use of mathematics, many further analytical problems have kept on being clarified, in a literature that has been expanding. Let me mention, among other upshots, the association of basic and non-basic commodities with the structure of irreducible and reducible matrices; the (Marxian) problem of (analytical) transformation of 'values' into prices of production and the opposite (symmetric) process of transformation of prices of production into 'values'; the reduction of prices to dated quantities of labour; the substantial development of the analysis of joint production;[8] the analytical subdivision

---

[7] See Pasinetti, 2003.
[8] See Manara, 1968, and then, much more extensively, Schefold, 1971.

of an economic system into as many subsystems as there are final commodities; and their relation to an equal number of vertically integrated sectors.[9] And the list could go on. Moreover, it must at least be mentioned that a slim (seven-page) last chapter of his book has proposed a highly original analysis of the switching and reswitching of technique. Precisely this short chapter was the igniting spark of a vast and heated debate on capital theory in the 1960s and 1970s. At the same time, his Introductions to Ricardo's *Works* have opened up the way to a clearer and deeper understanding than has ever been the case before of classical economic theory.

But precisely because his analysis was not preceded by a presentation of his conception of the historical evolution of economic thought and by his critique of marginal economic theory, his constructive efforts are still far from being fully understood. Many economists, even among those basically sympathetic to his approach, remain in a state of dissatisfaction.

Most of all, the part of Sraffa's analysis that would seem to have remained incomplete is the one concerning the role of the physical quantities of the commodities that are produced, and of their movements through time. One can understand quite well how prices and physical quantities remain separated in classical economic theory and, consistently, how they remain separated in Sraffa's theoretical scheme. But Sraffa refuses to go ahead on these problems. In his published 'propositions', the physical quantities are taken as given. So much so that some critics have (mis)interpreted his system as being only a half-system (concerning the price side but not the quantity side of the economy). To dispel this misinterpretation, one should face the problem of dealing with the physical quantities. In a much-quoted letter to a student who was asking illumination from him on this point, Sraffa replied that his analysis was limited to taking a 'photograph'

[9] See Pasinetti, 1973.

of an economic system, as this actually can be observed at a certain point of time.[10] Yet one cannot refrain from asking what conception Sraffa had of the economic movements of physical quantities, i.e. more specifically, of the dynamics of an economic system. It is tempting to make comparison with von Neumann's scheme or with Leontief's dynamic model, to try to gather some clues. But in spite of the analytical similarities with Sraffa's 'Standard system', von Neumann's approach appears inappropriate, and so does Leontief's. Sraffa does not even mention von Neumann's model, nor does he mention Leontief. Those who had the opportunity of putting questions to him on these similarities know Sraffa's negative responses. Von Neumann's and even more Leontief's approaches are quite alien to his conception of the movements of an economic system through time.

What really then is Piero Sraffa's conception? It is not easy to give a satisfactory answer to this question. In Sraffa's early notes, one finds some hints at the problem of 'closing' the system, in terms of what wages and profits could buy. But these are passing and incidental remarks (or so they appear to me). My impression is that, on these aspects, the enormous mass of Sraffa's notes are still not sufficient to reveal any clear direction. It may well be that, in the end, he simply lacked time to apply his mind to these problems. Personally, I am convinced that, while remaining within the bounds of what Sraffa calls 'pure economic theory', it is not enough to take a stand-still photograph of an economic system as it appears at a given point of time. One should also be able to proceed, so to speak, to the 'filming' of the movements of the economic system through time.

There is not much choice among alternatives here. My personal conviction is that the only direction consistent with all this and with Sraffa's line of thought lies in a conception of the economic movements through time in terms of *structural*

[10] The letter is in *Sraffa Papers*, C294/2.

economic dynamics. This is the direction in which I consistently decided to go, since the very beginning of my association with the Cambridge School of Keynesian Economics.[11] But I must stress that the question remains wide open and, I fear, it goes beyond the reach of Sraffa's manuscripts.

8.   Final remarks (or Sraffa versus Keynes?)

The present 'bird's eye view' exercise on Sraffa's manuscripts may well suffer from a somewhat hasty drive to arrive at least at some sharp conclusions. But it has been difficult for me not to be deeply impressed by the realisation of the drama that must have been lived through by this remarkable man, in isolation and silence. And I thought that taking a clear, even if controversial, stand would be the most helpful option I could offer.

No doubt an evolution in Sraffa's attitudes did take place in the course of his life, but − I am now convinced more than ever − not in his basic thoughts and convictions. From his notes, one can clearly perceive the long process: from an early volcanic eruption of never-ending criticisms of current economic theory, within a solid conceptual framework of the historical development of economic thought − surprisingly concealed even to his friends − to more mature reflections and search for a distinction between those traditionally held propositions and concepts that could clearly be shown to be lacking logical foundations and those that should be treated with great circumspection, given the prevailing widespread hostility towards classical and Marxian views; to a final extra-cautious attitude that led him to concentrate his published work on a concise nucleus of unassailable analytical propositions. But his remarkable final results − it seems to me − point in a double direction: i) they can indeed be used, without being accused of ideological prejudices, for a critique of

---

[11] i.e. from my Cambridge PhD dissertation (Pasinetti, 1962).

marginal economic theory, as he explicitly states; but also: ii) they can provide a solid logical basis – the starting seed we might say – for a reconstruction of economic theory. Because of the strikingly wide contrast between the huge amount of information available from Sraffa's unpublished notes and the tiny concise material that he has decided to publish, in the end, the exercise so far carried out brings into sharp evidence the vital importance of Piero Sraffa's manuscripts.[12]

But precisely here lies the conundrum. Which relations can one see between the plenty (of notes) and the scarcity (of published results)? Quantitatively – as has been stressed above – the contrast is enormous. But is it also so *qualitatively*? My answer is a definite no. What has been published – it seems to me – fits perfectly well into the initial grand scheme. The overall, wide spectrum of subjects, historical interpretations, evaluations of approaches, criticisms covered by the notes, and finally the (limited) attempts at a reconstruction, can perfectly be put together in a logically comprehensive scheme, *provided that* we are prepared to step on to a methodological approach which seems to me of the greatest importance. We should note that Sraffa chooses to concentrate on a narrow but at the same time on the solidest and permanent part of his theoretical framework, i.e. on the strictly basic foundations of his analysis. In *Production of Commodities* he does not rely on any institutional set-up, he does not make reference to

---

[12] There are many signs that Piero Sraffa was aware of this importance of his manuscripts. Already in his mentioned letter (1974) to John Eatwell and Alessandro Roncaglia he states: 'As for any publication of my manuscripts after death, any decision will either be in my will or left to my literary executors' (see Appendix, document 1). But there was nothing in his will on this issue. A literary executor was designated later, in an additional codicil, but without explicit instructions. The only hint that has been found so far is an incomplete note on the back of a fragment of calendar loose sheet. It was noticed by Giancarlo de Vivo, while he was looking for something else in a file of correspondence with antiquarian book dealers. It may have ended up there by mistake. The note is written in Italian, in pencil, and has all the appearance of a part of a draft of instructions to be given to the prospective editor(s) of his unpublished manuscripts. It is reproduced here as document 7 in the Appendix.

any historical context, he does not mention any kind of 'economic agent'. He carefully avoids making any assumptions on human behaviour, on market structure, on competition, on returns to scale. He even avoids taking a specific stand on the distribution of income, for which he does not commit himself to the way in which the rate of profit (or alternatively the wage rate) is determined. The rate of profit is simply considered as an independently determined variable. Because his basic 'pure economic theory' is one that does not depend on particular institutional assumptions, it enjoys a life of its own, at the very *foundation level* of economic theory. And Sraffa is confident: 'If the foundation holds [he states in his Preface] the critique – but, we may also add, the reconstruction of economic theory – can be attempted later.' There is no concealing that what is hinted at here is a really formidable task. Logically, it is not even one single task; it consists of at least two separate tasks. The 'impossibly grand programme', as I have called it above – that can be detected at the beginning of his mass of notes – is really spanning round 360 degrees: over history, over the evolution of economic thought, over the economic institutions. It is in fact – as we may now realise – a task which we can constantly find in the background of all the efforts attempted by his Cambridge colleagues, at various stages, in various parts, through many aspects – by Keynes *in primis*, but also by all the members of the Keynesian Cambridge group. Not surprisingly, their efforts never could satisfy Sraffa. Towards his colleagues – as well as towards his own thoughts – he was always exercising the most critical, and the so much appreciated, powerful force of his intellect.

And yet – from the point of view at which we have put ourselves here – this is by no means the whole story. If the analysis carried out above is correct, there is the task concerning also the *foundation aspects* of economic analysis that still remains to be completed. We should not be complacent about this, nor should we nurture illusions. This is the less satisfactory part of any work that may be carried out by an exclusive reliance on the *Sraffa Papers* because — as hinted at above — it seems to go beyond the content of the *Papers* themselves. Whatever investigation one may carry out on the *Sraffa Papers*, one cannot pretend to find in them what is not there.

It is up to the economists of the post-Sraffian generation to construct that part of the *foundations of economic theory* that Sraffa could not complete.

Appendix – selected documents from Sraffa's unpublished papers

Document 1
— Letter of Piero Sraffa to John Eatwell and Alessandro Roncaglia

Trinity College
20 Sept. 1974

Dear Eatwell and Roncaglia,
    Thank you for your letter dated 8 August. It is most kind of you to take an interest in my old papers.

As regards the English translation of my article in *Annali* 1925, it seems to me impossible to present to a new public in one's lifetime an article without implying that one still agrees with all that it contains, or else pointing out which are the points or aspects on which he has changed his mind. I do not feel that I could do this. I would therefore not wish the article to be published again in my lifetime.

Concerning quotations from my letters or other MSS, I am opposed to quotation from, or incomplete publication of, unpublished manuscripts.

As for any publication of my manuscripts after death, any decision will either be in my will or left to my literary executors.

Yours
Piero Sraffa

Document 2

– Sraffa Papers D3/12/11, f.35 (attributed date November 1927)

Impostazione del libro

L'unico sistema è di far la storia a ritroso e cioè: stato attuale dell'ec.; come vi si è giunti, mostrando la differenza e la superiorità delle vecchie teorie. Poi, esporre la teoria. Se si va in ordine cronol., Petty, Fisiocr., Ric., Marx, Jevons, Marsh., bisogna farlo precedere da uno statement della mia teoria per spiegare dove si 'drive at': il che significa esporre prima *tutta* la teoria. E allora c'è il pericolo di finire come Marx, che ha pubblicato prima il Cap., e poi non è riuscito a finire l'Histoire des Doctr. E il peggio si è che non è riuscito a farsi capire, senza la spiegazione storica. Il mio scopo è: I esporre la storia, che è veramente l'essenziale II farmi capire: per il che si richiede che io vada dritto all'ignoto, da Marshall a Marx, dalla disutilità al costo materiale

Translation

Layout of the book

The only way is to make history in reverse that is: present state of ec.; how it has been reached, showing the difference and superiority of the old theories. Then, present the theory. If I go in chronol. order, Petty, Physiocr., Ric., Marx, Jevons, Marsh., it is necessary to make first a statement of my theory to explain where I 'drive at': which means to present first all the theory. And then there is the danger to end up like Marx, who published Cap. and then did not succeed in finishing the Histoire des Doctr. And the worst is that he has not succeeded in making himself understood without historical explanation. My purpose is: to present history, which is really the essential thing. To make myself understood: for which what is required is that I go straight to the unknown, from Marshall to Marx, from disutility to material cost.

Document 3

– Sraffa Papers D 3/12/4, f.14 (dated November 1927)

. . . . .

It is terrific to contemplate the abysmal gulf of incomprehension that has opened itself between us and the classical economists. Only one century separates us from them: [then the following sentence, here reproduced in italics, is added as a footnote] *I say a century; but even half a century after, in 1870, they did not understand it. And during the preceding century an obscure process of 'disunderstanding' had been going on.* How can we imagine to understand the Greeks and the Romans? [then the following sentence, again here reproduced in italics, is added as a footnote] *Or rather, the extraordinary thing is that we do understand, since we find them perfect, Roman law and Greek philosophy.* The classical economists said things which were perfectly true, even according to our standards of truth: they expressed them very clearly, in terse and unambiguous language, as is proved by the fact that they perfectly understood each other. We don't understand a word of what they said: has their language been lost? Obviously not, as the English of Adam Smith is what people talk today in this country. What has happened then?

Document 4
– Sraffa Papers – D 3/12/4 f.10 (dated November 1927)

History
Classical Political Economy (The age of Ricardo) or A. Smith?

From Petty to Ricardo – right conception, fundamental assumptions
                    Primitive, rudimentary technique
(A. Smith had strong 'vulgar' tendencies: he can truly be said to be the 'founder of modern economics'!)
Vulgar Political Economy (The age of Mill)
From Malthus to Stuart Mill – All wrong here: they have the
                    wrong conceptions of modern
                    economics and the rudimentary
                    technique of the classical

Period dominated by Mill:
Marx stands here
towering as the last of the
classical amongst the vulgar,
just as Smith stood isolated

among the classicals, being the
first of the vulgar.

Economics (The age of Marshall)
   Since Jevons & Co to Marshall – highly refined technique,
                                    rotten conceptions and
                                    fundamental assumptions
   But technique so highly perfected
that sometimes compels them
unconsciously to modify their conscious
assumptions (justly contradicting
themselves) and thus reaching partially
true conclusions.

Note that at the end of the classics developed primitive socialism (Owen, Hodgskin) and *caused* vulgar P.E. At the end of vulgar
period came Marx and *caused* economics.

Document 5
– Sraffa Papers – D 3/12/4 f.12   (attributed date: November
1927)
Principio
   I shall begin by giving a short 'estratto' of what I believe is the
essence of the classical theories of value, i.e. of those which include
W. Petty, Cantillon, Physiocrats, A. Smith, Ricardo + Marx. This
is not the theory of any one of them, but an extract of what I think
is common to them. I state it of course, not in their own words, but
in modern terminology, and it will be useful when we proceed to
examine their theories to understand their portata from the point
of view of our present inquiry. It will be a sort of 'frame', a machine,
into which to fit their own statements in a homogeneous pattern,
so as to be able to find what is common in them and what is the
difference with the later theories.
   Then I shall go over these theories very cursorily, dealing with
them, not at all exhaustively, but examining only those points
which are relevant to my present purpose. So, of the Physiocrats,
I shall not talk of . . . the physiocratie, but only of one of its basic
points.

Document 6
– Sraffa Papers – D 3/12/43 f.4   (attributed date: post-1945)

? *Preface*

I intended at one time to add, to include in this work both an introduction which explained its relation to the work of earlier classical
econ (writers), (some anticipation of this I have given in Secs . . . .
of the Introduction. . . .) and a number of controversial notes on
views held by modern economists. I have decided however to send
it forth bare as it is and let it be judged on its own merits: if it is
found of any interest there will be time to [. . .] there may be other
opportunities of publishing those additions.

Slogans not used

The St. Syst provides tangible evidence of the rate of profits as a
non-price phenomenon.

A Dividend could be declared before knowing what is the price
of the company's product.

Document 7
Sraffa Papers H2/89, f.56,   (date uncertain)

. . . che le eventuali introduzioni e note alla pubblicazione di miei
MS dovrebbero essere limitate a fornire gli elementi di fatto nec-
essari alla comprensione dei MS stessi lasciando da parte il più
possibile commenti e interpretazioni di idee.

Per quanto riguarda lavoro di studiosi che avessero accesso ai
miei MSS sono contrario alla citazione incompleta di MSS inediti.

Translation

. . . that possible introductions and notes to the publication of my
MS should be limited to supply the factual elements necessary to
the understanding of the said MS leaving aside as much as possible
any comment or interpretations of ideas.

As far as the work of scholars that were to have access to my MSS,
I am against the incomplete quotation of unpublished MSS.

Interlude: unwise behaviour

The foregoing biographical sketches on Kahn, Joan Robinson, Kaldor and Sraffa may help – I hope – to highlight the multifaceted and significant aspects of the Cambridge School of Keynesian Economics. I hope the reader may have been able to grasp the unity, in some basic sense, of their purposes and at the same time the intriguing disparities in their approaches in many other respects. The whole picture is bound to raise further questions. But I hope the set of essays is powerful enough to make the reader perceive the achievements of some definite landmarks.

At a superficial level, it is their determined opposition to the prevailing stream of economic theories and policies that immediately appears as a most striking common feature. But the basic problem remains that of identifying something deeper that can link the many strands of their separate works. This is essential, for clearly one could not build a new research programme merely on a destructive basis. Exercises in destruction (when necessary) can only be preliminary to a process of reconstruction. This also implies that one cannot pretend to do full justice to them if one were to stop at the destructive stage of their analyses, as alas has been done too often and too easily.[1]

---

[1] Assar Lindbeck (1985), as President of the Memorial Nobel Prize Committee for Economic Sciences, in reviewing the work of the Prize Committee

Yet it is a fact that they did not devote sufficient efforts in their interchanges to facing and discussing the fundamentals and the unity of purposes on which their arguments were based. This leaves a wide ground in their interchanges that needs to be brought to fruition and requires in-depth exploration and investigation. Even Kahn, who had witnessed in minute detail Keynes's early determined efforts to break with the Marshallian tradition, never faced the task of spelling out explicitly what Keynes's break with the Marshallian tradition actually consisted of. Forty years after the event, in his Milan Mattioli Lectures (1978), he was still referring to that break-away simply as 'the General Theory', for lack of a better term.[2]

This peculiar, and intriguing, aspect may give the superficial impression of a perturbing lack of communication. In fact, hints at this lack of communication, notably between Keynes and Sraffa and between Sraffa and the other members of the group, have emerged already at various stages in the preceding essays. They certainly neglected to consolidate the unifying basic features of their achievements, while each of them – in their immediate efforts – was concentrating on moving in his/her own direction, perhaps in ways that to each of them singularly appeared as more urgent or more important than others.

This curious state of affairs may not have had damaging consequences on the effectiveness and fruitfulness of the ideas that each one of them was developing only because, among them, there was no urgent need for confrontation. It may even have appeared to each of them as a way of sparing time. Differences could be left aside for later, while each one could concentrate on his/her present (more urgent) task.

---

up to the 1980s, stressed the point that contributions in the destruction direction were among those characteristics which the Committee considered as a reason for *not* awarding Nobel Prizes.

[2] See Kahn, 1984, in particular his lecture 5.

But at the same time, this very state of affairs was not without consequences. It had, in fact, devastating consequences on the other economists outside the group: on those colleagues of their generation who were sympathetic to their lines of thought, on the junior colleagues around them, and most of all on *potential* developers of the ideas they had contributed to shape.

We have already heard the remark that for an effective 'revolution' to take off, a dissemination of basic ideas and a booming of innovative contributions would have been required.[3] This did not take place. Why? This question keeps cropping up, in many different contexts. Partial answers and tentative hypotheses – some of them not incompatible with one another – have been sketched out already in the preceding essays. But at this point I shall concentrate, albeit briefly, on just one of them, which relates to a specific and peculiar aspect of the Cambridge group, namely the attitude of exclusiveness which somehow they chose to adopt *vis-à-vis* what was happening both outside Cambridge and, most significantly, in Cambridge itself outside the group.

This attitude had its advantages and played an important role in terms of continuity and fruitfulness of their exchanges in the development of their ideas. The notable, most visible expression of these fruitful interchanges was the running of that peculiar and, in Cambridge, rather notorious arrangement, the 'Secret Seminar'.[4] As already mentioned, it was organised by Richard Kahn and was held in his rooms in King's College. Kahn quite naturally considered it a continuation of the Cambridge *Circus* of the early 1930s. It played a major role in the development of new concepts and ideas, right from their very tentative early origin, in the direction of both destructive criticisms and constructive reconstruction, as they were emerging in Cambridge and outside Cambridge

---

[3] See above, pp. 17, 40–41.
[4] See above, pp. 63, 74.

(as outside scholars, even if temporarily visiting, were normally invited to attend the Seminar). This obviously gave stimuli and provided intellectual food for imaginative thinking. But it must also be said that one should have become conscious of the collateral damage that such a peculiar arrangement inevitably would generate, by the very way it was organised.

The secrecy of something which everybody knew about is a very peculiar feature. In fact, it was also used – some people suggested it was specifically used – as a device to exclude particular people. But this, unwittingly, had the consequence of making those who did participate feel a sort of *conditional* state of presence – an effect which at the time nobody, apparently, thought about. Yet, understandably, this state of affairs irritated many participants (especially the young). Even more importantly, it may have generated a kind of blockage to potential contributors, who otherwise might have helped the strongly sought 'revolution' to explode if they had met reasonable expectations of a more tolerant – even if not enthusiastic – reception.

These hints are made here to give an idea of some of the several unwise aspects and vicissitudes that characterised the Cambridge group of Keynesian Economics, even during the most productive and flourishing phases of the postwar golden period.

Moreover, one must not forget that persistent opposition to the Keynesian group never ceased in Cambridge itself.

There was, to begin with, what was regarded as the conservative old guard, who never gave up their disapproval of Keynes's ideas – even after Pigou's (1950) generous recognition of Keynes's contributions. This group of people constantly exerted their opposition, especially in the various committees, at all stages of university and college life, sometimes very effectively. The Cambridge group took this as an inevitable aspect of university life and (unwisely and incorrectly) tended to associate with this 'faction' unwelcome colleagues, who by no means deserved such treatment.

But, most importantly, at the other extreme there was the impatience of many brilliant young economists, who resented what they regarded as a sort of intellectual imposition, which they felt to be unacceptable. They tended to consider it as a sign of intolerance. The resentment induced in these young economists was perhaps the most damaging aspect of the Keynesian group's unwise behaviour, right at the favourable times of their domination, as it deprived the Keynesian School of its most natural ground for continuation and development. Such resentment was far from indicating lack of talent or of substantive and fruitful ideas – as demonstrated by the success that most of these younger people had elsewhere when they left Cambridge. It was rather a kind of instinctive reaction to the unwise behaviour of those who should have acted as responsible masters, but didn't.

There was then the intermediate generation that happened to be immediately junior to the Keynes's pupils of the first hour and were ready – simply as a matter of age – to be their successors. Very quickly this generation divided up into a 'Keynesian' group and a 'neoclassical' group. The latter sided with the 'neoclassical synthesis' proposed from overseas, thereby enjoying great advantages in terms of freedom of action, external support from a powerful overseas school and even internal support from the conservative old guard mentioned above. The 'Keynesians', on the other hand, who should have become, or were meant to become, the natural developers of the 'Keynesian revolution', paradoxically suffered the heaviest handicaps, precisely because of the behaviour of the 'revolutionaries' of the first hour, whom they were trying to follow but from whom they obtained scant or reluctant or – on some crucial occasions – no support at all. They came to face endless difficulties.

I shall not try to pursue this aspect further with guesses, comments or risky and complicated counterfactual statements. Rather, I shall try an indirect but, I hope, more effective way of expressing the 'tragedy' (to take Kahn's expression) that Keynes's pupils of the first hour faced in their twilight, by reproducing here a further (brief) biographical essay, which I wrote for the *Cambridge Journal of Economics* in the commemoration issue devoted to Richard Goodwin.

Goodwin was by no means a product of Cambridge, England. He came from Schumpeter's Harvard, *i.e.* from the *other* Cambridge. He was openly and fully on the side of the Keynesians. By his non-achievements rather than by his achievements in Cambridge, England, Goodwin may offer more than a glimpse at the vast potential of the Keynesian School that remained unfulfilled – a shining example of that sort of blocked scientific productivity which I have tried to describe. At the same time, rather amusingly, a quotation given at the end of the essay from a speech by Richard Stone – another notable Cambridge character – may help to bring to the fore the other side of the coin. Dick Stone – like James Meade – came to be regarded as having shifted from the Keynesian to the neoclassical camp. He was a solitary character, but in contrast with Goodwin and perhaps precisely because of his solitude, he suffered no blockage of scientific activity: he remained very productive until the end of his life. He may well be taken as the symbol – on a path that had already been chosen at 'the other place' by Roy Harrod and John Hicks – of the other way of reacting to the intricacies of the intellectual environment – stimulating and restraining at the same time – that enmeshed the Cambridge postwar Keynesian economics school.

Chapter VII

Richard Murphey Goodwin (1913–1996)
The missed Keynes-Schumpeter connection

Editorial note
This essay was written for the 'Cambridge Journal of Economics'
(1996, pp. 645–949) on the news of Goodwin's death. (For this
book, the subdivision in sections, with titles, has been added.)

Since I was asked to open the commemoration issue, as its
only surviving original patron, I may perhaps remind the reader
of what being a 'patron' of the CJE meant at the time of its launch.
The group of non-conformist young economists who started the
journal (in 1977) asked senior colleagues for support, without
interference, though of course welcoming suggestions and criti-
cism. Not one of the three who originally accepted (others refused
and others joined later) entirely shared the views and attitudes of
the editorial group (Goodwin, most of all, regretted the absence
of Schumpeter among the authors explicitly mentioned for inspi-
ration). But we prized freedom of thought and of initiative above
all, at a time when a heavy anti-Keynesian counter-revolution
was under way.

1. Foreword

Richard (Dick to his friends) Goodwin died unexpectedly in
a Siena hospital on 6 August 1996 at the age of eighty-three,
following an emergency heart operation. His departure has
deprived his pupils, friends, admirers and the economics
profession of a most remarkable, original, enigmatic, non-
conformist economist.

For me, the death of Dick Goodwin was a painful experience of mixed sorrow, sadness and regret. He was my first teacher in Cambridge. When, in October 1956, I arrived as a foreign research student almost ignorant of economics (and of English), innocent of all that had been going on, I noticed Joan Robinson's newly published book, *The Accumulation of Capital*, prominently on display in the bookshop windows. Goodwin was very impressed; he was convinced of its importance. But he also thought that what Joan Robinson was proposing, in order to be understood and to be convincing, would have to be put into a mathematical framework. He set me the task of reading, and reporting on, Knut Wicksell's *Lectures*, where he (rightly) thought the antecedents would be found. I also read Wicksell's controversy with Åkerman and we had long discussions. As to formalisation, however, we did not get very far, except in realising that Joan Robinson had uncovered some thorny problems. Part of those interchanges between Goodwin and me found expression much later in the papers that we (separately) presented at the Frostavallen Wicksell symposium (1977). I did not go beyond analysing the difficulties (Wicksell-effects and reswitching – see Pasinetti, 1978). Goodwin attempted the more constructive task of using new mathematical tools to gain some further insights ('capital theory in orthogonalised general coordinates' – see Goodwin, 1977).

This personal recollection is an example of the relations he must have had with scores of students who, from him, absorbed encouragement, stimulus and inspiration. There were also more humane asides to the meetings. Most of his supervisions took place at his home, not in college. Jackie, his charming wife, would join us during breaks for chat and remarks, comments and gossip on the latest artistic events – art exhibitions, musical and theatrical performances. My attention was attracted, while relaxing, by his 'abstract expressionist' paintings that were always lying

Plate 5 Richard Goodwin at Siena, in 1988. Photograph by
Dorothy Hahn. Reproduced by permission of Dorothy Hahn.

about, intriguing and raising mysterious challenges to one's
imagination. I was puzzled by the geometric forms and sharp
variation of colours, helpless in trying to find interpretations.

I did not have the slightest idea, at that time, of the past
vicissitudes of that tall, slim, athletic-looking, joyful American who, besides all the rest, knew so well how to make the
best musical recordings, enjoyed college entertainments and
drove with zest old vintage sports cars. To me, an American

he looked, and an American he remained for the whole of his life.

2.   Basic biography

His biographical details, in the available sources, are all very scanty. Richard Murphey Goodwin was born in Newcastle, Indiana, on 24 February 1913. He won a scholarship to Harvard (1930), where he read Political Science and graduated in 1934. As a Rhodes Scholar (1934–37), he spent three years at St John's College, Oxford, reading PPE and then gaining a BLitt. But he also travelled extensively in Germany and in Italy. On returning to Harvard (1938), he gained his PhD in economics and then became a member of the Economics Department (1938–50). He taught Economics and, during the war, also Physics to Army officers. He then came to Cambridge, England, in 1951. He was appointed Girdlers' Lecturer, then a Reader in Economics and a Fellow of Peterhouse. In Cambridge he remained until retiring age, sixty-seven (in 1980). But this was by no means the end of his career. He won the *concours* to a Professorship of Economics at Siena, Italy, where he continued his teaching until the (Italian) retirement age, seventy-five (in 1988).

3.   Intellectual landmarks

This sort of bureaucratic list is precisely what Goodwin would have hated. It was much more important for him, in the many autobiographical interviews he gave, to trace the origin of his ideas and the influence and inspiration he had received. He would begin by telling you that both his grandfather (a banker) and his father went bankrupt during the Great Depression (1930), a shock which contributed to his decision to read Political Science at Harvard and to write a thesis on Marxism. He would stress how strongly he was influenced by the philosophers, especially Whitehead, who had come to Harvard from Cambridge. At Oxford he was fascinated by the seminars of Jacob Marschak and then by the contacts with Roy Harrod, who was his tutor in his second year. With him he read the proofs of *The General Theory*, which Keynes had sent to Harrod. This great work, together with Harrod's *Trade Cycle* (1936), became the major sources of all his following efforts to understand the process of cyclical growth that characterises capitalist economies. The pursuit of this aim led him, for the rest of his life, to a multiplicity of efforts and a variety of attempts to explore macro-economic as well as inter-industry, linear as well as non-linear, oscillatory as well as discontinuous (catastrophe), probabilistic as well as deterministic (chaotic), models. He was never entirely satisfied and remained optimistically inquisitive to the end of his life. But his BLitt thesis in Oxford, under the supervision of Henry Phelps Brown, was on monetary policy. And he used his findings as a basis for the dissertation that earned him his PhD degree at Harvard ('Studies in Money. England and Wales 1919 to 1938'). The upshot of this immersion in monetary data and analysis was to convince him that the management of money provided only insufficient hints and basically no explanation to understanding the movements of a capitalist economy. He became convinced that the clue had to be sought in the influence of 'real' phenomena (hence his attraction to Keynes and Harrod).

In Cambridge, Massachusetts, the major influences on him came from the mathematician Philippe Le Corbeiller (the great theorist on oscillations), from Wassily Leontief's input-output scheme [see 1949], from MIT's Norbert Wiener, and most of all from Joseph Schumpeter, of whom he became a close friend. The two were on diametrically opposite sides in political matters, but Goodwin was fascinated by Schumpeter's vision and culture. When Schumpeter died, his widow, Elizabeth, asked Goodwin to sort out and edit for publication the manuscripts of the last (unfinished) part of Schumpeter's *History of Economic Analysis*.

4.   A Cambridge enigma

But at Harvard, Goodwin did not get tenure. Dick Stone, whom he met at the first Input-Output International Conference in Driebergen (Holland), suggested to him to come to Cambridge, England. He came first as a Fulbright Visiting Fellow (1951–52), then received a faculty appointment, with tenure, and settled.

The extraordinary thing is that Goodwin spent the central, almost entire time (thirty years) of his career as an economist in Cambridge. Yet in his interviews Cambridge is the place which he mentions least when he lists his intellectual debts. Cambridge was certainly most congenial to his temperament, as it was a place where he could teach what he wanted. He could devote much of his time to his artistic *penchants* (essentially painting), he could even become a connoisseur as wine steward of his college. Yet on economic theory this was the least productive period of his career. He did, of course, write some seminal articles – think of his paper on the 'growth cycle' in the Dobb *Festschrift* [1967] and his *Economic Journal* paper [1961] on the 'optimal growth path for an underdeveloped economy', reflecting his experience on planning in India – but they were so few that Mark Blaug's second edition (1983) of *Who's Who in Economics*, by relying on recent publications and citations, does not even include his name. (Even more surprisingly, he is not mentioned even in Arestis and Sawyer's *Biographical Dictionary of Dissenting Economists*, 1992.) The Cambridge colleagues whom he most tried to understand and pay attention to were Joan Robinson and Piero Sraffa, even if he did not entirely share their views. He always felt he should first express anybody's concepts in his own terms. With Joan Robinson, his efforts remained halfway. With Sraffa (at whom he looked more through the filter of the von Neumann model) he gave his own representation using simple geometric graphs, which he developed in his lectures and then published in his *Elementary Economics from the Higher Standpoint* [1970].

5. Italian renaissance

When he retired, he even moved out of Cambridge to live in a small village in the countryside. But just when no economist expected anything more from him, he bravely decided (with encouragement from his Italian pupils and friends) to apply, in an open competition, for a chair at Siena University. The point deserves mentioning. Similar appointments to professorships in Italy, that were made subsequently, took place under a different (and new) rule – the so-called 'chiamata diretta', i.e. the decision by a faculty to 'call directly' a foreign, already established, professor to a chair, specifically set up for him. In the case of Goodwin, this was not so. His was an open national competition, in which he took the risk of competing with a host of freshly prepared young people. The committee's verdict rewarded him.

Thus, what he did not get from Harvard in 1950, he got from Siena in 1980. And the effects were astonishing. Goodwin's scientific productivity literally exploded. Surrounded by young, admiring and at the same time challenging colleagues, by a host of puzzled but exacting students, who, as he said, 'made him work hard against his intentions', relaxed by a Tuscan landscape rich in Renaissance memories and works of art, exposed to beautiful views and enjoying good wine (and driving a carefully chosen sports car), his scientific output took off at an extraordinary rate.

He did not simply rearrange his thoughts, as he would claim, but absorbed new mathematical tools and concepts that became available. Besides collecting, prefacing and publishing three books of previous essays, surprisingly he wrote two *new* books: one on the application of a new mathematical tool (chaos theory) to economics [1990] and the other (with a second part written by Lionello Punzo) on *The Dynamics of a Capitalist Economy* (Goodwin and Punzo, 1987). Resuming original enthusiasm, he thus finally wrote the book that had been expected from him since his Harvard days.

Paul Samuelson, in the Foreword to the book (*ibid.*, pp. ix), summed it all up:

> His new work is an epic poem dealing with great issues: the class struggle à la Marx; predator-prey drama of the Lotka-Volterra type; von Neumann's magisterial model of autonomous growth, Harrodian and Sraffian development of Keynesian systems in their input-output aspects. (or accelerator-multiplier aspects)

Only a few years. Then came retirement for the second time (1988). Siena made him Professor Emeritus and he remained extraordinarily active. For some years he spent summer in England, spring and autumn in Siena and winter in India, as the guest of a generous friend (living in a beautiful Le Corbusier-designed house), who gave him the opportunity and pleasure to devote as much time as he could to painting. A life finally fulfilled? Not exactly.

6.   A puzzling halt in Goodwin's economics creativity: Cambridge problem?

All that is written above raises disconcerting questions. Why was it that such an explosion of creativity was so long delayed? Why did it not happen earlier? And perhaps more effectively? At Harvard, he gained the appreciation of Haberler and Schumpeter. Amazingly, these two senior economists even decided to attend lectures that he agreed to give, on mathematics. He was certainly not unsuccessful with his students. (Karl Brunner had said that he was the only faculty member, in the late 1940s, besides Haberler, to whom he could talk. Bob Solow has written that, when he entered Harvard in 1940, it was only after attending Goodwin's lectures that he decided that economics was a worthwhile subject to pursue.) An explanation of the weakness of his academic position in the US has been given by pointing out that, besides failing to deliver the book he had promised, he had been, earlier, a member of the Communist Party, and the late 1940s were McCarthy's years.

But what about Cambridge, England? Why, we may ask, was he left intellectually so isolated? If it was true that he suddenly lost interest in economics, was this what he wanted? He did take advantage of the privileges of a Cambridge college and of the pleasure of devoting time to his cherished artistic inclinations (painting most of all). But economics was his profession. One should at least explore also the possibility that the surroundings were not really favourable to stimulating his economist's genius. Certainly, the Keynesian group respected his views (he was a member of the 'Secret Seminar'). But how much did they do to promote, stimulate or take advantage of his potential? At the same time, his left-wing inclinations gained him no sympathy from the conservative-minded part of the faculty. But was this not a myopic view to take? It seems odd that, after thirty years' teaching, a distinguished scholar of the calibre of Goodwin was never granted professorial status.

Perhaps a dispassionate reconsideration from all sides (right and left, old and young) of Goodwin's Cambridge period might also be illuminating in explaining how economics at Cambridge, after being a world centre of attraction in the immediate post-Keynesian years, then fell so dramatically in the official rankings.

An interesting reflection to ponder on is the one expressed by Richard Stone in Siena, on the occasion of Goodwin's second retirement:

> When I look back on Richard Goodwin's career and mine I sometimes wonder why, friends as we are, we never collaborated. Our aims as economists are the same, our skills complementary and for over three decades we have lived in the same town. Together we might have produced some masterly works that would have astonished the world. On and off we have talked about it, but when it came to the point we never got down to it. Collaboration, of course, is a tricky business and perhaps some

Plate 6 Richard Stone, in 1958, when President of the
International Econometric Society. Reproduced by permission
of Lady Giovanna Stone.

instinct told us that remaining friends was more important than
astonishing the world. Still, it is odd that we never even tried.
(Di Matteo, 1990, p. 19)

Richard Goodwin and Richard Stone: two economists, of
exactly the same age, who both devoted their lives to trying to apply useful mathematics to relevant economics, who
worked in the same university for thirty years, who were
good friends, and yet never set up any real interchange
of ideas between themselves. Is this not astonishing? In

the end, Stone received international recognition (a Nobel Prize). Goodwin, who equally deserved it, was too far off the mainstream regression line even to hope to be considered. Temperamentally, they both were mild, humane, accommodating, supportive characters. Neither of them was directly associated with any radical fighting faction. They stayed out of controversies. Stone was by and large supposed to be associated with the 'neoclassical synthesis', Goodwin with the Keynesians. But surely this can be no explanation for them being kept apart from each other, or from the others. One should clearly go much deeper or further. Did they give up possible complications in order to remain friends? But what complications? The world could wait? But for whom, and till when?

Stone's closing sentences are revealing but at the same time unconvincing. Historians of economic thought will no doubt investigate. Meanwhile, the troubling questions remain.

7. Selected works of Richard Goodwin

1949, 'The Multiplier as a Matrix', *Economic Journal*, vol. 59, pp. 537–555.

1961, 'The Optimal Growth Path for an Underdeveloped Economy', *Economic Journal*, vol. 71, pp. 756–774.

1967, 'A Growth Cycle', in Feinstein, C. H., ed., *Socialism, Capitalism and Economic Growth, Essays Presented to Maurice Dobb*, Cambridge: Cambridge University Press, pp. 54–58.

1970, *Elementary Economics from the Higher Standpoint*, Cambridge: Cambridge University Press.

1977, 'Capital Theory in Orthogonal General Coordinates', Wicksell Symposium, Frostavallen, Sweden; printed in Goodwin, 1983, pp. 153–172.

1982a, *Intervista a un economista: Richard M. Goodwin*, with a biography, edited by Maura Palazzi. Bologna: Clueb.

1982b, *Essays in Economic Dynamics*, London: Macmillan.

1983, *Essays in Linear Economic Structures*, London: Macmillan.

1987 (with L. F. Punzo), *The Dynamics of a Capitalist Economy: a Multi-sectoral Approach*, Cambridge: Polity in association with Basil Blackwell.

1989, *Essays in Nonlinear Economic Dynamics: Collected Papers 1980–1987*, Frankfurt am Main: Verlag Peter Lang.

1990, *Chaotic Economic Dynamics*, Oxford: Clarendon Press.

Postlude: fighting for independence

The time came, inevitably, when Keynes's pupils of the first hour reached retirement age. They had not cared to appoint genuine successors. The event happened to coincide with a really bad time for Keynesian economics, an anti-Keynesian counter-revolution being under way and spreading from the other side of the Atlantic.

In the Cambridge Economics faculty, for the 'neoclassical' group the process of taking over all key positions was child's play. Very rapidly, the faculty lost its pre-eminence even among British universities, let alone among the world centres of economic research.[1]

The 'Keynesian revolution' did continue to ramify, in a somewhat uncoordinated way, around the world, but hardly in Cambridge.[2] By the 1980s, in Cambridge teaching and research, Keynesian – and in general non-orthodox – economists were confined to secondary places.

There is an important aspect of these vicissitudes that seems to have escaped attention. Improper or unwise as the behaviour of the Keynesian group may have been in the Cambridge environment of the 1950s and 1960s, it did have the important effect of keeping high the prestige, impetus and world reputation of the academic economic thinking of

---

[1] See above, p. 35.
[2] Again, see above, p. 45.

Britain (and one might even say, by extension, of the old continent in general). This aspect, especially at the time of the Cambridge controversies, was entirely neglected by the contemporary critics of the Keynesian School. Hostility towards the Keynesian group grew steadily from the 1970s, just as their academic power was waning. The opposition to the Cambridge Keynesians barely paid any attention to the outstanding aspects of their achievements. Ex post, this turned out to be a myopic attitude, also because it inevitably affected the younger recruits who were coming in to fill the void and who were absorbed, most of the time unawares, by the current widespread hostile attitude, that missed the point of reckoning with the importance of maintaining an independent economic thought in Britain and, by extension, in the old continent.[3]

Meanwhile, around the world, the term 'Keynesian revolution' continued to be used and even to spread, but as I pointed out earlier[4] it kept taking on very different meanings in different places and by different authors, giving rise to a wide spectrum of views, amazingly variegated and sometimes even opposing one another. The effect was that the views of the Cambridge Keynesian group appear to have remained almost

[3] It is interesting to find that Robert Skidelsky, just before publishing his third volume of Keynes's biography (Skidelsky, 2000), precisely realised, on a broader historical level, this aspect of Keynes's efforts and accordingly changed the subtitle of his book in progress from 'Economist as a prince' to 'Fighting for Britain' (against the US – see *ibid*, p. xv). Not surprisingly, this subtitle did not please his American reviewer (De Long, 2002), who severely criticised Skidelsky precisely for underlining this aspect of Keynes's stand, considering it no less than the 'major howler' in an otherwise 'outstanding intellectual achievement' (*ibid.*, p. 155). Surprisingly enough, Skidelsky has graciously bowed to the American publisher's pressure and has made a complete turnabout. In the US edition of the book, he has drastically changed the subtitle to a neutral 'Fighting for freedom'. But he had to add an entirely new Preface to the US edition in order to give an explanation of his change of mind! The devil seems to have played the trick though. In the same new Preface, perhaps inadvertently, Skidelsky indirectly contradicts himself by quoting Keynes as saying that his major aim was 'to leave us capable of independent action' (Skidelsky, 2000, Preface to the American edition).
[4] See the second of the Caffè Lectures, i.e. Chapter 2 above.

the only ones to have maintained the original genuinely 'revolutionary' character (at least if one takes this term in its literal sense, i.e. in the sense of a *break* with the tradition), the conviction being that the whole economic theory should be shifted and firmly placed on an objective foundational framework, which is alternative to the prevailing one. Precisely for this specific characteristic, it may be worth making, at this point, a daring effort to single out its most important basic features.

To people like myself, who has been associated with the Cambridge Keynesian School for many years, a series of essential building blocks belonging to an alternative economic paradigm, with respect to the neoclassical one, appeared quite clearly from the beginning.[5] I shall try to expound the way in which I perceived them. It should be stressed that precisely because of this personal perception, the list need not be an exhaustive one; even less need it be one that would be found in the works of the members of the group (who neglected this aspect), or one that all of them would have endorsed at first sight. But it is precisely this heterogeneity of feelings and attitudes among the various members of the group that explains their difficulties in acknowledging a comprehensive scheme, which reason and logic would have required from them. Nevertheless, I think the effort must be made, in order to bring these characteristics into sharp relief, before making any attempt at picking up and trying to sew together the threads of their unaccomplished endeavours.

Let me therefore venture the following list of, to me, quite clear characteristic features (even at the cost of not always sharing all of them entirely):

1. *Reality (and not simply abstract rationality) as the starting point of economic theory.* This was a typical characteristic taken up from Keynes, who had the courage

---

[5] See the Preface to Pasinetti, 1981.

to say, 'When the facts change, I change my mind'.[6] The whole school always showed a strong aversion to a purely imaginary world of rationally behaving individuals, that, though fulfilling the rules of logic, does not show respect for facts. The conviction has always been that any theory needs to be based on factual evidence, to be evaluated right from the start and not only to be empirically tested at the end. This feature becomes crucial when the reality under investigation is that of industrial societies, with their tendency towards change and an evolving structure, as against the more static conditions of pre-industrial societies. Keynes expressed this feature by stressing that his analysis refers to a 'monetary production economy', in contrast with more primitive types of economies (which he saw as fundamentally based on the phenomenon of 'exchange' or even barter).[7] In Kaldor, this preoccupation took the form of singling out what he called 'stylised facts' – a vivid device conveying the need for simplification and abstraction, and yet the necessity of never losing contact with the most important and concrete features of the industrial world. With the term 'stylised facts', he meant some empirical regularities that are sufficiently general and persistent as to be able to capture the corresponding objective features of reality. It is worth remembering that the Keynesian 'revolution' itself grew out of this feature. Keynes certainly would not have changed his mind and written *The General Theory*, without the dramatic events of the Great Depression.

2.   *Economic logic with internal consistency (and not only formal rigour).* Economic theory does not only need to respect facts from the very start. It also needs to maintain close contact with economic reality, while the

---

[6] This is how Keynes is reported to have replied to a colleague accusing him of reversing a previous statement. See Malabre, 1993, p. 220.

[7] See Keynes, 1973a, pp. 253–255.

analysis is carried on. This is because any economy is a typically complex and evolving system, in which it is important to single out – and not lose sight of – the underlying emerging patterns. A good economic analysis cannot be built exclusively on abstract deductive logic. Keynes, Kahn and Joan Robinson always stressed that economics is an art, which requires qualitative judgements about what sometimes appears seemingly contradictory evidence; it requires intuition to organise a maze of ideas and phenomena into a coherent whole. It then needs caution to draw policy implications. Yet the deductive logic that is used must be absolutely waterproof. The basic theoretical framework can never be allowed to violate internal consistency. This feature has taken clear prominence in the elaborations of Sraffa's *Production of Commodities* – a masterpiece in this respect. Saying that a theory needs internal consistency is not the same as saying that it needs 'formal rigour', a term today adopted to mean the combined use of mathematical language, axiomatic deductive logic and formal proofs.[8] It should be borne in mind that Sraffa's masterpiece was not written in purely mathematical language – a choice that Sraffa made even against the advice of the distinguished mathematicians with whom he was in consultation at Cambridge.

On the concrete problems concerning actual measurements, a synthesis of Sraffa's stand may be found in his

---

[8] Giorgio Israel, an Italian mathematician, has recently criticised the widespread tendency among many economists to identify the concept of 'axiomatisation' with the concept of 'scientific rigour'. This is quite in opposition, Israel remarks, to the conception of rigour that was adopted by the great applied mathematicians, such as Henri Poincaré, Vito Volterra and Albert Einstein. For them, 'rigorous' meant consistent with a substrate of empirical results. Its opposite was not 'informal' but *unconstrained* by empirically confirmable interpersonal observations (see Israel, 1981, and the wider debate carried out by Weintraub *et al.*, 1998, in the *Economic Journal*). I find this conception very close to that adopted by the Cambridge group.

brief but profound statements made at the Corfù Conference on the theory of capital, where he contended that
any measurement of economic magnitudes – even when
approximate by practical necessity – must never violate
logic.[9] It may be useful to recall, in this respect, that
the controversy on capital theory of the 1960s between
the two Cambridges was won by the UK Cambridge
economists precisely on a question of logical consistency.[10]

3.   *Malthus and the Classics (not Walras and the Marginalists) as the major inspiring source in the history of economic thought.* The break with the prevailing (Walrasian) orthodoxy has been hinted at repeatedly in the
present book. Usually this feature of the Cambridge
School has been interpreted unilaterally as a purely
negative connotation. This is not correct. I should like
to stress that this characteristic should also be considered from the other side, which includes many positive
connotations. In particular, a positive connotation has
been the revival of classical economic thought (especially that of Smith, Malthus, Ricardo, Marx). Keynes
was an admirer of Malthus and considered him as
the forerunner of the principle of effective demand.
He was so fascinated by Malthus's contribution as to
assert, with some exaggeration, that the whole history of economic thought would have been very different if Malthus's ideas had prevailed.[11] It was then
Sraffa, with his eleven-volume critical edition of the

---

[9] Sraffa, 1961, pp. 305–306.
[10] The Levhari-Samuelson non-switching theorem, purported to give an ana-
     lytical basis to the notion of a neoclassical production function, was
     proved to be false because of an analytical error (see, originally, Pasinetti,
     1966, 1969, and then the useful survey by Harcourt, 1972).
[11] This is the reason Keynes defined all the economists after Malthus (includ-
     ing Ricardo) as 'classical'. By taking symbolically Say's law as the discrim-
     inant element, he (confusingly) made no distinction (on the basis of other
     elements) between the classics and the marginalists.

Collected Works of David Ricardo, that provided the crucial path to this revival of classical economics. In addition, with his (1960) slim book, he not only revived the classical method of analysis but made full use of it, first of all by drawing a set of propositions that could 'serve as the basis for a critique' of marginal economic theory, and then by suggesting an alternative direction in which to go. The reappraisal of the ideas and methodology of the classical economists seems therefore central to understanding the core contributions of the Cambridge School and to framing them in a 'production' rather than in an 'exchange' economic paradigm. This connection with the classical economists suggests that the break with neoclassical economics cannot be considered exclusively in negative terms, as it carries with it the positive connotation of revamping classical economic theory in a modern guise, which entails not only the immediate recovery of different theoretical principles but also the resumption of very different theoretical roots in the history of economic thought.

It is here that one finds the explanation of Keynes's very firm condemnation, quite early in the debate, of the dangerous effects of too conciliatory attitudes towards the prevailing views, from which he was determined to break away. One may recall that, slightly before the publication of *The General Theory* (27 August 1935) he was rebuking Harrod for his easy concessions.[12]

And again – slightly after the publication of *The General Theory* – precisely as a comment on the paper presented by Harrod at the 1936 Oxford meeting,

---

[12] 'I am frightfully afraid of the tendency, of which I see some signs in you, to appear to accept my constructive part and to find some accommodation between this and deeply cherished views which would in fact only be possible if my constructive part has been partially misunderstood' (Keynes, 1973a, vol. XIII, pp. 548).

where Hicks proposed his IS-LM model, Keynes was reiterating:

> You don't mention *effective demand* or, more precisely, the demand schedule for output as a whole, except in so far as it is implicit in the multiplier. To me, regarded historically, the most extraordinary thing is the complete disappearance of the theory of demand and supply for output as a whole, i.e. the theory of employment, *after* it had been for a quarter of a century the most discussed thing in economics. One of the most important transitions for me, after my *Treatise on Money* had been published, was suddenly realising this. It only came after I had enunciated to myself the psychological law that, when income increases, the gap between income and consumption will increase – a conclusion of vast importance to my own thinking but not apparently, expressed just like that, to anyone else's. Then, appreciably later, came the notion of interest being the measure of liquidity preference, which became quite clear in my mind the moment I thought of it. And last of all, after an immense lot of muddling and many drafts, the proper definition of the marginal efficiency of capital linked up one thing with another. (Keynes, 1973b, vol. XIV, p. 85)

Earlier he had specified that:

> [. . .] my definition of marginal efficiency of capital is quite different from anything to be found in his [i.e. Marshall's] work or in that of any other classical economist [. . .]. I emphasise this, because the discovery of the definition of marginal efficiency of capital looks very slight and scarcely more than formal, yet in my own progress of thought it was absolutely vital. (Keynes, 1973a, vol. XIII, p. 549)

One may notice here that Keynes is stressing all the major constituent concepts of his revolutionary work: effective demand, the gap between income and consumption, the multiplier, a new theory of the rate of interest, the marginal efficiency of capital. None of these

concepts was incorporated without previous manipu-
lations into Hicks's 'suggested interpretation'.[13] They
were all distorted so as to be inserted into a Walrasian
simultaneous equations model, which is in contrast to
Keynes's original *General Theory* model.[14] A battle to
vindicate Keynes's original ideas was therefore legitimate and perfectly justified; one might even say that it
was necessary in order to draw a sharp watershed line
between the tendencies inclined to reconciliations –
not only with Marshall's but most of all with Walrasian
economics– and the firm determination to break away
from orthodoxy, which was the basic starting point of
Keynes's explicitly advocated 'revolution'.

4.   *Non-ergodic*[15] *(in place of stationary, timeless) eco-
     nomic systems.* The Cambridge School was convinced
     that any economic system should be analysed in a
     framework of historical time and that this time dimen-
     sion could not be removed from the analysis. This is
     true not only for the long run but also for short-run
     analysis. The recognition of the importance of histor-
     ical time is connected with the belief that the economic
     systems do not have a point of rest, nor do they allow
     turning back the clock – a notion which is summarised
     here with the rather technical, but capturing, word *non-
     ergodic*. To put the matter more simply, this means that
     the future, though connected with the past, can never
     coincide with it. This characteristic emerged among
     the members of the Cambridge School in various ways.

[13] I have had the opportunity to come back on at least two of these basic
concepts: i) the marginal efficiency of investment, showing how it is something totally different from the neoclassical concept of marginal productivity of capital, with which Hicks (and all neoclassical economists) has
confused it (see Pasinetti, 1997a); and ii) the concept of effective demand
as a really fundamental feature of monetary production economies (see
Pasinetti, 1997b).
[14] See also the fourth point in the list, below.
[15] The usage of this clinching term is due to Paul Davidson, 1983.

Keynes stressed the role of uncertainty and the unpredictability of future events. Sraffa thought that an evolving unpredictable economic system would have forced economic theory to take only still pictures of reality at a specific point in time, so as to avoid counterfactuals.[16] Joan Robinson perhaps more than anybody else emphasised this characteristic by making a sharp distinction between historical time and logical time: while the former is crucial to the understanding of economics because it allows the flow of events to be organised from an irreversible past to an unknown future, the latter may become a misleading concept precisely because human history is not like a hydraulic system, that can be turned back or forth indifferently.

5.   *Causality vs. interdependence.* The notion of historical time opens up the question of causality. This notion is mentioned here to underline the conviction that economic relations should not necessarily all be forced into systems of simultaneous equations. The point is more than a methodological one. There are relations, in economics, that are genuinely interdependent. But there are other important economic relations that are characteristically asymmetrical, as far as the chain of causality is concerned. They should not be artificially forced into a logical frame in which everything depends on everything else, which is tantamount to introducing an unjustified sharp distinction which considers any specific variable as *either* totally unimportant (and in this case to be neglected) *or* of some importance and in this case to be considered exactly on the same level as, and symmetrically to, any one of the other variables, no matter how important these latter variables may be relative to the former. Keynes and the whole Cambridge Keynesian group always considered it necessary to bring out

---

[16] See above, p. 191.

first of all those variables and relations that are factually most important, leaving the others to a second stage of approximation and yet never losing 'reserves and qualifications' for them to be kept 'at the back of our heads' (Keynes, 1936a, p. 297). This implies the recognition of the existence of chains of relations that are of the 'causal' type, which nevertheless do not exclude subsets (sometimes quite substantial subsets) of relations of the interdependent type.[17] Causality and interdependence are thus both present in the works of the members of the Cambridge School of Keynesian Economics. Kaldor was even more emphatic in stressing the dynamic aspect of the causal relations, by recognising that many variables are connected through time with a reinforcing chain of causes and effects. He defined this phenomenon with the notion of *cumulative causation*, a process that leads to the polarisation – rather than the convergence – of the economic outcomes.[18]

6. *Macroeconomics before microeconomics.* The Cambridge School proposed an analysis in which the macroeconomic dimension always comes first with respect to the microeconomic dimension. The theoretical propositions of each member of the school normally avoided starting from subjective behaviour (or preferences) and from the study of the behaviour of single individuals. The Cambridge economists caught very clearly the principle that the behaviour of the economic system as a whole is not reducible to, in the sense that it does not emerge as the exclusive result of, the sum of its single individual parts, except under very restrictive conditions. So many times, what emerges is that the sum of the single parts has to *adapt* to independently determined macroeconomic outcomes or constraints.

[17] On these points I have had the opportunity of giving some enlarged and argumented details (Pasinetti, 1965, 1974, Chapter 2).
[18] See in particular Kaldor, 1966, 1977, 1981.

Sometimes, at the macroeconomic levels, some relations emerge that are entirely new. This does *not* mean a denial of the role of microeconomics as a genuine field of economic investigation, but it *does* mean the impossibility of explaining crucial macroeconomic phenomena on the sole bases of microeconomic behaviour.

There are many examples of fallacy of composition that the Cambridge School have highlighted, as against the attempts to extend what is true for the single individual to the behaviour of the economic system as a whole. No one could have more assertively stressed the difference between macro- and microeconomics than Keynes himself. '[There is a] vital difference between the theory of economic behaviour of the aggregate and the theory of behaviour of the individual unit' (from *The General Theory*, Keynes, 1936a, p. 85). It may also be argued that Sraffa (1960), in his treatment of income distribution, looked at the economic system from a macroeconomic perspective, showing the non-monotonicity between changes of the single prices and changes in the distribution of income. In this way, he also established the non-reducibility of the economic system to the characteristics of a simplified one-commodity world. In any case, the whole Cambridge group always shared the perception of some crucial macroeconomic relations and magnitudes that cannot simply be derived from the sum or aggregation of sectoral and/or microeconomic magnitudes.

Keynes, to begin with, and then all the Cambridge Keynesian school, pursued the search for relations and magnitudes which we may define as *genuinely* macroeconomic. This term is meant to define relations and magnitudes that are macroeconomic *as such*, independently of how their single constituent elements may have been decided upon. This attitude is in sharp contrast with what, later on in the economic literature, has too easily been called the search for the 'microeconomic foundations of macroeconomics', intending by such expression the adoption of the Walrasian set of hypotheses on individuals' maximising behaviour as the sole set of hypotheses admissible in economic analysis, a view that cannot be accepted as general. Clearly, the Walrasian hypotheses on individual behaviour are only one of many sets of hypotheses on which economic-behavioural relations can be built. To conclude, the imposition of the Walrasian behavioural model as the exclusive economic model to be accepted is tantamount to denying the possible existence of *genuinely* macroeconomic relations, in the sense defined above. And this cannot be accepted. It could very simply be rejected even on the basis of the well-known principle of the possibility of *emerging characteristics* in the analysis of any complex system.

7. *Disequilibrium and instability (not equilibrium) as the normal state of the industrial economies.* This characteristic, which has been prominent in Kahn, Joan Robinson and Kaldor, expresses the conviction that a modern production economy can never be in a position of perfect equilibrium. Kaldor, to take a notable example, entirely based his 'Okun Memorial Lectures' (1983) at Yale University on this characteristic, by revealingly calling it 'economics without equilibrium'. This is, of course, a very wide issue but a very basic one. It entails the rejection of what was for a century known as 'Say's Law', namely the proposition that at any initial structure of productive capacity, whatever this may be, the competitive market mechanism is able to generate a set of equilibrium prices that elicits a corresponding demand which is equal to potential production thus generating full employment of labour and full utilisation of existing resources. Keynes began by overturning this proposition and stressing that it is the amount of *effective demand* that generates a corresponding production and that this actual production might well turn out to be below the

size that corresponds to full employment of labour and full utilisation of existing resources. These questions have never been properly settled. The point is that there appears to be something very basic and intrinsic in the dynamics of industrialised economies (as opposed to more primitive, tendentially static economies) that cannot allow us to rely on a spontaneous and automatic tendency to the full use of the existing resources and to the full employment of the labour force. But where can we detect the source (or more likely the sources) of this inherent instability? In *The General Theory*, Keynes's concentration of emphasis on the slump problems of his times attracted everybody's attention to the short run. And this caused a neglect of the problems of the long run. This attitude was accentuated by the abuse of a quotation that became famous ('in the long run we are all dead'), which is *not* to be found in *The General Theory* and is almost always cited out of context. The passage comes from the *Tract on Monetary Reform*, where, in a slightly wider context, it reads:

> In the long run we are all dead. Economists set themselves too easy, too useless a task if in tempestuous seasons they can only tell us that when the storm is over the ocean is flat again. (Keynes, 1923, p. 88)

Thus Keynes contemplates both the short and the long run. The instabilities during the 'storm' – typical of the short run – have been almost invariably the only ones to attract attention and have generally referred to the financial markets. The point is that firms, households and financial institutions in general can hold and even multiply huge amounts of abstract purchasing power, without taking any decision on *how* and/or *when* this purchasing power may be converted into effective demand for goods and services. Nowadays they can even shift them round the world in a matter of seconds. However, this important source of instability is not the only one. Even less is it the exclusive source of the upsetting forces at work. Without minimising or even less neglecting these forces, we must stress that another source of instability is lying at a more profound level and thus carries a heavier relevance. This crucial source of instability emerges very clearly when the time horizon is even slightly widened to include decades and not only days or months. It concerns the unavoidable necessity of the changes that take place in the physical structure, in the price structure and in the employment structure of any industrial economic system as time (and technical knowledge) are moving on.

To resume Keynes's image, in the long run there is no 'flat ocean', neither before nor after and not even during any temporary 'storm'. The flat ocean is a misleading image coming from the idea of the stationary equilibrium of traditional economics. In a monetary production economy the fundamental terms of reference are themselves always and consistently in motion and, most of all, they are undergoing uneven and continuous transformations. This is a much deeper source of instability, which is due to the inherently *structural* dynamics, typical of all the economic systems that have undergone the industrial revolution. Too little attention has been paid to this vital point, even among Keynesian economists, let alone outside Keynes's economics.[19]

---

[19] To this context also belongs the (mis)use of Keynes's concepts in what is called the 'neoclassical synthesis', where Keynes's theory is regarded as the leading model of short-run economic fluctuations, while claiming that, in the long run, when the ocean is 'flat again' neoclassical general equilibrium theory comes back to rule the roost. To adopt Solow's words: '[. . .] one can be a Keynesian for the short run and a neoclassical for the long run, and this combination of commitments may be the right one' (Solow, 1997, p. 594). This statement, it seems to me, has a sense only in the context of economic dynamics of the *proportional* type, which is never the case in industrial systems.

8. *Necessity of finding an appropriate analytical frame-work for dealing with technical change and economic growth.* It is important to recall that a few months after the publication of *The General Theory*, in a letter to Roy Harrod, Keynes confirmed the need to extend his theoretical framework into dynamics.[20] Harrod himself (1939, 1948), was the first to take up the challenge and move in this direction. He proposed a coherent frame-work to place the Keynes theory into a dynamic set-ting. Soon after, the topic of economic growth became one of those which saw the whole Cambridge group involved most passionately (though with the ostensible reluctance of Sraffa). The members of the group carried on their research on this topic very expeditiously and, to a certain extent, coherently. From the beginning they found a close connection between the growth of income and its distribution, and in these two fields they made many important contributions. At the same time, Sraffa reopened the Pandora's box of Marxian inconsistencies and offered an entirely new framework (along classi-cal lines) where the whole issue of income distribution could be placed, thus opening the way to considering the role of history and of institutions in the determi-nation of the distribution of the social product. With Harrod's *Towards a Dynamic Economics*, Joan Robin-son's *Accumulation of Capital* and Kaldor's various ver-sions of a Keynesian growth model (Kaldor 1956, 1957, 1961, 1962, the latter including a 'technical progress function'), and moreover with Kaldor's 'Keynesian' the-ory of income distribution,[21] the topics of economic growth, technical progress, increasing returns entered

[20] Keynes was commenting on Harrod's draft of 'Mr. Keynes and Traditional Theory' (1937) and was asserting: 'I think that you have re-orientated the argument beautifully. I also agree with your hints at the end about future dynamic theory' (Keynes, 1936b).
[21] It is interesting to see the way in which Kaldor's distribution theory – by picking up the 'causal chain' inherent in Keynes's theory of effective

the scene and became essential ingredients of the whole Keynesian economic approach. If at all, one could even add that this concern with technical progress was not pushed far enough.[22]

Of course, technical progress was not a central issue in Keynes's *General Theory*, this book being focused on the effects of a major slump. But it would be wrong to argue that technical progress was absent in Keynes's mind. It is still amazing to discover today the remarkable flashes of Keynes's intuition when, in one of his most brilliant essays (written, it must be stressed, in the very depth of the 1930s depression), Keynes could look so far ahead, with such extraordinary calm and detachment as to 'predict', in the midst of the widespread gloomy views of the moment, that:

> ... assuming no important wars and no important increase in population, the *economic problem* may be solved, or be at least within sight of solution, within a hundred years ... [when] ... the standard of life in progressive countries one hundred years hence will be between four and eight times as high as it is today. (Keynes, 1930b, pp. 325–326)

He could even clearly foresee the social difficulties that were going to be implied by such dramatic changes:

> We are being afflicted with a new disease of which some readers may not yet have heard the name, but of which they will hear a great deal in the years to come – namely, *technological unemployment*. This means unemployment due to our discovery of means of economising the use of

demand, and thus by reversing the 'causal chain' behind Ricardo's theory of income distribution – could show that all benefits of technical progress are bound eventually to go to labour, once the requirements of both primitive capital accumulation and full employment investments have been fulfilled.

[22] I have had the opportunity to investigate the origin of this shortcoming, which concerns all growth theorists, in Pasinetti, 1999.

labour outrunning the pace at which we can find new uses for labour (*ibid*, p. 325). [. . .] I think with dread of the readjustment of the habits and instincts of the ordinary man, bred into him for countless generations, which he may be asked to discard within a few decades. (*ibid*, p. 327)

Most of all, he could see the fascinating possibilities offered by the process of structural change:

> Thus for the first time since his creation man will be faced with his real, his permanent problem – how to use his freedom from pressing economic cares, how to occupy the leisure, which science and compound interest will have won for him, to live wisely and agreeably and well. (*ibid*, p. 328)

So much for the reductively attributed Keynes's attitude that 'in the long run we are all dead'!

One may admit that in postwar Cambridge the potentialities of these intuitions have been only partly fulfilled. It must also be admitted that equally unfulfilled or squandered have remained the advantages that might have come from the presence of Richard Goodwin, who was bringing with him the potential richness of his close acquaintance with Joseph Schumpeter (see above, p. 213).

9. *A strong, deeply felt social concern.* This feature is very characteristic of the whole Cambridge School of Keynesian Economics and is in sharp contrast to that kind of uncritical *laissez-faire* attitude which has always been so widespread in mainstream economics, in the form of a blind reliance or faith in the spontaneous equilibrating forces of the market mechanism, taken as a *deus ex machina*, unwittingly leading a society of self-interested, competing individuals to the best of all possible positions. Keynes quite sharply expressed his opposition to this widespread conviction many years before writing *The General Theory* (see Keynes, 1926).

For the Cambridge Keynesian School, social concern has always been placed at a foremost place, the conviction being that if, or when, social order could be safeguarded by the free interaction of households, firms and existing government institutions (a situation that cannot be excluded at some particular fortunate junctures), this should be encouraged. But the conviction equally being that, in any monetary production economy, equilibrium is *not* normally the case because of the cumulative interaction of the two types of instability-generating sources mentioned above (point 7). Fundamentally, it was felt that stability can never be taken as achieved. The scope of Keynesian economics was precisely that of giving substantiation to these propositions. An overall monitoring of the working of the economic system as a whole – with reference both to its real aspects and to its monetary/financial aspects – was seen to be the task of the economic institutions (or, rather, of a set of coordinated institutions) created, constantly adapted and, at times, newly to be invented, both at the national and at the international level.

If a synthesis of this deep socially concerned attitude is to be searched for, one may simply refer to the very concluding sentences of *The General Theory*, where Keynes sums up: 'The outstanding faults of the economic society in which we live are its failure to provide for full employment and its arbitrary and inequitable distribution of wealth and incomes . . .' (Keynes, 1936a, p. 372). We may presume: both at the national and at the international level. And, as soon as we go just beyond the developed world, we may well add the dramatic problem of the appallingly widespread poverty, in a world of potential plenty.

The really deep conviction of the Cambridge School of Keynesian Economics was that, on these problems, mainstream (neoclassical) economics is helplessly powerless, precisely because it is intrinsically embedded into a theoretical scheme which, at its very foundations, is not appropriate to interpreting the essential evolving features of the industrial world, where the mentioned social problems are being generated.

* * *

What else can one do if not invoking, and very strongly searching for, an 'alternative economic paradigm'? The list of building blocks reviewed above is a rough but appealing starting point. I hope these blocks may contribute to capturing the basically common ground on which Keynes and the Cambridge School of Keynesian Economics have been moving. Yet it must be recognised that a coherent theoretical framework cannot simply grow out of a list, no matter how rich, of building blocks if these remain unconnected with one another.

The emerging challenge should have been faced long ago by selecting and shaping the theories of Keynes and Sraffa and the developments of Kahn, Robinson and Kaldor (and Goodwin, and whoever else have made contributions in the same direction at Cambridge or elsewhere) into a coherent, solid, overall framework. A grand operation of this type has not been accomplished so far. Is this because it is impossible? Or is it because the appropriate time (from any point of view) has been slow to arrive?

At the same time, one must admit that the dominant (neoclassical) theory, though surreptitiously changing under the pressure of too many factual events, is bulging into numerous but amazingly restrictive channels, while finding increasing difficulties and deficiencies, both at its core and in its outstretching branches.[23]

---

[23] This is recognised even by major economists who have contributed to its development (see the quotation from Arrow, on p. 49).

The time really seems to be ripe for giving up asking a theory, basically born to explain an 'exchange economy', to answer questions and to face problems concerning the evolving structural dynamics of an industrial world.

References for Book Two

Anderson, Perry, (1976), *Considerations on Western Marxism*, London: New Left Books.

Arestis, Philip and Sawyer, Malcolm, (1992), *A Biographical Dictionary of Dissenting Economists*, Aldershot: Edward Elgar.

Blaug, Mark and Sturges, Paul, eds, (1983), *Who's Who in Economics: a biographical dictionary of major economists 1700–1981*, Brighton: Wheatsheaf.

Bortkiewicz, Ladislaus, von (1907), 'On the Correction of Marx's Fundamental Theoretical Construction in the Third Volume of *Capital*', *Jahr. Nationalökonomie Statistik*, vol. 34 (3), pp. 370–385. English translation in Appendix to P. Sweezy, ed., (1949), *Karl Marx and the Close of his System*, New York: Augustus M. Kelley.

Cannan, Edwin, (1929), *A Review of Economic Theory*, London: King and Son.

Chamberlin, Edward, (1933), *The Theory of Monopolistic Competition*. Cambridge, Mass.: Harvard University Press.

Dardi, Marco, (1983), 'Introduction' to *L'Economia del Breve Periodo* (Italian translation of Kahn, 1929), Torino: Boringhieri, pp. 9–26, and in English in Pasinetti (1994).

Davidson, Paul, (1983), 'Rational Expectations: A Fallacious Foundation for Studying Crucial Decision-Making Processes', in *Journal of Post Keynesian Economics*, 1982–83, vol. 5, pp. 182–197.

De Long, J. Bradford, (2002), 'Review of Skidelsky's *John Maynard Keynes: Fighting for Britain*', in *Journal of Economic Literature*, vol. XL, pp. 155–162.

De Vivo, Giancarlo, (2004), 'Da Ricardo e Marx a *Produzione di Merci a mezzo di Merci*', in *Atti dei Convegni Lincei*, n. 200, International Conference on 'Piero Sraffa', Rome, 11–12 February 2003, pp. 215–234.

Di Matteo, Massimo, ed., (1990), 'Celebrating R. M. Goodwin's 75th Birthday', *Quaderni del Dipartimento di Economia Politica*, n. 100, Siena: Department of Economics.

Dmitriev, Vladimir Karpovich, (1974) *Economic Essays on Value, Competition and Utility*, (D. M. Nuti ed.), Cambridge: Cambridge University Press (originally published in Russian, 1904).

Graaff, Johannes de Villiers, (1957), *Theoretical Welfare Economics*, Cambridge: Cambridge University Press.

Harcourt, Geoffrey C., (1972), *Some Cambridge Controversies in the Theory of Capital*, Cambridge: Cambridge University Press.

Harrod, Roy F., (1936), *The Trade Cycle – An Essay*, Oxford: Clarendon Press.

Harrod, Roy F., (1939), 'An Essay in Dynamic Theory', in *The Economic Journal*, vol. 49, pp. 14–33.

Harrod, Roy F., (1948), *Towards a Dynamic Economics*, London: Macmillan.

Hayek, Friedrich A., von, (1931), *Prices and Production*, London: Routledge.

Israel, Giorgio, (1981), 'Rigor and Axiomatics in Modern Mathematics', *Fundamenta Scientiae*, vol. 2, pp. 205–219.

Kahn, Richard F., (1929), *The Economics of the Short Period*. Fellowship dissertation, submitted to King's College, Cambridge, in December 1929; published, with the addition of thirteen-page Acknowledgements, by Macmillan, London, 1989; also published as *Economia del breve periodo* in Italian by Boringhieri, Torino, 1983, with an Introduction by Marco Dardi.

Kahn, Richard F., (1984), *The Making of Keynes's General Theory* (The 'Raffaele Mattioli Lectures', delivered at Università Bocconi, Milan, 1978), Cambridge: Cambridge University Press.

Kaldor, Nicholas, (1956), 'Alternative Theories of Distribution', in *Review of Economic Studies*, vol. 22, pp. 83–100.

Kaldor, Nicholas, (1957), 'A Model of Economic Growth', in The Economic Journal, vol. 67, pp. 591–624; reprinted in Kaldor [1960–1979, vol. 2, pp. 259–300].

Kaldor, Nicholas, (1961), 'Capital Accumulation and Economic Growth', pp. 177–222, in Hague, Douglas C. and Lutz, Friedrich, eds, The Theory of Capital, London: Macmillan; reprinted in Kaldor [1960–1979, vol. 5, pp. 1–53].

Kaldor, Nicholas, (1962), (with J. A. Mirrlees), 'A New Model of Economic Growth', in Review of Economic Studies, vol. 29, pp. 174–192.

Kaldor, Nicholas, (1966), 'Causes of the Slow Rate of Economic Growth in the United Kingdom', inaugural lecture at the University of Cambridge, Cambridge: Cambridge University Press.

Kaldor, Nicholas, (1977), 'Capitalism and Industrial Development: Some Lessons from Britain's Experience', in Cambridge Journal of Economics, no. 2, pp. 193–204.

Kaldor, Nicholas, (1981), 'The Role of Increasing Returns, Technical Progress and Cumulative Causation in the Theory of International Trade and Economic Growth', in Economie Appliquée, vol. 34 (4), reprinted in Targetti, F. and Thirlwall, A., eds, (1989), The Essential Kaldor, London: Duckworth, pp. 327–350.

Kaldor, Nicholas, (1985), 'Economic without Equilibrium', the Okun Memorial Lectures delivered at Yale University, 1983, Armonk, New York: M. E. Sharpe Inc.

Kaldor, Nicholas, (1986), Ricordi di un economista, (Maria Cristina Marcuzzo, ed.), Milano: Garzanti.

Keynes, John Maynard, (1923), A Tract on Monetary Reform, London: Macmillan.

Keynes, John Maynard, (1926), The End of Laissez-faire, London: Hogarth Press; reprinted in Essays in Persuasion, (1931), London: Macmillan and New York: Harcourt, Brace and Company, pp. 312–322.

Keynes, John Maynard, (1930a), A Treatise on Money, 2 vols, London: Macmillan.

Keynes, John Maynard, (1930b), 'Economic Possibilities for Our Grandchildren', in The Nation and Athenaeum, (11 and 18 October 1930); reprinted in Essays in Persuasion, (1931), London: Macmillan and New York: Harcourt, Brace and Company, pp. 358–373.

Keynes, John Maynard, (1936a), *The General Theory of Employment, Interest and Money*, London: Macmillan.

Keynes, John Maynard, (1936b), Letter to Harrod, 30 August 1936, in Besomi, Daniele, ed., 'The Collected Interwar Papers and Correspondence of Roy Harrod', electronic version.

Keynes, John Maynard, (1973a), 'The Collected Writings of John Maynard Keynes', (Donald Moggridge, ed.), vol. XIII, *The General Theory and After, Part I: Preparation*, London: Macmillan and Cambridge University Press for the Royal Economic Society.

Keynes, John Maynard, (1973b), 'The Collected Writings of John Maynard Keynes', (Donald Moggridge, ed.), vol. XIV, *The General Theory and After, Part II: Defence and Development*, London: Macmillan and Cambridge University Press for the Royal Economic Society.

Keynes, John Maynard, (1979), 'The Collected Writings of John Maynard Keynes', vol. XXIX, *The General Theory – A Supplement*, (Donald Moggridge, ed.), London: Macmillan and Cambridge University Press for the Royal Economic Society.

Keynes, John Maynard, (1983), 'The Collected Writings of John Maynard Keynes', vol. XII, *Economic Articles and Correspondence: Investments and Editorial*, (Donald Moggridge, ed.), London: Macmillan and Cambridge University Press.

Kuhn, Thomas S., (1970), *The Structure of Scientific Revolutions*, 2nd edition, Chicago: University of Chicago Press.

Lindbeck, Assar, (1985), 'The Prize in Economic Science in Memory of Alfred Nobel', in *Journal of Economic Literature*, vol. 23, no. 1, pp. 37–56.

Luxemburg, Rosa, (1951), *The Accumulation of Capital*, transl. by A. A. Schwarzschild, with an Introduction by Joan Robinson, London: Routledge and Kegan Paul, (originally published in German in 1913).

Malabre, Alfred L., (1993), *Lost Prophets: An Insider's History of the Modern Economists*, Boston: Harvard Business School Press.

Manara, C. F., (1968), 'Il modello di Sraffa per la produzione congiunta di merci a mezzo di merci', in *L'industria*, no. 1, pp. 3–18, transl. into English as 'Sraffa's Model for the Joint Production of Commodities by Means of Commodities', in Pasinetti,

Luigi L. ed., (1980), *Essays on the Theory of Joint Production*, London: Macmillan, pp. 1–15.

Marx, Karl, (1867, 1885, 1894), *Capital*, vol. I–III, Moscow: Progress Publishers and Harmondsworth: Penguin, 1959.

Ministero della Pubblica Istruzione [Ministry of Education], (1926), *Bollettino Ufficiale*, no. 9, March, 4.

Modigliani, Franco, (1944), 'Liquidity Preference and the Theory of Interest and Money', *Econometrica*, vol. 12, pp. 45–88.

Morishima, Michio, (1973), *Marx's Economics*, Cambridge: Cambridge University Press.

Pasinetti, Luigi L., (1962), 'A Multi-sector Model of Economic Growth', a Ph.D. dissertation submitted to the Faculty of Economics and Political Science of the University of Cambridge, England, September.

Pasinetti, Luigi L., (1965), 'Causalità e interdipendenza nell'analisi econometrica e nella teoria economica', in *Annuario dell'Università Cattolica del S. Cuore, 1964–65*, Milano: Vita e Pensiero, pp. 233–250.

Pasinetti, Luigi L., (1966), 'Changes in the Rate of Profit and Switches of Techniques' (leading article of 'Paradoxes in Capital Theory: A Symposium'), in *The Quarterly Journal of Economics*, vol. 80 (4), pp. 503–517.

Pasinetti, Luigi L., (1969), 'Switches of Techniques and the "Rate of Return" in Capital Theory', in *The Economic Journal*, vol. 79, pp. 508–531.

Pasinetti, Luigi L., (1973), 'The Notion of Vertical Integration in Economic Analysis', in *Metroeconomica*, vol. 25, pp. 1–29.

Pasinetti, Luigi L., (1974), *Growth and Income Distribution – Essays in Economic Theory*, Cambridge: Cambridge University Press.

Pasinetti Luigi L., (1978), 'Wicksell Effects and Reswitchings of Technique in Capital Theory', in *The Scandinavian Journal of Economics*, vol. 80, pp. 181–189.

Pasinetti, Luigi L., (1981), *Structural Change and Economic Growth – A theoretical essay on the dynamics of the wealth of nations*, Cambridge: Cambridge University Press.

Pasinetti, Luigi L., (1987), 'Kahn, Richard Ferdinand', an entry in *The New Palgrave. A Dictionary of Economics*, vol. 3, pp. 1–3, London: Macmillan.

Pasinetti, Luigi L., (1989), 'Address', at King's College Chapel Kahn Memorial Service, 21 October 1989, King's College, Cambridge, pp. 6–11.

Pasinetti, Luigi L., ed., (1994), *Italian Economic Papers*, vol. II, Bologna: il Mulino and Oxford: Oxford University Press.

Pasinetti, Luigi L., (1996), 'Joan Robinson and "Reswitching"', in Marcuzzo, M. C., Pasinetti, L. L. and Roncaglia, A., *The Economics of Joan Robinson*, London: Routledge, pp. 209–217.

Pasinetti, Luigi L., (1997a), 'The Principle of Effective Demand', Chapter 3 in Harcourt, Geoffrey C. and Riach, Peter, eds, *A 'Second Edition' of the General Theory*, vol. I, London and New York: Routledge, pp. 93–104.

Pasinetti, Luigi L., (1997b), 'The Marginal Efficiency of Investment', Chapter 11 on Harcourt, Geoffrey C. and Riach, Peter, eds, *A 'Second Edition' of the General Theory*, vol. I, London and New York: Routledge, pp. 198–218.

Pasinetti, Luigi L., ed., (1998), *Italian Economic Papers*, vol. III, Bologna: il Mulino and Oxford: Oxford University Press.

Pasinetti, Luigi L. (1999), 'Economic Theory and Technical Progress' (given as the *Economic Issues* Lecture at the Royal Economic Society Annual Conference, Nottingham, England, March 1999), in *Economic Issues*, vol. 4, part 2, pp. 1–18.

Pasinetti, Luigi L., (2003), 'Sraffa e la matematica: diffidenza e necessità – quali sviluppi per il futuro?', in *Atti dei Convegni Lincei*, no. 200, International Conference on 'Piero Sraffa', Rome, 11–12 February 2003, pp. 373–383.

Pasinetti, Luigi L., Levhari, David, Samuelson, Paul A., Bruno, Michael, Burmeister, Edwin, Sheshinski, Etyan, Morishima, Michio and Garegnani, Pierangelo, (1966), contributions to 'Paradoxes in Capital Theory: A Symposium', in *Quarterly Journal of Economics*, vol. 80 (4), pp. 503–583.

Patinkin, Don, (1989), 'Different Interpretations of the "General Theory"', British Academy Keynes Lecture in Economics, in *Proceedings of the British Academy*, vol. 75, pp. 201–242.

Pigou, Arthur Cecil, (1950), *Keynes's General Theory: a retrospective view*, Two Lectures, London: Macmillan.

Quesnay, François, (1972), *Tableau Economique*, in Kuczynscki, Marguerite and Meek, Ronald, L., eds, 'Quesnay Tableau Economique' (containing Quesnay's 3rd edition of his *Tableau Economique*, 1758), London: Macmillan.

Ricardo, David, (1821), *On the Principles of Political Economy and Taxation*, 3rd edition, London: John Murray.

Robertson, Dennis H., Sraffa, Piero and Shove, Gerard F., (1930), 'Symposium on Increasing Returns and the Representative Firm', in *The Economic Journal*, vol. 40, pp. 79–116.

Robinson, Joan, (1933), *The Economics of Imperfect Competition*, London: Macmillan.

Robinson, Joan, (1956), *The Accumulation of Capital*, London: Macmillan.

Samuelson, Paul A., (1947), 'The General Theory (3)', in Harris, S. E., ed., *The New Economics*, London: Dennis Dobson, pp. 145–160.

Samuelson, Paul A., (1967), 'The Monopolistic Competition Revolution', in Kuenne, R. M., ed., *Monopolistic Competition: Studies in Impact*, New York: Wiley & Sons.

Samuelson, Paul A., (1971), 'Understanding the Marxian Notion of Exploitation: a Summary of the So-called Transformation Problem between Marxian Values and Competitive Prices', in *Journal of Economic Literature*, vol. 9, pp. 339–431.

Schefold, B., (1971), *Piero Sraffas Theorie der Kuppelproduktion des Kapitals und der Rente*, PhD dissertation, republished in *Mr. Sraffa on Joint Production*, London: Unwin Hyman, 1989.

Schumpeter, Joseph A., (1954), *History of Economic Analysis*, New York: Oxford University Press.

Skidelsky, Robert, (2000), *John Maynard Keynes, a Biography*, vol. Three: *Fighting for Britain 1937–1946*, London: Macmillan; published in the United States as *John Maynard Keynes, a Biography*, vol. Three: *Fighting for Freedom, 1937–1946*, Viking Press, 2001.

Solow, Robert M., (1955–56), 'The Production Function and the Theory of Capital', in *Review of Economic Studies*, vol. 23 (2), pp. 101–108.

Solow, Robert M., (1997), Entry on 'Trevor W. Swan', in Cate, Thomas, ed., *An Encyclopedia of Keynesian Economics*, Aldershot: Edward Elgar, pp. 594–597.

Sraffa, Piero, (1925), 'Sulle relazioni fra costo e quantità prodotta', in *Annali di Economia*, vol. 2, pp. 277–328.

Sraffa, Piero, (1926), 'The Laws of Returns under Competitive Conditions', in *The Economic Journal*, vol. 36, pp. 535–550.

Sraffa, Piero, (1960), *Production of Commodities by Means of Commodities: Prelude to a Critique of Economic Theory*, Cambridge: Cambridge University Press.

Sraffa, Piero, (1961), Comment made at the Discussion of Professor Hicks's paper 'The Measurement of Capital in Relation to the Measurement of Other Economic Aggregates' at the I. E. A. Corfù Conference, 1958, in Lutz, Friedrich and Hague, Douglas C. eds, (1961), *The Theory of Capital*, London: Macmillan, pp. 305–306.

Steedman, Ian, (1977), *Marx after Sraffa*, London: New Left Books.

Swan, Trevor W., (1956), 'Economic Growth and Capital Accumulation', in *Economic Record*, vol. 32, pp. 344–361.

Tabor, David, (1989), 'Address' at Kahn's burial ceremony, on 12 June 1989 (mimeo).

Targetti, Ferdinando, (1992), *Nicholas Kaldor – The Economics and Politics of Capitalism as a Dynamic System*, Oxford: Clarendon Press.

Thirlwall, Anthony P., (1987), *Nicholas Kaldor*, Brighton: Wheatsheaf Books.

von, Neumann, John, (1937), 'Über ein ökonomisches Gleichungssystem und eine Verallgemeinerung des Brouwerschen Fixpunktsatzes', in *Ergebnisse eines Matematischen Kolloquiums*, Vienna, vol. VIII, pp. 73–83, English transl. 'A Model of General Economic Equilibrium', in *Review of Economic Studies*, vol. XIII(l), 1945, pp. 1–9.

Weintraub, Roy E., (1998), 'Axiomatisches Mißverständnis', in *The Economic Journal*, vol. 108, pp. 1837–1847.

Wicksell, Knut, (1934), *Lectures on Political Economy*, vol. I, (Lionel Robbins, ed.), London: Routledge and Kegan Paul,

1934 (originally published in Swedish in 1901 and 1906 – 2nd part).

Wittgenstein, Ludwig, (1922), *Tractatus Logico-Philosophicus*, London: Routledge and Kegan Paul Ltd.

Wittgenstein, Ludwig, (1945), *Philosophical Investigations*, Oxford: Oxford University Press.

Wright, George Henrik, von, (1958), 'Biographical Sketch', in Malcolm, Norman, *Ludwig Wittgenstein, A Memoir*, London: Oxford University Press.

Book Three

**Towards a production paradigm
for an expanding economy**

Chapter VIII

Beyond neoclassical economics

1. Two connected 'revolutions'

The end of Book Two has brought to the surface the crunching question: do we really need an alternative economic paradigm? And, if so, can this alternative paradigm be built on the foundations laid by Keynes and the Cambridge Keynesians?

Let it be recalled that the Cambridge Keynesians were firmly convinced that, to pursue the Keynesian project, one should not attempt to make compromises with 'pernicious' (this epithet is Kaldor's) neo-classical economics. The insights that can be perceived from Keynes's *General Theory*, and the research efforts that in Cambridge originated from them, or parallel to them, were aimed at a break – not a reconciliation – with traditional neoclassical economics. But in what sense, and to what extent, may this conviction be justified?

The bio-bibliographical sketches presented in Book Two were meant to bring evidence and substantiation to the Keynesian claim. When, as in the case of Sraffa, the role played by Keynes himself appears less central, the differences do not refer to the break itself (which, in Sraffa's view, is even sharper), but to the question of whether and how such a break should be placed in a wider historical and theoretical context. The Cambridge School was in fact successful to a considerable extent in pursuing the critique part of the project and in beginning to develop Keynes's scheme for a 'monetary production economy'. They were less successful in coordinating their works and in placing their efforts into a clear, well-organised and comprehensive alternative paradigm. The Keynesian revolution has thus remained unaccomplished (as was argued in the 'Caffè Lectures' above).

In facing this problem, I shall now follow a more personal approach and try a rather different, but I feel more basic, method of resuming Keynes's claim concerning the necessity of a revolution in economics. I shall attempt to do so in two steps. The first one is an appeal to awareness of the impending, indeed dramatic, reality that has been shaping the external world around us – a reality that concerns the phase of human history that has started since the industrial revolution and is continuing unabated in impetus and penetration into all aspects of our life. The second step is an appeal to search for that kind of economic analysis which is appropriate to investigate this new historical phase. The revolution that has taken place in economic history cannot be disjointed from the search for the analytical tools appropriate to investigate it. In short, a revolution in economic history cannot be disjointed from a parallel revolution in economic analysis.

2.   The historical background of economic analysis

I have thought for some time that the most convincing way to present the need for an alternative economic paradigm, basically grounded on the phenomenon of production (and technical change), as against the prevailing paradigm, basically grounded on the phenomenon of exchange (and the scarcity of resource endowments), is to draw attention to the process through which the modern world has been taking shape in the past few centuries, during which the perspectives of human societies have changed profoundly (in fact radically). A new paradigm should firmly place the dynamics of the modern world at the base of economic analysis. In a work which I carried out in Cambridge at the time of my association with the Cambridge School of Keynesian Economics (Pasinetti, 1962, 1965, 1981), I tried to briefly present this historical background through a passage which in its basic lines (see Pasinetti, 1981, pp. 1–4) remains topical. I think it is worth representing it here.

If we consider the historical context in which economic analysis has come into being, we may say that this context is represented by the 'modern world', namely, the stage of our history which is known as the age of experiment and science, because of the dominating idea that mankind, by using its own critical intellect, by observing nature and by experimenting, can *learn* in a systematic way and can pass on his improved knowledge to the following generations. The idea that mankind can systematically progress, simple though it may seem today, took a long time to assert itself, but once discovered it has, in a few centuries, revolutionised the whole prospects of humanity and has pervaded every activity involving human ingenuity.

In economic terms, the direct consequence has been a process of unprecedented increase in material wealth. The process may be divided, for analytical purposes, into two distinct phases, which may be called the phase of trade and the phase of industry. There is no clear-cut distinction between the two, as they have a common origin and are intermingled, but they appear nevertheless on the historical scene with very definite characteristic features of their own.

The phase of trade is the first to break through. It can be perceived even as early as the turn of the first millennium, with the rise of the Mediterranean maritime republics, but it can be seen more clearly later on, after the Renaissance 'opening of the minds' towards the outside world. A few basic improvements in the technique of transportation led to the discoveries of new lands and extended the horizon of the known world to include countries with climates and products previously unknown. New possibilities of trade were opened up, with a profound impact on the economic conditions of the whole world. The trading nations were suddenly better off, not because of a rise in the world's production but because of better utilisation of the production which was already taking place. Each nation kept its own institutions and organisational structure of production, but could now advantageously exchange the products which were proper to its particular climate or localised resources for products which it could never produce or which it could produce only at much higher cost. The material wealth of all nations was increased just by exchange, by a better spatial allocation of existing resources and products. This is the merchant era, which represents perhaps the most outstanding example of how all people can gain from trade.

Much slower to reveal itself is the phase of industry, which requires the existence of, and thus presupposes, trade. Industry is a process of augmenting wealth through a material increase in the quantity and number of products, to be achieved by the practical application of the advances of science, division and specialisation of labour, better organisation, invention and utilisation of new sources of energy and new materials. Unlike trade, industry requires changes in the organisational structure of society. Therefore, it comes about slowly, but progressively. It requires long and painful social changes in the relations between men and the means of production before it can fully break out in the industrial revolution that England experienced in the eighteenth century. Of course, trade remains the natural and necessary complement to industry, but as a cause of *further* increases in wealth, it is bound to subside. Industry, however, is bound to remain a permanent cause of increase in wealth and to become pre-eminent as time goes on, owing to the very nature of its cumulative process.

Even with crude simplifications, these two aspects of the modern world seem to me very helpful in indicating the directions in which the emergence of the modern era has stimulated economic analysis.

The concept of trade is, so to speak, a *static* concept. It is associated with a situation in which a plurality of economic systems (or of individuals) is endowed with particular resources or products and tries to gain advantages through exchange. The interest that such a situation arouses in an economist concerns the problem of how to make the best use of what is already available, namely of how to reach the best allocation of given resources. We may imagine a situation in which a plurality of economic systems has reached an internal equilibrium, but the systems do not trade among themselves, and then another situation in which the same economic systems, besides having reached an internal equilibrium, also trade with one another. It is easy to show that the passage from the first to the second situation – i.e. a *once-and-for-all* change from no trade to trade, to be maintained thereafter – normally brings about gains for all. What is involved is *a problem of rationality*, which may be expressed by a mathematical function to be maximised under certain constraints.

The concept of, and the problems entailed by, 'industry' – to be intended of course in a wider sense, which goes well beyond the original one of 'manufacture' – are quite different. Industry is, so to speak, a *dynamic* concept. It implies production, i.e. the engagement and the application of human ingenuity to make and shape the products that people want. But since, by doing and experiencing, mankind learns, it is implicit in the very nature of carrying on a production activity that new and better methods of production will be discovered. Of course, to find new methods takes time, and takes time in a persistent way. The economist is faced here no longer with a problem of rationality but with a *process of learning*. Any mathematical formulation of it cannot but be made with reference to time. There may well be phases of sharp breaks with the past and phases of small but persistent improvements, which are, however, cumulative. The process cannot in any case be shaped but in the form of functions of time. In the phases of continuous changes, it may well make short steps at a time and may therefore appear almost negligible in the short run, but as it goes on incessantly, it is inevitably bound to become more pronounced the longer the period which is considered.

The contrast between this complex process characterised by learning and continuous movement and the simpler concept of trade should now be evident. The passage from a position of no trade to a position of trade induces a jump, which may well be quite large but which is temporary, as it ends when the new equilibrium situation has been reached. The process of learning associated with industry, by contrast, implies a *persistent* movement − not a once-and-for-all change but a *rate of change* in time, a cumulative and indefinite movement. Clearly, these are two distinct series of concepts and problems. A particularly important difference between the two, for theoretical analysis, is that they acquire an opposite practical relevance in relation to time, the former being relevant (at a given point in time) just when the latter is practically irrelevant and the latter becoming relevant (as time is elapsing) just when the former has become irrelevant.

This opposition carries with it profound consequences for theoretical analysis, as it has inevitably induced economic theorists to adopt diametrically opposite attitudes to the type of hypotheses to choose.

It should appear quite evident from this synthetic sketch how, historically, the 'phase of trade' may appear to have stimulated and to have framed the bases of the economic paradigm, which I earlier called the 'model of pure exchange', of which the neoclassical scheme of general economic equilibrium represents the most elegant and complete expression.[1] At the same time, it should appear equally evident how the unfolding of the historical 'phase of industry' may have

---

[1] See my Caffè Lectures above (pp. 16–21) and the references given there.

stimulated and framed the bases of the economic paradigm which, in the same Lectures, I called 'model of pure production', of which the Physiocrats first, then the Classics, and lately the streams of thought which have been inspired by Keynes and Schumpeter represent the most obvious expression.

The interesting point is that it has precisely been the evolution of history, more specifically of two particular phases of the major historical events of the last millennium, that has stimulated two quite different and contrasting ways of elaborating economic theory, even if both of them appear justified by the events of the historical phase to which they can be related. But the process has taken rather intricate and round-about paths, which deserve a few further reflections.

3.   From mercantilism to neoclassicism

After what has just been said, it cannot be surprising to find that the immediate response from the economists, at the inception of the modern world − with its early prominence of the 'phase of trade'− was of a 'mercantilist' type. Mercantilism, with its central tenet that a nation, in order to increase her wealth, should aim at an excess of exports over imports and at accumulating precious metals (i.e. purchasing power), dominated economic thought in the sixteenth, seventeenth and first half of the eighteenth centuries. The mercantilists' arguments and their over-enthusiasm about the benefits of trade have subsequently been proved faulty and their famous policy *recipés*, that were also interpreted as an urge for the advanced countries to dominate, even by military force, the rest of the world,[2] have been proved to be based on deficient

---

[2] Landes (1998, p. 143) quotes the following passage by Jan Pieterzoom, the young and forceful proconsul in Batavia (now Jakarta) of the Dutch East India Company, at the beginning of the seventeenth century: 'Your Honours should know by experience that trade in Asia must be driven and maintained under the protection and favour of Your Honours' own weapons,

or false arguments. But this only underlines how strong must have been the impact of the benefits from trade on the minds of those scholars who, during those centuries, tried to analyse and understand the relevant economic aspects of the commercial environment of the time.

The mercantilists lacked the appropriate analytical tools to support their discovery of the importance of worldwide trade. A theoretical scheme that could have been used to evince the positive economic achievements of the 'trade phase' of modern history did not exist at the time and the mercantilists were unable to provide it. Curiously enough, a scheme that could have fulfilled such a function was formally developed much later in economics, by the marginalists, in the 1870s, as we will see in a moment. Mercantilism had long since fallen into disrepute. At the time of the Classics, Ricardo could already show – against the mercantilists – how international trade would bring benefits to all traders concerned through specialisation in production. But the marginalists, though within a more restrictive vision, succeeded in proposing a far more elegant theoretical scheme, attractively and beautifully expressed in mathematical terms. Unlike Ricardo, they proposed a scheme which was consistent with the more primitive mercantilists' concept of wealth as a given stock of natural resources. At the same time – contrary to the (especially earlier) mercantilists' beliefs – they could show that international trade is a non-zero-sum activity, that could potentially benefit *all* traders. Their analytical achievement was to prove that, under certain conditions, trade could lead to a better (ideally an optimum) allocation of the given endowments of natural resources, within a given, static, technological and institutional framework. It

and that the weapons must be paid for by the profits from the trade; so that we cannot carry on trade without war nor war without trade.' The connection between wealth and power has been stressed by practically all scholars who investigated mercantilism; see Hecksher (1955), especially part II.

may appear paradoxical that the general equilibrium scheme which thereby emerged, squarely built on static premises, should happen to be developed simultaneously and in striking contrast with an unprecedented development that was meanwhile taking place in the real production structure of the external world. This is a curious but fascinating story that deserves ampler investigation.[3]

Of course, the other economic aspect of the modern world – the aspect connected with industry and production – could not fail to progressively emerge. Already in the second half of the eighteenth century, physiocracy, which came to submerge mercantilism, centred the attention precisely on *production* and – understandably enough in the eighteenth century – on agricultural production, singled out as the real source of wealth of a nation. It is to the physiocrats that we owe the first table representing the circulation of commodities in an economic system (François Quesnay's celebrated *Tableau économique*). The crucial step forward taken by this *Tableau* consisted not only, and in fact not so much, in its attempts at a quantitative analysis, as in the change it brought about in the very concept of *wealth*. No longer was the appropriation of natural resources and in particular of precious metals (all *stocks* concepts) indicated as the real source of the wealth of a nation, but rather her annual net production: her *produit net* (a *flow* concept).

The physiocratic analytical innovations were quickly picked up by the British Classical economists. To Quesnay's idea of agricultural production, as a surplus above subsistence and reproduction requirements, Adam Smith made the addition of industrial production. By stressing the pre-eminence of the 'skill, dexterity, and judgement with which labour is applied . . . [w]hatever be the soil, climate and extent of territory' (Smith, 1976, p. 10), he effectively singled out what nowadays we call the forces behind the growth

---

[3] For further details, see Pasinetti, 1981, pp. 8–23; also see below, pp. 261–262.

of labour productivity, as constituting the basic cause of the wealth of nations, to be achieved by specialisation and division of labour, *independently* of the given endowment of scarce natural resources. He also thought he could single out the appropriate economic institution – free trade among competitive, self-interested individuals – that could make market prices and quantities produced converge towards their 'natural levels'. Ricardo enriched Smith's analysis, though on a narrower basis. He drew two distinctions that are also crucial to our purposes. He stated, with a clearness and sharpness that Adam Smith and the physiocrats had not achieved, the distinction between *scarce* commodities[4] and *produced* commodities,[5] and he drew an equally sharp distinction between the investigations concerning the 'natural' prices[6] and those concerning the 'market' prices.[7] Moreover, the importance of the *net product* of the economy (considered as the surplus above subsistence and replacements) became, in Ricardo's analysis, so pre-eminent as to induce him to think of the problem of its distribution between 'rent, profit and wages' as 'the principal problem in Political Economy' (Ricardo, 1821, p. 5). His attention shifted to the accumulation of profit as the major propeller of economic growth, and to international trade as a major source of gains through specialisation in manufacturing, which he considered the dynamic sector, agriculture being thought to suffer from decreasing returns to scale. A

[4] '[. . .] commodities the value of which is determined by scarcity alone', to which Ricardo attributed minor importance, as they 'form a very little part of the mass of commodities daily exchanged on the market' (Ricardo, 1951, p. 12).

[5] 'By far the greatest part of those goods, which are the object of desire, are procured by labour, and they may be multiplied, not in one country alone, but in many, almost without any assignable limit, if we are disposed to bestow the labour necessary to obtain them' (*ibid.*, p. 12). It is on these 'produced' commodities that Ricardo concentrated his analysis.

[6] They are determined, Ricardo says, by factors that are 'primary and natural' (*ibid.*, p. 88).

[7] These are 'disturbed by accidental and temporary deviations', due to the inevitable non-correspondence at every time between the possibilities of production and temporary whims of market demand (*ibid.*, p. 88, as to Smith, 1976, see pp. 74–75). But Ricardo concentrated the bulk of his analysis on the determination of the 'natural' prices.

further notable feature of Classicism, which at the time was neglected and then remained in the shadows until Keynes, was the problem of overall expenditure. The issue was perceived by Malthus with the well-founded fear that the abundance of production potential could be frustrated by lack of 'effectual demand'.[8]

The whole set of the Classical economists' contributions was astoundingly rich in concepts, with a strong awareness of the relevant problems brought into existence by the emerging industrial society. But these problems proved too complex to be dealt with through their primitive economic analysis. They fell into theoretical difficulties, which they were unable to solve. They dramatically underestimated the unprecedented possibilities of technological development. Most of all, they failed to foresee that the evolution of technology itself was producing major changes in the relations between a growing population and the economic and social organizations of the society of their time.

We must nevertheless acknowledge their substantial achievements. To conceive, construct and develop the bases of a new ('production') paradigm, which after all they did basically grasp, was a huge step forward. They were insufficiently equipped, but the historical challenge they had to face was unprecedented. The abundance of concepts which they did nevertheless produce would have needed to be cleared of ambiguities, adapted, reshaped, polished and more clearly specified, while new concepts were badly needed in the light of the extraordinary historical evolution of knowledge, technology and institutions which was taking place.

The inability of the Classical economists to perceive the fact that – unlike what had happened in the previous 'phase of trade' – institutions themselves were being profoundly affected by the 'phase of industry' spelled disaster for their doctrines. The surge of Karl Marx on the scene of economic discussions brought their deficiencies to the surface in a

---

[8] Details on Keynes's 'effective', as against Malthus's 'effectual', demand may be seen in Pasinetti, 1974, pp. 29–31.

dramatic way. On a strict level of economic analysis, Marx inherited the basic elements of Classical economics theory. He was indeed able to move with surprising ease within the relevant 'production' economic paradigm, which the Classics had perceived and placed at the basis of their enquiries.[9] Unlike the Classics, he then concentrated most of his analysis on what I am going to call the institutional stage of economic (and social) investigation. He placed the new social problems at the fore of his concern, denouncing unconditionally all existing (capitalist) institutions. But he was not able to propose a viable alternative to them, as against the established (bourgeois) society of his time. He went to the opposite extreme and called for a radical social revolution. Marx perceived precisely the profound *institutional* implications of the new industrial age, which the Classical economists had missed. The 'phase of industry', unlike the 'phase of trade', required deep changes *in the institutions* of society. By re-elaborating the concepts inherited from the Classics, Marx turned their 'innocent' conclusions upside down and reshaped them to serve his revolutionary purposes.[10] What would have been so badly needed was a new economic theory. Though advocating revolution in practice, he failed to give substantial constructive improvements to that revolution in economic theory which the Classical economists had only intuited. From this point of view, his works sadly turned out to be utterly destructive. His critique should not be underestimated, yet the development of a constructive fully fledged 'production' economic paradigm has remained unfulfilled ever since.

What turned out to be so devastating was the social impact of his writings. The immediate practical effect of Marx's call

---

[9] Remember Marx's intuitive but conceptually profound definition of mankind as a species that, unlike animals, which simply look around and pick up the food they find for their subsistence, *produces* what it needs (see references given in Chapter I of Pasinetti, 1977).

[10] See Pasinetti, 1981, pp. xi–xii.

for a social revolution was to elicit a strong social reaction. The establishment of the Western nations, at the end of the nineteenth century, became scared by Marx's revolutionary call. This by itself explains a lot of the fortune that in academic circles blessed marginalism in the 1870s, whose success was essentially analytical. By simply going back to the pre-industrial age concept of wealth considered as a set of given endowments of scarce natural resources (a *stock* concept), the marginalists succeeded in reaching an *analytical* breakthrough, against which Classical economic theory had nothing to compare. They elaborated a formally sophisticated and elegant scheme capable of dealing with the problems of a simpler society — a society in which the more traditional concept of wealth, as consisting of a stock endowment of resources provided by nature in given and, for most components, *scarce* quantities, could be placed at the very centre of the whole investigation. Hence, not the dynamism of a changing society as, paradoxically, could be observed all around, but the problems of managing efficiently the wealth that existed already became the crucial subject of economic investigation, through the assumption of a perfectly rational behaviour of the single individuals, in a perfectly competitive, strictly *atomistic* stationary society.

In academic circles, this no doubt represented a radical change, but not in the strict sense of a scientific 'revolution', though some historians of economic thought later hastened to call it so (the 'Marginal Revolution').[11] Conceptually, it was a 'counter-revolution', an anachronistic achievement, yet a beautiful one, reached with the most sophisticated tools of economic analysis (precisely what the Classical economists had lacked).[12]

---

[11] See Collison Black *et al.*, 1973.
[12] No doubt, one of the circumstances that contributed to its attractiveness and strength was also the weakness of Classical economic theory in dealing with demand. The marginalists developed an entirely (subjective) theory of value, elegantly based on individual choice, relative scarcities and

At the end of the nineteenth and the beginning of the twentieth century, marginal economic theory led to conclusions which were pleasing to the establishment, especially in terms of a splendid detachment from the hot social issues that were boiling up in the real world, and in terms of arguments that could easily be used for the advocacy of unrestricted *laissez-faire* policies, supposedly leading, in ideal conditions, to optimal positions. On strict substance, the implications were for no revolution at all, on any plane: i) not in the real world, where the distribution of wealth was portrayed as one to be accepted as it was; ii) not in the economic investigations, which tended to abandon emphasis on the phenomenon of production – i.e. on the really novel feature of industrial societies – and to resume emphasis on the typical features of an erstwhile relevant 'exchange' paradigm, now framed in such a way as to produce the static conception of an elegant 'general economic equilibrium' (proposed by Walras and Pareto in the nineteenth century and then perfected half a century later by Arrow and Debreu, 1954); and iii), most important of all, not in the fundamental institutions of society, which, though acknowledged as 'imperfect', were taken as the basic institutions to be accepted as they had thus far evolved.[13]

What appears as extraordinarily relevant for us here is that this type of economic analysis has achieved astonishing academic success. Its supporters are claiming that it has proved to be 'flexible enough' as to be able to absorb into itself all the developments that in the meantime have been taking place in many other directions. It is in this all-embracing guise that it has been called neoclassical economics and has surged to the

rational maximising behaviour, which appeared as perfectly alternative to the formally more rudimentary Classical (objective) theory of value, based on division of labour and cost of production. (For a comparison of these two alternative foundational bases of the theories of value, see Pasinetti, 1986.)

[13] This assertion is not meant to deny the deeply felt social concern that authors such as Walras, Wicksell and Arrow always entertained, not sparing criticisms of the market-oriented institutions of their times.

point of dominating economic teaching and research on a vast scale across the world. It has resisted and contrasted Keynes's revolutionary ideas by widening the scope of the exchange paradigm, with the aim of grafting on to it all aspects of economic reality, including those of production and, more recently, in a peculiar sort of way, even those of technical change. Its advocates are convinced that it can also absorb the contributions of Keynes and of the Keynesians themselves.

Can this be true? If what is said above is correct, the argument sounds, to say the least, counter-intuitive. To choose a theoretical scheme built on the characteristics of the early 'trade phase' of modern economic history and pretend to use it as the very basis on which to graft all the evolutionary events that have characterised the subsequent revolutionary phase of modern industrial history sounds illogical. Elementary logic would suggest doing precisely the opposite; namely to concentrate first on constructing a theoretical framework appropriate to the newly emerging, industrial phase of our history and then – only then – to look back and recoup, if and where possible, whatever aspects of the previous phase could still be considered to be relevant and/or helpful.

4. Methodological reductionism of neoclassical economics

I think that one should not underestimate the achievements of mainstream neoclassical economics. To say that it succeeded where mercantilism failed should not be taken as a perfunctory statement. To have shown that *all* (individuals and countries) can gain from trade, and particularly from international trade, was a major achievement. This was possible precisely through its association with the pure exchange model, which provided a scientific basis for the analysis of the phenomenon of exchange and of the conditions under which it may lead self-interested, rationally behaving individuals to achieve optimal positions, in a world in which technology and institutions are given. Marginalism succeeded in providing a scientific basis for the 'trade phase' of the modern world.

But we have outgrown that phase, however significant it may have been. The fault of neoclassical economists is to have remained enmeshed in it. More specifically, we may say that neoclassical economists are at fault when, from the enthusiasm generated by their beautiful analytical scheme, they go on to the claim that they have obtained a model of *general* validity. This claim is not justified and should be sharply rejected.

It is true that they have not been inactive. They have indeed become quite conscious of a world in which the 'exchange' characteristics, while continuing to be relevant, are progressively becoming less and less so, relative to the increasing relevance of the 'industry' characteristics. And they have persistently concentrated their efforts on reshaping and adapting the general equilibrium model in many ways, with the aim of absorbing into it the process of production. Yet by doing so, neoclassical economists have inexorably been falling into what is termed *methodological reductionism*. More specifically, rather than attempting to explain reality, they have forced themselves into a self-indulgent (no matter how attractive) intellectual exercise, which consists in constructing *by assumption* – sometimes by extreme assumptions – an increasingly *hypothetical* world, which is conceived and shaped in such a way as to be amenable to be fitted into the pre-conceived general equilibrium scheme.

The unsatisfactory outcome of this reductionist pursuit can be seen in two major directions: i) in preventing us from singling out and uncovering the basic *foundations* of the monetary production economies that have emerged from the industrial revolution, and ii) in a biased and prejudicial exploration of the characteristics of the actual institutions appropriate to the industrial world.

At the foundational level, the failures are associated with an intrinsic inability to absorb the fundamental problems of an evolving production and consumption structure, typical of the economies that have emerged from the industrial revolution. With the pure exchange model in its background, neoclassical theory is intrinsically looking at any economic phenomenon through the lens of the principle of scarcity. Such a logical scheme is badly suited to deal with the problems of production. Reproducible goods are treated as if they were always in short supply, which is not only a distortion of reality but basically a misinterpretation of it. It ignores the fact that in the industrial societies most economic difficulties that tend to arise do not come from problems of scarcity but from problems of oversupply of produced goods. As a consequence, in their forced artificial adaptations of the pure exchange model to tackle the characteristics of the industrial world, neoclassical economists are compelled to transform *by assumption* – i.e. by a purely mental exercise – the process of production into a sort of artificial exchange through time.

It is true that enormous efforts have been made recently, first to construct neoclassical models of growth and then to introduce technical progress into them. This trend has been considered as a great step forward. But precisely the nature of the efforts that have been carried out in this direction indicates clearly the *reductionist* character of the whole operation. When trying to go into dynamics, neoclassical economists are forced into a contradiction between the reductionist requirements of an intrinsically artificial approach to the dynamics of production and the *methodological individualism* which is at the very basis of the neoclassical approach, whose admissible 'micro-foundations' are drastically but inevitably limited to those of the Walrasian theoretical scheme. On the first aspect, they are forced into hypothesising an unstructured, basically a one-commodity, world – not as a first-step simplification, but as a necessary and unrelaxable characteristic of the model concerned. To indicate an analytical tool that perhaps best highlights this reductionist neoclassical characteristic I may mention the almost inevitable reliance on a macroeconomic Cobb-Douglas production function, a purely hypothetical instrument of convenience, requiring the accumulation of an incredible number of restrictive assumptions, made only in order to avoid logical inconsistencies.[14] But then, paradoxically, comes the second aspect, which compels them to the equally trivial assumption of a world in which there is one single individual, or else – to make the pill more digestible – a series of individuals assumed to be all exactly like one another so as to reduce them, for all analytical purposes, to one single 'representative agent'.[15] This sort of exercise shows quite strikingly the remoteness of the purely hypothetical world that is assumed. At a dynamic level, the basic shortcoming concerns the inability to deal with heterogeneity – of goods, on the one side, and of individuals, on the other side. The macroeconomic consequence is quite logical – the so-called

---

[14] See Pasinetti (2000), Sylos Labini (1995), where it is shown that the widespread assertion that the Cobb-Douglas production function enjoyed empirical success is not true; actually it is far from the truth. The great majority of empirical tests are negative.

[15] Essentially Alan Kirman has also arrived at these same conclusions in a very accurate critical analysis of the mathematical foundations of the general equilibrium model. Kirman has been pursuing a different route from the one mentioned here. He has put under scrutiny the required properties of uniqueness and stability of the general equilibrium model. And his conclusions have been devastating: '. . . It is not mere chance that one assumption that leads to strong results as to uniqueness and stability is that society should behave as an individual. Yet we know that to obtain such behaviour, individuals' behaviour must be very similar. Thus demand and expenditure functions, if they are to be set against reality, must be defined at some reasonably high level of aggregation. The idea that we should start at the level of the isolated individual is one which we may well have to abandon. There is no more misleading description in modern economics than the so-called microfoundations of macroeconomics, which in fact describe the behaviour of the consumption or production sector by the behaviour of one individual or firm' (Kirman, 1989, p. 138; see also Kirman, 1992). Kirman's analysis has practically remained without refutation. Interestingly enough, mainstream economists have ended up by reacting to it in exactly the same way as they have finally decided to react to the results of the Cambridge critique on the neoclassical theory of capital: by simply ignoring it.

'fallacy of composition', generated by the forced assumption that the whole system always and exclusively is generated by the sum of the independent actions of all the single individuals; a complete negation of any truly macroeconomic dimension, so essential in the investigations of industrial economic systems.[16] Basically, economic analysis is deprived of the possibilities of any reasonable enquiry into the process of the *structural* evolution of output imposed by technological change and by the evolving changes in consumers' choices, all phenomena which are at the very foundations of industrial societies.[17]

However, it is not only at the foundational level, but also at the level of the exploration of the specific institutions of our economies that the *reductionist* character of neoclassical economics is forcing it into serious oversimplifications. Precisely because of the trap represented by its basically *static* conceptual characteristics, this requires the scheme to be framed with an exclusive reference to very specific institutions. The inevitable hypotheses have been those of assuming market institutions – not only for the determination of commodity prices (which is what the pure exchange model is conceived for) but also of *all* other economic variables of the economic system. Most of all, the scheme is constrained by the assumption of *perfect* market institutions. The essentiality of these assumptions is imposed by the fact that the model cannot otherwise produce those ideal situations of optimum allocation of existing resources, which is what gives a justification and confers beauty and intellectual attraction on the whole economic general equilibrium scheme. But to be compelled to make such assumptions, for a world where institutions are in a continuous reorganisation, is tantamount to being

---

[16] All the immense literature on so-called 'endogenous growth', appreciable as it may have been for the fresh wind of novelty it has introduced, is in one way or another suffering from the two contradictory aspects mentioned in the text.

[17] See above, pp. 227–234, for hints at the reaction of the Keynesian group.

compelled to enormously – in fact crucially – reduce the interpretative power of the whole model.

It must be added that economists of original neoclassical extraction have recently developed plenty of schemes dealing with non-perfect competition conditions and using various – not necessarily optimising – techniques and also attempting the introduction of non-market institutions. This is a welcome opening, though all such tendencies are still strongly resisted, precisely because they inevitably bump into serious difficulties of compatibility with the very logic of the inherited schemes. First of all, the analyses are becoming increasingly fragmented. We witness the development of a whole series of little models, each of which relates to a specific phenomenon that is, at a particular time, appearing on the world economic scene. The models normally start as very simple, but they quickly become rather complicated, even at their early stages of elaboration. Moreover, by necessarily deflecting from the originally perfect competition model, they are bound to come into contradictions with the early (individualistic and atomistic) characteristics of the original model. One loses sight of, or has to abandon claims to, the achievement of optimality positions, i.e. precisely those features that have been originally and remain the major source of attraction of the general economic equilibrium scheme.

For a neoclassical economist, there is, it appears to me, an inescapable dilemma here. Either one gives up any attempt at any new opening and retreats into assuming hypothetical, imaginary worlds of atomistic, overall knowledgeable, perfectly competitive individuals, which means falling into the methodological reductionist trap described above. Or one takes the jump ahead and goes on to analysing the more realistic aspects of the actual institutions of the industrial world, to be considered not as deviations or as 'market failures' – as it has become customary to say, with the (misleading) implication that the (practically impossible!) solution would be to eliminate the market 'failures' – but as the normal way in which the present institutional set-up is working. In this case, however, one is compelled to abandon not only any claim to but actually any clear idea on how to proceed in the evaluation of a world in which equilibrium or non-equilibrium situations are entirely disconnected from optimum, or reasonably optimal, or even reasonably acceptable, actual situations. More precisely, one may indeed pursue the positive task of reaching results that reflect reality, but in this case one is compelled to abandon any idea to claim them to be good or satisfactory or acceptable, simply because the connections with the most beautiful properties (the properties of optimality) of the fascinating but dynamically irrelevant general equilibrium, pure exchange, perfect competition model have vanished. By losing the 'optimality' frame of reference, one is left to wander in the darkness.[18]

It is precisely here that one reaches the crucial point. Which other framework of reference can we look for? Traditional theory does not provide another one. It leaves us in the wilderness, at a complete loss. To solve the riddle one must really stop the patching-up. One must genuinely go back to Keynes's initial exhortation for a really radical change – for a genuine breakaway from the reductionist constraints of neoclassical economics. Time has come to sail widely and freely beyond.

5.   The ideal task of Keynesian economics

If the exhortation is justified and the arguments so far developed are correct – i.e. if Keynes and the (Cambridge) Keynesians were right in claiming that a break with neoclassical economics is inevitable – the question that once again

---

[18] An indication, from many sources, that something new must be invented can be perceived by the use, still in an inappropriate sense, of the term 'paradigm', which some of the most perceptive, originally neoclassical economists have begun to do (e.g. Phelps, 1994, Stiglitz, 2001). The real solution lies in the radical *break* with tradition, as advocated by Keynes, and as will be argued below (see pp. 331–334).

emerges is why Keynes's revolution has remained unaccomplished.

At this stage, the question must be answered on a more substantive basis than earlier. An explanation seems necessary, quite apart from, and besides, the simple ones already described. My guess is that something really substantial may have escaped attention, pertaining to the very nature of the basic task that Keynes and the whole Keynesian School were ideally supposed to carry out.

I shall be bold and make a rough attempt to state plainly such a basic task myself, at least in the way I have perceived it.

If the characterisation of the 'modern world', as depicted in the previous pages, is correct, one might say that Keynes and the Cambridge Keynesians, and all the economists that have genuinely followed them, when they proclaimed the necessity of a revolution with respect to the theoretical framework that had been erected with great care by the marginalists and then by the general equilibrium theorists, were in fact ideally called upon to carry out a task similar to the one which the marginalists had carried out with respect to the economics of the mercantilists. More precisely, and with reference to the substance of their undertaking, they were called upon to carry out, with reference to the 'industrial phase' of our economic history, a task similar to the one which the neoclassical economists had successfully carried out with reference to the earlier 'trade phase'.

The marginalists, as has been pointed out, had shaped the analytical tools that allowed them to erect a theoretical construction based on the traditional concept of wealth conceived as a *stock* – an endowment of scarce natural resources. Accordingly, they placed the search for the optimum allocation of given and scarce resources at the centre and foundation of economics and they found an appropriate analytical tool (maximisation under constraints) which allowed them to deal in general with the economic problems that they chose to investigate. Contextually, the same analytical scheme led them to single out a unique and exclusive institutional mechanism, the free market, in the particular (let me stress this adjective) form of the behaviour of a set of atomistically competing, self-interested, independent, maximising individuals, that would, under certain ideal conditions, drive the economic system to the achievement of relatively optimum allocative positions.

Symmetrically, we might say that Keynes and the Keynesians have ideally been called upon to erect a theoretical construction based on the (post-industrial revolution) concept of wealth conceived as a continuous *flow* of net output – i.e. as a flow of goods and services produced and becoming available in each period of time. Accordingly, they have been called upon to concentrate on the investigation of the causes and nature of the production process, the laws that underlie the distribution of the national output, the factors that govern its evolution through time.

But let us be aware: while this task of the Keynesians may conceptually appear symmetrical in essence to that of the marginalists, the extent of the efforts necessary to accomplish it is much greater, in fact dramatically greater, both in size and in scale. The conception of a 'production paradigm' is by far more complex than the conception of an 'exchange paradigm'. To begin with, it requires a dynamic framework, not a static one. Secondly, it would miss its central problems if it pretended to rely exclusively on an atomistic analysis of society. The production activity, while indeed relying on individual initiative, is also, typically, a social process, and in more than one sense. Thirdly, it could no longer abstract, as the models of exchange usually do, from historical specificities, since the kind of institutions that shape an industrial society, besides being far more complex, are inherently subject to changes induced by the evolving historical events, much more extensively than those that shaped the era of trade.

From this point of view, a mere reference to the free market mechanism becomes insufficient and must itself be called into question. Neoclassical economics has ended up by monopolising the concept of a free market as an institution characterised by the function of an optimum allocation of resources. The idea in itself is not 'wrong' – it is awfully reductive. First, because the conditions of a truly workable perfect market are very stringent and second because, in any dynamic setting, the social function of free markets may go far beyond the function of the optimum allocation of given resources. Furthermore, because free market competition may not be enough. In any case, and most fundamentally, simply equating free competitive markets with neoclassical economics is *not* a permissible equation. The conception of a much wider institutional framework is needed.

Here again going back to the Classical economists becomes essential as the very starting point. We must be careful not to squander what they achieved. We should resume, and take advantage of what they had already discovered – relevance of population growth, of the progressive division of labour, of the improvements of techniques, of the ever-present risk of a lack or a drop in 'effectual demand'; most of all, relevance of the typically dynamic approach of investigation they adopted and of linking together economic relations and social changes.

Yet this is not all. It can only be, it should be stressed, the beginning. The analytical scheme that is needed will have to move widely forward, into the investigation of those phenomena that the Classical economists had underestimated (such as the long-run effects of technical progress, the structural differentiation of consumption, production and employment) and also of those phenomena which they could not, at the time, understand or had missed altogether simply because they had not yet materialised. Think especially of the startling impact of the diffusion of knowledge, of the process of learning in shaping the behaviour of people (of *all* people), with regard to both the evolution of technology and the evolution of the size and structure of overall demand.

In the end, we should be able to place the whole of these evolving phenomena within a framework of compatibility with the appropriate, or at least with the achievable, social institutions that are by themselves evolving or must be made to evolve.

Does this sound an impossibly complex research programme? Maybe. But that is no reason for not attempting it or for giving it up before it is started. I hope that others, like myself, will not refrain from feeling the excitement and spur arising from the challenges it is positing.[19]

[19] One useful reflection that may be added is that the ideal 'Keynesian task' that lies ahead would seem to require, at its root, an underlying radical change of *vision*. The investigation of a stationary economy must give way to the investigation of a permanently evolving economy. This sort of radical shift of vision is similar – to take a different field as an example, even if the comparison may appear impossibly ambitious – to the one that brought the astro-physicists to break away from the conception of a stationary universe – indeed perfectly logical and self-contained – and jump to their present, intrinsically dynamic conception of an ever-expanding universe.

Chapter IX

The stage of pure economic theory

1. A *separation theorem*

Max Planck is quoted as saying that he had considered studying economics but found the subject too complicated and opted for physics instead. Alas, economic analysis lost a most beautiful mind, but the justification that Planck is supposed to have given is not a joke.

If the foregoing analysis is correct and, accordingly, if the task to be undertaken is that of going down – much deeper behind what Keynes called a 'monetary production economy' – to search for the place to lay the foundations of a comprehensive 'production paradigm', there is a real problem of complexity that cannot be dodged. It simply becomes no longer possible to rely on a closed model – as has been the case with the pure exchange scheme of the general equilibrium theory, where the essential features of the economic system and the set of behavioural rules that are appropriate to achieve them are inextricably linked.

A separation becomes necessary. But where, and how? Once more it is to the Classical political economy that we must return. When the Classical economists specifically dealt with the theory of value (but the issue is obviously general!), they drew a sharp distinction[1] between what they called the 'natural' prices, which they investigated in their own right,

---

[1] For details, see especially Pasinetti, 1981 (pp. 6–8) and 1986.

and what they called the 'market' prices, i.e. the prices which emerge from the actual state of market demand, within the existing institutional set-up under consideration. This Classical distinction, inherited from the Physiocrats, appears to me as an embryonic but powerful methodological device that permits economic analysis to open up to the investigations of the industrial world, with a freedom of approach which the neoclassical economists, confined to their closed model, have effectively denied to us (thus falling into the reductionist trap referred to above).

To put the matter another way, I might say that a real methodological breakthrough in dynamic economic analysis, which the Classics had intuited, can be achieved by adopting what I shall now call for simplicity a *separation theorem*.

This theorem states that we must make it possible to disengage those investigations that concern the foundational bases of economic relations – to be detected at a strictly essential level of basic economic analysis – from those investigations that must be carried out at the level of the actual economic institutions, which at any time any economic system is landed with, or has chosen to adopt, or is trying to achieve.

The former type of investigation is of a foundational, essentialistic type. They are aimed at discovering basic relations, which the Classical economists called 'natural', i.e. in their view aimed at determining the economic magnitudes at a level which is so fundamental as to allow us to investigate them independently of the rules of individual and social behaviour to be chosen in order to achieve them. At this level, economic analysis is in a sense autonomous (as it remains at a stage which – to use a term adopted by Sraffa – is of 'pure economic theory'). This is a stage kept free from specific geographical and historical circumstances. Then, one is able to proceed to a second stage of investigation, which concerns how the economic magnitudes are actually determined, within the bounds and constraints of the institutions characterising the economy at the time it is investigated. When this

second stage is entered upon, a further dimension of freedom is gained in our analysis, which concerns the choice
of assumptions on individual and/or social behaviour, and
even as to the particular institutions to submit to investigation. *Any* type of observable behaviour becomes open to
investigation, within any particular economic institutional
set-up that may actually be observed, or detected by empirical observations, or aimed at by ideally thought-out patterns.
The crucial point here is that the problem of the desirable
or 'ideal' positions – if we may call them so, to the extent
that they exist – must have been faced already at the first,
the 'natural', stage of investigation. Thus, problems concerning normative positions must have been solved already and
the analysis that follows at the institutional stage becomes
free from any pre-imposed, restrictive, and thus reductionist, assumptions.[2]

There is an important consequence that economists must
accept. From this two-stage approach, it follows that, while
the 'natural' stage of investigation remains a typical field for
pure economic theory, the (institutional) stage of investigation, though normally requiring plenty of economic analysis, can no longer be claimed to be exclusive to economists.
The whole field of enquiry about institutions in specific
economies must open up to the possible contributions and
investigations coming from other social sciences as well. Economic analysis, at this second stage, is no longer autonomous.
Hypotheses on individuals and social behaviour become relevant, whatever the source or approach they may be coming
from, provided only that they are empirically justified and
analytically correct.

It should thus also become clear, as a consequence, that the
theoretical schemes erected at the first stage of investigations

---

[2] Of course, the class of 'normative' rules or problems already to be solved
may include a whole list of other basic rules for an orderly society, which
go well beyond basic 'normative' rules strictly referring to the economic
systems (see section 4 below).

cannot be closed. They must contain a sufficient number of degrees of freedom to allow the insertion of whatever type of rules of behaviour that may then emerge from carrying out the second (the more practically oriented, more down-to-earth) stage of investigation.

It has been hinted at already that it is among the Classical economists that we find the early intuitively based attempts at applying this methodological approach. We may now also add that such a methodological approach is acquiring unexpected strength from recent events concerning the explosion of highly dynamic economic systems, which have nullified, or severely limited, the empirical relevance of stationary equilibria.

At the same time one must admit that the members of the Cambridge School of Keynesian Economics, while implicitly taking advantage of this methodological, Classically inspired, *separation* approach, have not explicitly acknowledged it, which seems to me to go a long way to explain why they found it so difficult to face (and in the end preferred to escape) the task of sketching out that comprehensive theoretical scheme that would have been needed to give a common frame to the endeavours that each of them was individually pursuing. Yet I should like to stress that the separation of the 'natural', and at the same time 'normative', relations from the relations concerning the actual determination of the economic variables in any economic system[3] is precisely the essential methodological device that allows us to grasp and clearly see the common *vision* that lies behind their efforts, even when in their works the two mentioned stages of investigation are inadvertently, sometimes even unawarely, mixed up with each other. In my view, the Classically inspired *separation theorem*, had it been explicitly acknowledged and pursued, would have contributed substantially to overcoming that lack of

---

[3] This is a conviction, derived especially in the course of daily talks and discussions with each of them. See Pasinetti 1981, p. xiv.

communication among them at which I hinted earlier,[4] and even more their lack of communication with the outside world of economists.

Although I might simply refer the reader to my past proposals,[5] I shall here be bold and make a heroic effort of synthesis within the limits of the present work and try to give some distilled substantiation to what I mean by the first stage (the pure theory stage) of investigation. I shall do so by starting from the hints made earlier in this book to Piero Sraffa's scheme[6] and juxtaposing the simplest dynamic models which I have had the opportunity to develop – namely the model of a pure labour evolving economy. I hope that the rather sharp device I am choosing here of presenting this dynamic model may provide the simplest means to illustrate the foundational framework into which the works of *all* members of the Cambridge School of Keynesian Economics may be inserted. I shall simply add that Sraffa's *production of commodities by means of commodities* scheme and my own *production of commodities by means of labour* scheme are not only complementary but actually susceptible to being integrated into each other through the analytical device of vertical integration (Pasinetti, 1973), which eventually leads to an interpretation of the pure labour scheme as representing the most essential foundational version of the whole production paradigm.

It goes without saying that it is not the purpose of the synthetic sketch that I am going to present now to give a detailed exposition of the most general pure production paradigm which I intend to refer to. The purpose here is purely instrumental, i.e. using the simplest and most basic of all schemes in order to give an idea of the direction in which to proceed, and at the same time giving an illustration of what I mean by the separation theorem involving the advocated Classically

---

[4] See above, pp. 61–63, 169–171, 200–201.
[5] Especially, Pasinetti 1981, 1986, 1993a, 1993b, *passim*.
[6] See pp. 191–194.

inspired, two-stage approach to economic reality. The conviction is that this two-stage approach is the key to conferring upon the works of the whole Cambridge School of Keynesian Economics that unity which its members have failed to convey.

2. The simplest version of the 'natural' economic system

The original idea of a pure labour production economy (a community of individuals for whom the process of production requires labour alone) goes back to Adam Smith. He thought he could refer it to a primitive economy (a device which, by making 'labour embodied' and 'labour commanded' coincide, allowed him to overcome all objections against his strongly cherished pure labour theory of value).

But Smith's ingenious device may be taken well beyond his original purposes. With a minimum of abstraction, it can equally well be applied to an *advanced* economic system, with extensive division of labour and specialisation of jobs, so that each individual (or household) contributes to the production of only one good or even a fraction of one good (or service) and at the same time exerts demand (as a consumer unit) for *all* goods and services produced in the economy.

The easiest approach to labour in this connection is the one used by Sraffa, who supposes 'labour to be uniform in quality or, what amounts to the same thing, any difference in quality to have been previously reduced to equivalent differences in quantity, so that each unit receives the same wage' (Sraffa, 1960, p. 10).

What is added here with respect to Sraffa (though not entirely with respect to Smith) is the presence of human *learning*, a process which is going on incessantly and which, as time goes on, causes all technical (labour) coefficients to diminish, though at different rates for different production processes. This makes it possible for *per capita* physical consumption to increase, most naturally at different rates from one good or service to another. There is nothing in this scheme against – on the contrary there is a most natural inducement to – a persistent activity of invention of *new* goods and services, so that the production processes (and hence the available goods and services) will be increasing in number (while some of them may become obsolete and disappear). At the same time, the kind, and quality, of goods may continually be improving, changing, diversifying.

But before beginning the presentation of the simple pure labour model, let me give a provisional answer to at least three objections or hesitations which I have found most frequently raised against such a scheme:

a)   First of all, it may be instructive to take note of at least a substantial aspect of recent empirical evidence. The recent progress of knowledge in information technology, with the rising importance of software (vs. hardware) techniques, coupled with the invention of new materials, has substantially diminished the relative importance of what used to be traditionally considered the essential raw materials necessary to industrial production. Some economists have even begun to talk of 'dematerialised' or 'weightless' economies.[7] Thus the idea of an economic system with labour alone as a factor of production no longer appears today as far-fetched as it might have appeared only a few decades ago.

b)   In any case, I should like to stress that the model is far from being meant to be confined to a world in which material goods are not used as means of production. Extensions of the model to a scheme with capital goods must be made and have actually been made.[8] For the present purposes, the pure labour model has the great

---

[7] See, for example, Quah, 2001, and 2002.
[8] I may simply refer to my own works (Pasinetti 1962, 1965, 1981, 1973, 1988).

advantage of extreme simplicity, flexibility and conge-
niality to stressing basic features.

c)   Thirdly, the *process of learning*, which is absent in
Sraffa but is embryonically present in Smith (through
his emphasis on the division of labour) and in other
Classical economists as well (e.g. in Ricardo, as
'improvements' in the methods of cultivation), has subsequently emerged as crucial in the historical evolution
of industrial societies. It is placed here at the very centre of the pure labour scheme, as the essential engine
of the structural economic dynamics that is necessarily
generated therefrom. For analytical purposes, the easiest attitude to take is to conceive of the society concerned as one in which a minimum degree of education
(appropriate to the current state of knowledge) is considered to be a public duty, which the community as a
whole has to assure to all its members.[9] When this is so,
Sraffa's conception of qualified homogeneity of labour
continues to make good sense.

3.   A succinct presentation of the model

I have gathered the essential features of the model of a pure
labour economy in a single table (Table IX.1), which reproduces algebraic formulae used in Pasinetti, 1993a. (In some
cases, more than one alternative algebraic expression is given
for the same relation, to facilitate comprehension.) For convenience, a list of the notation used is added at the end of the
table.

Using *continuous* time and supposing exponential movements of all magnitudes, for simplicity the exogenous
hypotheses for the time movements are represented by

---

[9] We shall have an opportunity to return to this point at the very end of this
work.

Table IX.1 *A pure labour model*

Basic hypotheses on exogenous magnitudes		
[1] movements of labour coefficients	$l_i(t) = l_i(0)e^{-\rho_i t},$	$i = 1, 2, \ldots m.$
[2] movements of per capita consumption	$c_i(t) = c_i(0)e^{r_i t},$	$i = 1, 2, \ldots m.$
[3] population growth	$N(t) = N(0)e^{gt},$	
[4] structural dynamics	$\rho_i \neq \rho_j,\ r_i \neq r_j,\ r_i \neq \rho_i,$	$\left.\begin{array}{l}\rho_i \\ r_i \\ g\end{array}\right\} \gtrless 0$

Physical quantity and price systems

[5] physical quantity system

$$
\begin{bmatrix}
1 & 0 & \cdots & 0 & \cdots & 0 & -c_1(t) \\
0 & 1 & \cdots & 0 & \cdots & 0 & -c_2(t) \\
\vdots & \vdots & \ddots & \vdots & & \vdots & \vdots \\
0 & 0 & \cdots & 1 & \cdots & 0 & -c_i(t) \\
\vdots & \vdots & & \vdots & \ddots & \vdots & \vdots \\
0 & 0 & \cdots & 0 & \cdots & 1 & -c_m(t) \\
-l_1(t) & -l_2(t) & \cdots & -l_i(t) & \cdots & -l_m(t) & \mu(t)\nu(t)
\end{bmatrix}
\begin{bmatrix}
Q_1(t) \\ Q_2(t) \\ \vdots \\ Q_i(t) \\ \vdots \\ Q_m(t) \\ N(t)
\end{bmatrix}
=
\begin{bmatrix}
0 \\ 0 \\ \vdots \\ 0 \\ \vdots \\ 0 \\ 0
\end{bmatrix},
$$

[6] commodity price system

$$
\begin{bmatrix}
1 & 0 & \cdots & 0 & \cdots & 0 & -l_1(t) \\
0 & 1 & \cdots & 0 & \cdots & 0 & -l_2(t) \\
\vdots & \vdots & \ddots & \vdots & & \vdots & \vdots \\
0 & 0 & \cdots & 1 & \cdots & 0 & -l_i(t) \\
\vdots & \vdots & & \vdots & \ddots & \vdots & \vdots \\
0 & 0 & \cdots & 0 & \cdots & 1 & -l_m(t) \\
-c_1(t) & -c_2(t) & \cdots & -c_i(t) & \cdots & -c_m(t) & \mu(t)\nu(t)
\end{bmatrix}
\begin{bmatrix}
p_1(t) \\ p_2(t) \\ \vdots \\ p_i(t) \\ \vdots \\ p_m(t) \\ w(t)
\end{bmatrix}
=
\begin{bmatrix}
0 \\ 0 \\ \vdots \\ 0 \\ \vdots \\ 0 \\ 0
\end{bmatrix},
$$

Solutions and further developments

[7] structural dynamics of physical quantities	$Q_i(t) = c_i(t)N(t),$ $Q_i(t) = c_i(0)N(0)e^{(g+r_i)t},$	or, more specifically:
[8] total labour to be employed	$Q_n(t) = \mu(t)\nu(t)N(t),$ $Q_n(t) = \mu(t)\nu(t)N(0)e^{gt},$	or, more specifically:

Table IX.1 *(cont.)*

[9]	sectoral employment	$E_i(t) = l_i(t)c_i(t)N(t)$, or, more specifically: $E_i(t) = l_i(0)c_i(0)N(0)e^{(g+r_i-\rho_i)t}$, with $\sum_{i=1}^{m} E_i(t) \le Q_n(t)$.
[10]	sectoral rate of change of employment	$\varepsilon_i = g + r_i - \rho_i \gtrless 0$,
[11]	structural dynamics of natural prices	$p_i(t) = l_i(t)w(t)$, or, more specifically: $p_i(t) = l_i(0)w(0)e^{(\sigma_w - \rho_i)t}$.
[12]	movement of wage rate	$w(t) = w(0)e^{\sigma_w t}$,
[12bis]		with $\begin{cases} w(0) = \bar{w} \\ \sigma_w = \bar{\sigma}_w. \end{cases}$
[13]	aggregate condition of full employment and of full expenditure	$\frac{1}{\mu(t)v(t)} \sum_{i=1}^{m} c_i(t)l_i(t) - 1 = 0$, or, more specifically: $\frac{1}{\mu(t)v(t)} \sum_{i=1}^{m} c_i(0)l_i(0)e^{(r_i-\rho_i)t} - 1 = 0$,
[14]	proportion of sectorally employed labour to total labour	$\lambda_i(t) = \frac{1}{\mu(t)v(t)} c_i(t)l_i(t)$,
[15]	'standard' rate of growth of productivity	$\rho^*(t) = \sum_{i=1}^{m} \lambda_i(t)\rho_i(t)$,
[16]	adoption of the dynamic standard commodity as *numéraire*	$p_{h^*}(t) = \sum \alpha_i^*(t)p_i(t) = 1$, with $\begin{cases} p_{h^*}(0) = 1, \\ \sigma_{h^*} = 0, \end{cases}$
[17]	aggregate condition for stable prices	$\sigma_w = \rho^*$,
[18]	rate of monetary inflation	$\sigma_M = \bar{\sigma}_w - \rho^* \gtrless 0$,

(cont.)

Table IX.1 *(cont.)*

[19]	sectoral rate of change of each commodity price $\Big\}$	$\sigma_i = (\bar{\sigma}_w - \rho_i) = (\bar{\sigma}_w - \rho^*) + (\rho^* - \rho_i) =$ $= \sigma_M + (\rho^* - \rho_i),$
[20]	'natural' rate of interest, with stable prices $\Big\}$	$i_{h^*}^* = \rho^*,$
[21]	'natural' rate of interest (in general) $\Big\}$	$i^* = \rho^* + \sigma_M = \sigma_w.$

Legend of symbols ($i = 1, 2, \ldots m$)

$Q_i(t)$: physical quantities of produced commodities

$Q_n(t)$: total quantity of labour to be employed

$N(t)$: total population

$E_i(t)$: sectoral employment

$\varepsilon_i(t)$ sectoral rate of change of employment

$p_i(t)$: 'natural' commodity prices

$w(t)$: wage rate

$l_i(t)$: labour coefficients (labour input per unit of output)

$c_i(t)$: per capita consumption

m: number of production sectors and commodities

n: $m + 1$

t: time

h: commodity chosen as *numéraire* of the price system

h^*: dynamic 'standard' commodity

μ: proportion of active to total population

v: proportion of working time to total time

g: rate of growth of population

ρ_i: rate of growth of labour productivity in sector i

ρ^*: 'standard' rate of growth of labour productivity

r_i: rate of change of per capita consumption of commodity i

σ_i: rate of change of price i

σ_w: rate of change of the wage rate

λ_i: proportion of sectorally employed labour to total labour

α_i: weight coefficients (for a composite commodity)

i^*: 'natural' rate of interest, whatever the *numéraire* of the price system

$i_{h^*}^*$: specific 'natural' rate of interest when the 'dynamic standard commodity' is chosen as *numéraire*

σ_M: rate of monetary inflation

expressions [1]–[4].[10] At any given point of time, $\bar{t}$, they may be framed in the form of a closed Leontief model as is done by expressions [5] and [6], which yield solutions for physical quantities and for commodity prices respectively. When t is allowed to elapse, each single magnitude, and thus the two equation systems and their solutions, are evolving through time. The two equation systems being linear and homogenous, a formal requirement is the fulfilment of the necessary condition of a zero determinant for each of the two matrices in [5] and [6] respectively. This must be so both at time zero, when our analysis is supposed to begin, and through time; this is expressed by condition [13], which, remarkably enough, turns out to be the same for both systems. Note the essentially macroeconomic nature of condition [13], not so much because of the sum of the m sectors, but more fundamentally because all sectors are linked – even when, as here, there are no inter-industry relations – by the effect of overall effective demand. Each worker may contribute to a very tiny fraction of the production of any particular good (a sectoral contribution), but at the same time, with his/her family, contributes to demand for virtually *all* the goods and services produced in the economic system. Through this channel, owing to the all-embracing effect of overall demand, the set of all production processes forms a true economic 'system'. Condition [13] is indeed a single relation, but it concerns the *whole* system, i.e. it is a single truly macroeconomic relation, independent of the number and structure of the sectors and irrespective of all the movements both of technology and of consumers' demand.

Note now that the fulfilment of condition [13] by no means entails an automatic self-adjusting process. The spontaneous forces operating behind it are in fact tending to make it *not*

---

[10] Let me stress simplicity. The exponential shape given to these movements is *not* a necessity. Any other types of movements – continuous or discontinuous – may be hypothesised, though with some obvious complications (see Pasinetti 1980, 1981, 1993a).

satisfied. The reason is that in each single production sector, two opposite movements are constantly at work – a technology-generated movement, which affects the l_i coefficients, and a sectoral, physical-quantity movement, generated by effective demand, which affects the c_i coefficients. In general, the two movements do not match (see [4] and hence [10]). The resulting sectoral effect is either the urge (when $\varepsilon_i < 0$) to expel labour from, or the need (when $\varepsilon_i > 0$) to absorb further labour into, the sector concerned. But there are m such sectors! Each of them has its own specific dynamics. Moreover, number m itself (which should be written $m(t)$, though t is omitted here for brevity) is changing as time goes on: new processes are added, others are closed down. Here lies the crux and drama of a complex inherently structural instability, which is thus revealed to have sectoral origins, but whose effects are building up, inevitably, to affect the dynamics of the economic system as a whole.[11]

Yet the 'natural' economic system requires both the recomposition of sectoral imbalances and the achievement and maintenance of full employment in the economic system as a whole. Analytically, this means that it requires the fulfilment of condition [13], which thereby emerges as a genuine and stringent *macroeconomic* condition, which links the economic system as a whole.[12] Keynes's intuition is proved right and the implications are far reaching. Condition [13] is *not* a once-and-for-all condition, except in the extreme trivial case of a perfectly stationary economic system (i.e. when, in [4] all ρ_is and all r_is are zero). In general, i.e. in a *dynamic* system, each single component of [13] is moving. The changes to be generated are therefore manifold and complex. Since they may go in opposite directions, they will compensate one another to a certain extent – sometimes to a great extent – but

---

[11] This effect belongs to the sort of deep instability hinted at in the *Postlude*, pp. 229–230.
[12] Again, see *Postlude*, ibidem.

never completely, in any systematic way. Yet condition [13] requires compensation in the aggregate. This *must* be brought about if the 'natural' system is to be achieved.

There are in fact multiple ways through which the tendencies to disequilibrium may be counteracted, which means that, from the strict point of view of the 'natural' economic system, the problem of fulfilling condition [13] is left wide open in many directions, which are not mutually exclusive, as they may operate in combination. I may recall at least the most obvious ones among them, as they clearly emerge from the model itself: i) increase of per capita demand in already operating sectors; ii) creation of entirely new sectors; iii) progressive diminution over time of parameter $\mu_i(t)$ (i.e. of the ratio of active to total population, e.g. through earlier retirements, etc.); iv) progressive diminution over time of parameter $v_i(t)$, i.e. of the fraction of total time devoted to work (and corresponding increase of part-time employment, leisure time), etc.

All these movements obviously require structural dynamics of employment, with inter-sector labour mobility so as to enact a process of economic growth in which some sectors are closed down (declining industries in a process of economic growth), other sectors expand and others are created. Schumpeter seems to have been the only earlier economist who had some intuitive glimpses at these typical effects of structural growth.

In any case, if we suppose for the moment that condition [13] is satisfied, one of the variables, in each of the two equation systems, may be fixed exogenously, both at time zero and at each point through time. In fact, this means that in each equation system, the whole time *movement* of one of the variables must be fixed from outside the respective system, which in turns means (all the movements being supposed for simplicity to be of the exponential form) that in each of the two equation systems, there are *two* degrees of freedom that have to be closed. For the single magnitude which is chosen as exogenous, we must fix both its initial value and its rate of change through time.[13]

This procedure is quite straightforward for the physical quantity system, where the movement to be considered as exogenous is obviously population, $N(t)$, so that the solutions are given by [7]. From these solutions, one can see the full, indeed very complex, structural dynamics of sectoral physical quantities and their repercussions on the structural dynamics of employment in the whole economic system (see [9]). Notice that, in some sectors, employment may be decreasing even if the physical quantities produced are growing. Expressions [8] and [9]–[10] show explicitly on the one side the evolution of total available labour and on the other side the evolution in time of the structure of sectoral employment, as a direct consequence of the structural dynamics of productivity (i.e. the rates of growth ρ_i's) and demand (i.e. the rates of growth r_i's). Each sector i will be (relatively) expanding or contracting, in terms of employment, according as $\varepsilon_i \gtrless 0$ (see [10]). Full employment (i.e. fulfilment of macroeconomic condition [13]) requires that overall availability of labour and the sum of sectoral employment are brought together.

For the price system, the solutions are given by [11]. Here, however, the choice of the exogenous movement is by no means straightforward, since it takes up the meaning of fixing the *numéraire*, the choice of which is typically arbitrary. We are therefore faced with a full range of alternatives. In a pure labour model, one obvious alternative would be that of choosing the wage rate as the *numéraire* of the price system. This means fixing from outside the movement in time

[13] Non-fulfilment of necessary condition [13] does mean non-existence of *equilibrium* solutions, but it does not exclude existence of non-equilibrium solutions. In fact, owing to the simplicity of the model, when necessary condition [13] is not fulfilled, in each of the two equation systems, the first m equations continue to hold. What breaks down is the last $(m+1)^{th}$ equation, which in economic terms means less (or pressure for more) than full employment, in the physical quantity system, and less (or tendentially more) than full expenditure of national income, in the price equation system, respectively. (For details see Pasinetti 1981, 1993a.)

of $w(t)$, as is done in [12]–[12bis], which confers on the price system a perfect symmetry with respect to the physical quantity system – a feature that has many analytical advantages. First of all, it shows explicitly that, when one abandons a static scheme (where the price system contains one degree of freedom) and goes over to deal with a dynamic economy, the price system contains no longer one but *two* degrees of freedom. It requires fixing the wage rate at the initial time, let us say at time zero ($w(0) = \bar{w}$), and then fixing its *rate of change* through time (e.g. $\sigma_w = \bar{\sigma}_w$), as shown by [12bis]. Second, this way of closing the price system shows explicitly how a production economy with structural dynamics cannot but be a *monetary* economy. Fixing initially the unit of the price system – and thus its purchasing power at time zero – is done most conveniently by expressing w in terms of a nominal unit (the dollar, or the euro, or the pound sterling, or the yen, etc.), but then the real purchasing power of such a nominal unit will change through time. A monetary production economy entails a *moving* unit of measurement (in real terms) of the price system which the present model is capable of incorporating.[14] In this respect, notation [18] expresses the rate of monetary inflation. Thereby, solutions [11] show the full, again complex, structural dynamics of the system of commodity prices, while expression [19] shows a breaking up of the *movement* of each price into its two components: a structural component – yielded by the differentiated rates of productivity changes – and an inflationary component – yielded by the excess of the rate of change of the nominal wage rate over the rate of growth of overall productivity.

We could, of course, choose, not the wage rate, but any physical commodity h (call it *gold*) as *numéraire*. And we

---

[14] This is a point not always entirely understood. It may sound strange at first to talk of a moving 'unit of measurement', but this is precisely what happens in a monetary production economy (as any houseperson realises when she goes shopping and finds she can buy less – or, usually in fewer cases, more – with the same nominal monetary units, especially when the weighted *average* of prices, as is usually the case, is moving up).

could choose its physical unit (a specified quantity of gold) as fixed for all times. This would mean fixing the price of h (i.e. of gold) equal to unity, both at time zero *and* through time. In the present model, this would be expressed by $p_h(0) = 1$ and $\sigma_h = 0$ (which shows explicitly, by the way, that the degrees of freedom to be closed are indeed 2, in any case). We should notice immediately however that if each single relative price is moving through time in its own way, as it happens according to our hypotheses [4], no single *physical* commodity exists which, if chosen as *numéraire*, would be able to keep the (average) price level constant through time. For the (weighted) average of prices would be increasing if the commodity chosen as *numéraire* is produced at a rate of productivity change below average, and would be decreasing if the commodity chosen as *numéraire* is produced at a rate of productivity change above average. To achieve a perfectly stable level of prices, one would have to find a particular physical commodity that is characterised by a rate of change of productivity that is exactly the (weighted) average of all rates of productivity change.

As may intuitively be imagined, a physical commodity possessing such 'price stability' property when used as *numéraire* does not exist in reality (and even if it were to be found by fluke at a specific point in time, it would no longer enjoy the same price stability-generating property at the immediately following point of time). It can however be 'constructed' analytically. It will have to be a 'composite' physical commodity, whose composition is changing as time moves on. It can be shown that it may be concocted in such a way – using expressions [14] and [15] – as to be associated with a virtual production process characterised by the overall rate of growth of productivity, that is to say the (weighted) average of all the rates of productivity changes in the whole economic system. By adopting such a commodity as *numéraire*, as in [16], we would strike precisely that middle point, among all rates of productivity changes, that will cause the overall level of prices to remain perfectly constant through time. I have called such a (composite) commodity the 'dynamic standard commodity'[15] and I have called the corresponding (weighted) average rate of growth of productivity the 'standard' rate of growth of productivity. It is an interesting property of the present model that it makes it unnecessary to explicitly 'construct' such a peculiar commodity, or to know exactly what its actual composition is. There is an indirect way, as with Sraffa's 'standard commodity', to single out such a commodity and fix it as *numéraire*. This can be done by using movement [12] as exogenous and closing its two degrees of freedom by setting $w(0) = \bar{w}$ (the wage rate equal to whatever nominal, i.e. monetary, unit one may wish to choose at the initial time) and $\sigma_w = \rho^*$, as indicated by [17] – i.e. a rate of change of the wage rate equal to the standard rate of growth of labour productivity.

But this is not the end of our story. There is another way of looking at the centrality of macroeconomic condition [13] in the system – another side, so to speak, of the same coin. Each addendum $(l_i c_i \frac{1}{\mu v})$ in [13] expresses – as just seen above – the *proportion* of total employment in sector i. But it also expresses the *proportion* of total demand for the outputs of sector i. Obviously, the sum of all these proportions must be equal to unity, to ensure full employment. This simply expresses the proposition that the totality of national income must be spent; and this – as will be realised – is an expression of Keynes's principle of effective demand. In our pure labour model (in which there are no capital goods) this also means that total income (wages) must be spent on consumption goods. In each period of time, total consumption must absorb the totality of national income. There can be no overall savings in a pure labour economy. Total savings, in Keynesian

---

[15] This (composite) commodity turns out to be the dynamic counterpart of Sraffa's 'standard' commodity and, jointly with it, gives a complete solution to Ricardo's idea of an 'invariable standard of value' (see Pasinetti, 1981, pp. 104–106, 1993a, pp. 70–72).

terms, must be zero. Yet this condition imposes no constraint on *individual* savings. The only proviso it entails is that, if some individuals save, some other individuals must dissave to the same extent. The implication is that, in a monetary production economy, individuals, and groups of individuals, directly or through intermediaries, may stipulate debts and credit relations among themselves, i.e. inter-temporal transactions in terms of any specific *numéraire*. This implies the coming into existence of *financial* assets and liabilities, i.e. financial *stocks*, even if, by assumption, there are no physical stocks of capital goods in the pure labour economy we are considering. The *numéraire*, in terms of which the financial stocks are reckoned, will normally be (and we take it here to be) the same *numéraire* as the one chosen for the price system. In this case – i.e. when people stipulate inter-temporal debt/credit transactions in terms of the current *numéraire* – an *additional* economic variable necessarily appears in the economic system, namely the *rate of interest*. In the present pure labour model this happens through the appearance of an additional (a third!) degree of freedom which, of course, must now be closed precisely by fixing the rate of interest. *Any* rate of interest may be fixed, from outside the production system, in terms of the currently chosen *numéraire*. Such actual rate of interest – once chosen and fixed – finally determines both the size of the purchasing power of the flows of incomes (wages, in our case) and the actual size of the purchasing power of the cumulated stocks of (inter-temporal) financial assets. At this stage, all degrees of freedom are closed and the financial structure of the monetary production economy we are considering is completely specified, while it obviously adds another dimension (a financial dimension) to the complex problem of bringing macroeconomic condition [13] into fulfilment.

But this closure of the monetary and financial part of the economy raises a crucial problem: which rate of interest should be chosen in order to preserve a 'natural' economic system? To put the problem in different terms: from all possible (alternative) rates of interest that may exogenously be chosen from outside the production system, is there a particular rate of interest that can be singled out as deserving the appellative of the 'natural' rate of interest?

The answer to this question is straightforward in the present model. In a pure labour production economy, the 'natural' rate of interest cannot but be that rate of interest that possesses the property of keeping constant in time the purchasing power of labour. This means a zero rate of interest *in terms of labour*.

Note the immediacy of such a basic principle, which – in its most general form – can even be stated *independently* of the *numéraire* which is chosen. In other words, it may simply be stated as follows: *the natural rate of interest* is that rate of interest which is equal to the percentage rate of change of the wage rate.

But, of course, in a structural dynamics context, in which all prices are changing relative to one another and relative to the wage rate, once the actual *numéraire* is specified, the natural rate of interest will take up a *numerical* specification which is different according to the *numéraire* that is adopted. This must be so in order to generate, in all cases, the same real effects *in terms of labour*.

It may be instructive to consider explicitly the interesting cases:

i)   when the *numéraire* chosen is labour, i.e. when we fix $w(t) = 1$, the natural rate of interest is zero, by definition;

ii) when the *numéraire* chosen is any physical commodity h, i.e. when we fix $p_h(t) = 1$, the natural rate of interest is equal to ρ_h, the rate of growth of productivity in sector h. This is so because the purchasing power of all financial assets, when expressed in terms of commodity h, devalues over time, in terms of labour, at rate of change ρ_h. The actual (natural) rate of interest in this case acts as a compensation for this devaluation, so as to keep the value of existing financial assets constant in time in terms of labour;

iii) when the *numéraire* chosen is that particular commodity which we have called the 'dynamic standard commodity', which implies a *constant* general level of prices, the natural rate of interest, as indicated by [20], is equal to ρ^*, the 'standard' rate of growth of productivity;

iv) when the *numéraire* chosen is a nominal (monetary) unit, the natural rate of interest, as indicated by [21], is equal to the standard rate of growth of productivity plus the rate of inflation – a sum which, in turn, we have indicated by $\bar{\sigma}_w$ (see [12bis]), as this rate of change enters the definition of the (nominal) unit in terms of which the wage rate, and hence all prices, are expressed.

In real terms, all these alternative numerical expressions for the natural rate of interest are equivalent. They express alternative ways, in the presence of alternative choices of the *numéraires* fixed for the price system (and at the same time for the unit of account of debt/credit relations), to achieve exactly the same real effects (i.e. a zero rate of interest in terms of labour).[16]

---

[16] It may be worth mentioning that, in an economic system with structural dynamics of prices, there is a whole series of further effects that the choice of any particular rate of interest also generates (whatever it may be and whatever the *numéraire* that is chosen), namely a whole series of *own* rates of interest – in fact, as many own rates of interest as there are differentiated movements of prices. The simplest and easiest way to see this is to consider the particular case of a zero natural rate of interest with labour as the *numéraire*. In this case, the actual zero rate of interest generates a series of m own-rates of interest, which coincide with the m rates of productivity growth. For the value of all financial assets is indeed absolutely constant in time in nominal terms (as they all are expressed in terms of labour) but their purchasing power is increasing at rate ρ_1 in terms of commodity 1, . . . at rate ρ_h in terms of any commodity h, . . . at rate ρ_m in terms of commodity m. In all the other cases, with other *numéraires*, and with a natural, or non-natural, rate of interest, the relations are more complex. But the actual rate of interest, whatever it may be, is always generating a corresponding series of m *own* rates of interest. (For details, see Pasinetti, 1993a, pp. 88–89.)

In any case, among all the various alternatives mentioned above, we may note the particularly interesting properties of the two basic cases of choice of *numéraire* that emerge immediately from the present model of a production economy, namely: case i) (labour as the *numéraire*) and case iii) ('dynamic standard commodity' as the *numéraire*). In case i), the natural rate of interest is zero and all financial assets maintain their values constant in time, in terms of labour, while *all* prices decrease in time according to the corresponding rates of productivity changes: a general movement of price deflation. In case iii) ('dynamic standard commodity' as *numéraire*), the natural rate of interest is equal to the standard rate of growth of productivity, ρ^*, while the (weighted) average price level remains absolutely constant (though not, of course, the price of any specific commodity expressed in terms of the standard commodity). All financial assets devalue in time, in terms of labour, at a rate of change equal to the standard rate of productivity growth (which is precisely what the payment of a natural rate of interest equal to ρ^* is meant to offset). In both cases the implications for *income distribution* are straightforward. In a pure labour 'natural' economic system, the distribution of income (the 'natural' distribution of income, as we may call it) is proportionate to labour (both 'embodied' and 'commanded'): that is to say all national income, in real terms, goes to labour. But the important point is that this happens *both* at any given point of time, thanks to the 'natural' wage, *and* through time, thanks to the 'natural' rate of interest. We may indeed call this a pure labour theory of income distribution.

It may be instructive to note how this same effect in real terms is obtained with the use of the two most interesting alternative *numéraires*: i) or iii); namely, by a continuous fall of the *general level* of prices (at a rate of change ρ^*) and a zero actual rate of interest, in the case of labour as *numéraire;* or by the growth of the wage rate (at rate ρ^*) and an actual rate of interest also equal to ρ^*, while the general level of prices remains constant, in the case of the dynamic standard commodity as *numéraire*.

Note the remarkable property of the case in which the 'dynamic standard commodity' is used as the *numéraire*. It avoids the deflationary price movement that would take place with labour as *numéraire* and at the same time, by keeping the price level absolutely constant, it produces a numerically positive *natural* rate of interest, equal to the 'standard' rate of growth of productivity, ρ^*. The meaning of such natural rate of interest, as we have seen, is that of a compensation (of the devaluation of all financial assets in terms of the purchasing power of the wage rate) for all creditors holding financial assets in terms of a stable level of prices.

At this point, the present (compact) presentation of the scheme of a pure labour economy may be considered completed for our purposes.

4.   Normative properties

Already at this stage, some clear properties of the variables characterising the 'natural' economic system we have been considering emerge straightaway.

Notice to begin with that, by simply starting from very few hypotheses on the movements through time of basic magnitudes given from outside economic analysis (population, technology, human learning, hierarchy of consumption needs, human preferences), a complete conceptual scheme has been conceived, concerning the movements of all the relevant variables of a dynamic economic system, together with a few basic macroeconomic requirements that must be satisfied. This conceptual scheme emerges as possessing basic normative properties from the very way it has been constructed. It is for this reason that I have thought it justified to call it 'natural', as it resumes methods and concepts anticipated by the Classical economists. Simplicity, essentiality and permanence appear as its most evident traits, in spite of its being framed within a complex context of structural economic dynamics.

Very simply, the pure labour version of the 'natural' economic system here presented exhibits the following features:

i) An evolving structure of commodity prices, each of which is moving in its own way, in perfect syntony with the differentiated learning processes which are taking place in the technological sphere. They incorporate a cost of production – specifically, in our case, a pure labour theory of value. They raise no analytical complications as, in the present case, 'labour embodied' coincides with 'labour commanded', a feature evincing a typically Smithian flavour. In a homogenised pure production labour context, in the sense of Sraffa (see above, p. 279), labour is the obvious standard at the basis of the concept of a 'just' price – a normative property. Moreover, the context gives a solution to Ricardo's problem of finding an *invariable standard of value* through time. The formulation of a 'dynamic standard commodity', if used as the term of reference both of the price system and of the financial stocks, has the property of maintaining perfect stability of the *general* level of prices, both for monetary flows and for financial stocks.

ii) An evolving structure of sectoral productions, activated by effective demand. This is Malthusian-Keynesian theory of effective demand at its purest. When inserted into a structural dynamics process, it incorporates a generalisation of 'Engel's law'. In such a dynamics context, demand is essentially governed by rising incomes in a differentiated way from product to product. Each sectoral demand is, in its specific way, eventually bound to reach saturation. This means that sectoral productions must continually be changing in their proportions, be redirected into new channels, new goods and new services, which may be an improvement on the old ones, or entirely novel as never experienced before. Thus, learning on the side of demand emerges to be equally essential as learning on the side of technology. But this also means that, in the long run, the influence of prices on sectoral demand and production is becoming fainter and fainter. It is the level of real income that eventually becomes, in economic terms, the all-important determining factor.[17] This is one of the most obvious points where the 'natural' system signals the necessity for economics to *open up* the enquiry to non-economic determining forces. As long as basic needs are prevalent (i.e. at low levels of real incomes), economic analysis may be offering the most obvious tools of investigation, but as real incomes increase, other sources of investigation, in the social sciences, may begin to have a lot to say and will then go on increasingly to have a lot to say. The model opens up to the possibility and richness of the formulation of theories of choice, both at the individual level and at the social level, as its degrees of freedom are leaving wide openings in these directions.

iii)   An evolving structure of sectoral employments, generated by the combined structural dynamics of i) and ii), i.e. by the interaction of the evolution of labour productivity on the one side and of per capita demand on the other side. Neither structural movements i), taken by themselves, nor structural movements ii), taken by themselves, can give a clear picture of what is happening to sectoral employments. It is the *combination* of the two that is vital. And this combination brings to the fore, very clearly, a 'natural', continuous process of labour *mobility:* from sector to sector, from old to new sectors, from long to shorter working weeks, from full-time jobs to part-time jobs, etc., lest the emergence of unemployment and thus of an (unrecoverable) loss of production,

---

[17] See, for details, Pasinetti, 1981, pp. 71–75.

through sheer waste, derived from unused potential production in the economic system as a whole.

iv) A uniform wage rate, the purchasing power of which, if evaluated in terms of any specific commodity i [$i = 1, 2, \ldots m(t)$], is increasing at the rate of growth of labour productivity in that specific sector i. But this of course would have little meaning if only a tiny fraction of w is spent on commodity i and if prices are all changing meanwhile. The model shows that in a production system, the wage rate, taken by itself, stands out as the counterpart to the whole system of prices. Commodity prices are sectoral concepts. The wage rate, by contrast, emerges as a macroeconomic concept. It necessarily must consist of an abstract amount of purchasing power over *all* that is produced in the whole economic system. It takes up the nature of each worker's share into the net national product – a typically macroeconomic concept.[18] In a structural dynamic context, the uniformity of the natural wage rate simultaneously fulfils two important functions: an income distribution function and an efficiency inducing function. It channels the distribution of the benefits of technical progress to labour in the whole economic system, independently of the differentiated changes in sectoral labour coefficients. At the same time, by virtue of its uniformity, it spurs productivity improvements in the below-average-productivity-growth sectors and puts pressure on prices to diminish (relative to average) in the above-average-productivity-growth sectors.[19]

v) A 'natural' rate of interest, which inevitably arises as soon as a series of financial assets, due to the

---

[18] Variable *w(t)* in the price system appears as formally symmetrical to variable $Q_n(t)$ in the physical quantity system, which is also a variable of *macroeconomic* relevance. As against quantities $Q_i(t)$, which are *sectoral*, it expresses the overall amount of required (full) employment in the economic system as a whole.

[19] For details, see Pasinetti, 1993a.

undertaking of inter-temporal debt/credit relations, among individuals or groups of individuals, come into existence. The model shows that this happens even with complete absence of any *physical* assets (i.e. even with no capital goods). Moreover, it shows that there exists a 'natural' level for such rate of interest that possesses the normative property of keeping constant in time the purchasing power of all financial assets in terms of labour.[20] Not only is this not in contradiction with a normatively grounded pure labour theory of income distribution (see requirement b) below), but the 'natural' rate of interest actually becomes part of a 'natural' pure labour distribution of income, since it maintains constant over time the purchasing power of all financial assets, in terms of labour.

This 'natural economic system' – expressed by i), ii), iii), iv), v) – emerges moreover as characterised by three macroeconomic requirements:

a) Achievement and maintenance through time of full employment, this requirement being expressed by the fulfilment of macroeconomic condition [13]. The justification of this requirement is strictly normative – macroeconomic efficiency. Any unemployment represents an unrecoverable loss of production (for ever) and thus an unrecoverable loss of income (for ever) in the economic system as a whole.

b) Achievement of an equitable distribution of income. In the present pure labour model, this macroeconomic conclusion is obvious and clear: all income goes to labour.[21] But this is only part of the story. There is a second aspect of income distribution that concerns the *personal* income distribution. In the present scheme, with

---

[20] There is also a whole structure of 'natural' but implicit own-rates of interest: see footnote 16 above.

[21] See below for hints at the more general case.

homogenised labour in the sense of Sraffa,[22] the uniform 'natural' wage performs the function of distributing income to the labourers, in each period of time, in proportion to (homogenised) labour contributed. And the 'natural' rate of interest performs the function of maintaining constant through time the purchasing power of labour, when inter-temporal debt/credit relations are involved. The interesting result is that we need both a natural wage rate *and* a natural rate of interest to achieve a normatively grounded pure labour distribution of income.

c) Price stability. On this subject, the problem is a more articulated one. In a structural dynamic context, all relative prices *must* change. No price can be 'stable' in the strict sense of being constant, except in the trivial case of absolutely constant technical coefficients (i.e. of no technical progress or regress). The concept of price stability, to have a sense, must therefore be referred to the (weighted) average of prices. The model actually yields a standard of reference (the 'dynamic standard commodity') which, if used as *numéraire* of the price system, has the property of keeping the (weighted) price average absolutely constant in time, i.e. of maintaining perfect (average) price stability. But this is not a strict necessity. On this point, the natural system is also compatible with (i.e. it is open to the existence of) a rate of inflation, as we have seen, provided that it is a steady rate of inflation. Each natural price, in such case, would move according to the sum of two components: an inflationary component, uniform for all prices, and a structural component, specific to each price (see above, p. 289, and Table IX.1, expression [19]).

I shall not attempt to go beyond the pure labour version of the natural economic system at this point, except for the

[22] See p. 279.

few brief hints, on the extensions that have been made already. I have tried to give the reader a perception of what the 'natural' economic system is meant to be and of how its normative properties *and* requirements are coming to characterise it, at what I have called the first stage – the pure theory stage – of economic investigation.

5.   On completing the 'natural' economic system

The above presentation of the 'natural economic system' has been carried out at the level of the simplest of all versions – that of a pure labour economy. But a lot of work has been done already in order to achieve a wider conceptualisation of it. And a lot of work remains to be done to complete the task. The scheme, which has been elaborated by Piero Sraffa (in *Production of Commodities by Means of Commodities*), and the (dynamic) pure labour scheme compactly presented here express at this stage two (different but complementary) points of view from which to look at the same economic system. Taken together, they should in the end come to express a fully fledged theoretical scheme of the natural production economic system. The Sraffa scheme is focused on exploring the essential characteristics of employing means of production (capital goods) in the inter-industry relations. The scheme succinctly presented here is focused on exploring the essential aspects of the evolution of the economic system, under the impact of technical knowledge, with its implications for the structural dynamics of prices, output and employment. The two schemes belong to the same basic framework. Among the works that have already been done to bring together these two schemes, I shall mention here only what I consider to be my own contributions: i) the elaboration of the concept of vertical integration, which is precisely aimed at making the analytical connection explicit between the inter-industry (Sraffian) scheme and the present structural dynamics scheme;[23]

23 These contributions are given in Pasinetti, 1973, 1998.

ii) the more explicit introduction of intermediate commodities (capital goods) into such a framework, by which one can see immediately how the elaborations yield – as expected – a series of relations of the Harrod-Domar type. Each of them is linking the sectoral rate of growth, sectoral investment and the sectoral capital/output ratio, each relation being specific to each (vertically integrated) sector;[24] iii) the consequential need to face the problem of the search for a 'natural' rate (in fact a whole *series* of 'natural' rates) of profit and their implications for income distribution;[25] iv) the applications and extensions of the whole pure production model to international economic relations.

This research has led me to discover an extraordinarily important property inherent in all industrial economies, which so far seems to have escaped the attention of economists and of the whole economic literature. I am referring to the remarkable closure of economic systems to the international distribution of the benefits flowing from the growth of technical knowledge, quite independently of the possible gains coming from international trade as such, with crucial implications for the diffusion, or rather for the lack of diffusion, of the process of economic development.[26]

I have always considered these contributions as coming out straight from the association I have experienced and enjoyed with the Cambridge School of Keynesian Economics. It is, of course, impossible to dwell, even briefly, on any of them here (although the interested reader may look up the references given below). In any case, let me, incidentally, point

---

[24] The details are in Pasinetti, 1981, pp. 85–86.

[25] For details, see Pasinetti, 1981, pp. 128–131, and Pasinetti, 1988. The latter work extends the concept of vertical integration to what I have called *vertical hyper-integration*. This conceptualisation uses the notion of 'natural' (sectoral) rate of profit to transform all intermediate (capital) goods into labour, thus ending up with the pure labour scheme no longer as a simplification but as the most general scheme of a pure production economy.

[26] For details on all these contributions, see Pasinetti, 1981, pp. 261–262, and 1993a, pp. 165–168.

out how naturally the whole scheme does in fact carry out both i) a complete *multi-sectoral* generalisation of what Harrod, Kaldor and Joan Robinson tried to obtain by extending Keynes's analysis to the long run, and ii) a dynamic extension, along classical (Smithian/Ricardian) lines of the inter-industry scheme conceived by Piero Sraffa.

The members of the Cambridge School of Keynesian Economics did not entirely realise how far reaching their undertakings were in carrying ahead Keynes's original break-through, both for short-run analysis and, most of all, for long-run – necessarily structural – dynamic analysis.

I am confident that the scheme succinctly presented above, the further indications I have given here and those that will incidentally emerge in the following pages may help to illustrate how numerous and complex the steps to be taken are when one tries, on the one side, to go beyond each single evolving sectoral production process and, on the other side, to follow the intricacies of their combined effects on the evolution of the economic system as a whole.

Chapter X

The stage of institutional investigation

1.   The role of institutions

Let me now come to whatever hints I may able to give, in a short space, at the second (i.e. the institutional) stage of economic investigation. This stage is inevitably much wider, more variegated, less compact, more heterogeneous than the stage of pure theory concerning the natural economic system (of which I have tried to give an idea in the previous chapter). I shall of course refer the reader to whatever contributions I have myself already tried to give.[1] But the task becomes here so huge and heterogeneous, in front of what has become a necessarily persistent process of institutional change in the evolving historical context of industrial societies, as to advise me to concentrate not so much on the enormous number of problems that have been faced or solved already as on those that remain open for investigation. They are so numerous and important that I cannot even hope to make an exhaustive list.

Let me begin by harking back to methodology and saying that the most obvious reason for which a separation of economic investigations becomes necessary is the juxtaposition that one can see between the rather clear configuration of the

---

[1] See especially Pasinetti, 1993a, where a whole chapter (Chapter VIII) has been devoted to this purpose. It happens to have been written within the framework of a pure labour economy. See also Pasinetti, 1981, Chapter VIII.

natural economic system on the one side and the efforts necessary to bring it into existence on the other side. The natural economic system, as I see it, does not come down to reality from heaven. It does not automatically come into being by itself. It *has* to be brought into actual existence – by us. But it is a *moving* framework (not a *stationary* one). This means that, within it, many profound tendencies are constantly at work, from its very foundations, which are continually making it evolve, i.e. *change* in its structure. Thus, even if, or when, the natural economic system were hypothetically to be perfectly brought into active existence at any specific point in time (which will never happen, also because some extant institutions, at any specific point, may become unsuitable), it would then soon change in size and, most importantly, in its proportions (i.e. in its structure) and hence the current economic magnitudes would have to be modified accordingly, as time goes on.

To bring the natural economic system into existence, to close its degrees of freedom and then to keep it going through time, a set of procedures, rules, regulations, administrative bodies is required, which for short I have called *institutions*. There is no escape from this. Essentially any society must face its 'institutional problem'. It must face the social responsibility of constructing its institutions, adapting and modifying them as time goes on, perfecting them and (now and then when it becomes necessary) even discarding some of them, while inventing new ones. To carry out the investigations concerning the setting up and the operation of these institutions is indeed such a huge field of economic enquiry (and, in fact, not only of economic enquiry) as to concern a process that is heavily affected by the actual flowing of historical events and by the stage of development which the economic system under examination has reached.

In the conception proposed here, therefore, the dynamically conceived framework of the natural economic system stands solidly in the background, as the firm term of reference and confrontation. In the foreground, we are called to examine and analyse the outcomes that can actually be achieved by means of the existing (historically evolving) institutions.

This means that the same set of economic variables, after being defined and examined at the natural level, should have to be subjected to scrutiny again from a different point of view, i.e. from the point of view of their actual chances of being achieved, or not achieved, through the operation of the existing institutions. At their natural level, they are conceived as ideal positions to be aimed at. At their institutional level, they come under examination as actual positions to be realised, entirely or partially, in practice. It is the comparison and confrontation of these *actual* outcomes with their corresponding *natural* configurations that provide the criterion for the justification or non-justification, and thus the urge towards modification, of the institutional mechanisms through which they are (or should be) pursued.

Another simplified, rough, historical attempt at bringing home the methodological importance and relevance of the distinction between the two stages of investigation will be made in a moment. Meanwhile, let me stress that the first really relevant point that immediately emerges is that, at the second stage of investigation, there can be no necessary pattern that may be proposed in general. Both the *type* of the actual institutions and the *analysis* of their (more or less) appropriate characteristics will normally be open to diverse, alternative, sometimes even diametrically opposite solutions. It is in this respect that we can see how the application of the *separation theorem* leads us to distinguish between the necessity of a pure theory, concerning the evolution of the natural economic system, and the freedom of choice inherent in the deployment of the actual institutional framework that any specific society has decided to adopt or has partially succeeded in adopting in the face of historical events. The important consequence that logically follows (as stressed already) is that, in suggesting ways to solve the institutional problems, economic analysis, at this second stage of investigation, can no longer claim exclusiveness. It cannot pretend to be alone. The institutions that take shape in any society, apart from their economic characteristics, are also the result of many other factors – historical, cultural, legal, religious, political, geographic, etc. All these factors contribute to shaping (through time) the social framework and thus the social institutions of the economic system with which we may be concerned. Indeed, the responsible construction of a newly conceived set of institutions that may aim at a normatively grounded, desirably shaped, industrial economic system is the really great challenge that the industrial revolution has brought to modern societies, with a compulsion unprecedented in history and that, alas, remains far from being not only matched but even entirely understood. In carrying out this task, any specific society may succeed in a reasonably acceptable way, or it may succeed in only a partial way, or it may fail altogether, sometimes with disastrous consequences.

In the century that has just come to an end, we have in fact sadly witnessed two striking experiences of really major *institutional* failures, in two opposite directions (besides others of somewhat lesser importance). I am thinking of the Great Depression that characterised the 'capitalist' economies in the 1930s and the collapse of the Eastern European 'real socialist' economies in the late 1980s.

2.   The institutional problem facing the challenge of history

To bring some substantiation to the foregoing assertions, I shall first make another compact effort, though with inevitably crude simplifications and at the cost of appearing naïve or even superficial to the well-prepared economic historians. I shall try to take a rather comprehensive, synthetic look, from a very high-up point of view (so high as to be spanning a few centuries), at that complex process of institution building that has been generated through the intricate channels of social intercourse, in response to the unfolding major historical events that have led to the final outlet of the industrial revolution.

We know quite well that, since time immemorial, it has been at the level of the organisation of the political systems that all the relations concerning the aspects of what today we refer to as economic life have been dealt with. In any country, the monarch or the dictator or whatever responsible authority of more variegated and/or more representative bodies has been administering not only law and order, war and peace but also a taxation system, public expenditures, the circulation of money, and has always been regulating external relations, through a cascading set of political, legal, administrative institutions that have continually been adapting themselves to the flowing course of history.

But something novel, in fact something dramatically novel, at the *institutional* level has happened in the past few centuries. The evolution of our institutions has been compelled to react in the face of those unprecedented macroscopic phenomena mentioned in the previous pages, in particular in reaction to the explosion of population, the introduction of machinery, the diffusion of technical knowledge, in general, which have brought with them an unprecedented increase in the aggregate wealth of a few leading nations. All these events have given prominence to the *economic* aspects of social life in a way that never happened before. It is not easy to trace the chain of effects and counter-effects, or to pinpoint the chain of causation of the many interlocking events. It is, however, a fact that these events have also created the favourable bases for the emergence of a new science: the *economic science*, which has cut its enclave in the more general field of moral sciences.

The interconnections between the macroscopic phenomena and what has been happening at the level of the single individuals are extraordinarily and intriguingly complex and have persistently been generating new tensions between individuals and society as a whole. Many scholars have become convinced that, parallel to and perhaps because of the evolution of technological knowledge, something remarkably new has taken place precisely *at the level of the single individuals*, and that it is from here that economic investigations have been inspired and have taken their first steps.

It is important to notice that the emergence of the Enlightenment era and the outbreak of the French Revolution in continental Europe, democracy in North America, the constitutional monarchy in the British Isles: all of them have not been extraneous but contextual to the industrial revolution and at the same time to the emergence of economic science itself. In spite of the instinctive, even unconscious, sometimes naïve tendency to look in a more primitive way at the new hordes of proletarians that the factory system in manufacturing was creating, the Charter of Rights that emerged from the French Revolution, the American Constitution, the unwritten constitutional innovations in England were all directed towards establishing fundamental *civil rights* for *all* individuals — whatever their social extraction. This could only be a process loaded with socially explosive implications.

Many scholars have seen an *economic* counterpart to all this complex social evolution in the growing impatience of a dynamically acting bourgeoisie to claim freedom of initiative, thus rebelling against the earlier consuetude of the nation leaders to try to regulate every aspect of social life. There was a need to break out of imposed regulations, while claiming that single persons should be left free to organise economic relations by themselves. Many moral philosophers and political scientists increased their efforts to stress the importance and uniqueness of the power of rationality and of the potential of inventiveness of single human beings. They began to demand from their governments a retreat from the tendency to regulate every social relation and pressed strongly for a practice of freedom in economic affairs.

It seemed natural to associate the emerging power of individuals' originality, rationality and inventiveness with the implementation of economic policies of *laissez-faire*, and this could not avoid having a strong social impact. It was precisely the necessity to look more deeply into these phenomena that generated the impetus behind physiocracy in France and Classical political economy in Great Britain.

Of course, this social process has been an intricate and slow one. Our schematisation of the two phases behind the emerging of the modern world may be of some help in this respect too. First, through the early exchange phase of modern history that brought to evidence the power of rationality, and then, through the industry phase that brought to evidence the power of improving knowledge, the intuition, sometimes only a suspicion, emerged of the existence and action of a spontaneous economic mechanism, acting in a diffused, decentralised way at the microeconomic level (as we say today), in a manner not clearly or entirely understood, under the powerful inherent spring of the individuals' *self-interest*. This had all the appearance of a true discovery in social relations.

This social mechanism belongs precisely to the stage of investigation that we have come to consider here: the stage of the shaping of social institutions. It is a process essentially based on *competition* among individuals in their attempts at the rational organisation of both manufacturing and market exchange and in the process of human learning. But it requires a reasonable expectation for the acting persons of being able to appropriate the fruits of their efforts. At the same time, it could not go so far as to undermine the bases of social cohesion. Precisely here has been the delicate point, because this process, in order to work, requires rights of property to be protected, within a regulated legal framework, but also, at the same time, it requires preventing the more active members of the community (usually an *élite*) for taking excessive advantage of their privileged positions and exploiting others. It means the assurance of non-prevarication of the basic human rights of all persons, with the safeguard of an equitable distribution of the benefits of the evolving economic process and a social coordination of all efforts to prevent the outbreak of social discontent and unrest and hence of social instability.

Thus, the gist of a satisfactory outcome of this complex process lies in the assurance of giving full expression to the originality and inventiveness of the single individuals, but at the same time keeping an overall economic and social order in the new industrial society, which meant protecting the (majority) of less well-off members of the community from the possible exploitation of those in privileged positions. If we push this argument ahead, up to our own days, it is quite easy to see where this process leads; how, as it widens and widens, eventually and inevitably it reaches a much wider horizon – up to the necessity of protecting the whole natural environment in which we live, entailing a global protection from the excesses and distortions imposed by population, technology and irrationality, on a worldwide scale. This seems inevitable, as soon as the economic problems grow to such a wide dimension as to impose the necessity of overall coordination both at the national and at the international level.

It is remarkable to notice how these conclusions seem to follow from apparently simple, pragmatic, common-sense arguments. Of course, one should not close one's eyes to the presence of all too evident tensions in multiple directions: between the social effects of the competitive mechanism and the individuals' tendency to cling on to already achieved privileged positions; between individuals' inventiveness in response to the compulsion of competition and the requirements of overall coordination, not to mention the necessary protection of the under-privileged lot, etc. There is the obvious temptation, that should be resisted, of thinking that the discovery of a spontaneous, all-pervasive, decentralised, individualistic institutional mechanism, such as the competitive social mechanism – exciting as it may have appeared to the early (and many present) authors of the economic science – could be something that is able to provide *the* final solution to all the institutional problems of the industrial age. It should have appeared little less than obvious from the beginning, on mere common-sense grounds, that the pretence of a complete *laissez-faire* society – where all individuals are left entirely free to act in whatever way they like, even within a minimal legal framework ensuring law and order – could not be but a utopian solution of the institutional problem – in fact, as simplistic and extreme as the opposite attitude of pretending to impose an overall metaphoric straitjacket in which all economic relations, in a society becoming more and more complex, could be regulated, in all its details, by a central authority. Unrestricted *laissez-faire* policies on the one side and entirely centralised decisions on the other should have appeared immediately as representing two opposite aberrations. A satisfactory institutional framework could not but be aimed at making a selection, and taking stock only of the favourable features contributed by each of the two extreme views, with an effort to tame the conflicting aspects of the interaction between individuals' initiatives and social requirements.

But to devise the appropriate institutions to achieve these ends is no easy task. Common sense is a strong (most of the time a vital) guide to discussions of social relevance, but by itself it provides too weak and uncertain (sometimes even misleading) a basis for sustaining convincing policies in complex situations. Something more profound (and intellectually more satisfactory) needed to be proposed. This, I think, may well help a lot to understand the urge that was felt, in the second half of the eighteenth century, to raise hopes for the emergence of a 'new' science concerning *economic* matters. After some remarkable insights by precursors, such as Richard Cantillon in France and William Petty in England, physiocracy on one side of the Channel and Classical political economy on the other side seemed to fulfil the expectations. Alas, their scientific basis was rough and still too primitive. Something more accurate, more rigorous, was needed. In this respect, what followed, in the second half of the nineteenth century, opened up much greater hopes, while adding feverish excitement. However, it also generated one of the most puzzling and disconcerting episodes in the history of economic thought. Dire consequences were alas to materialise in the following (the twentieth) century.

3. Disillusionment with extreme solutions and elusiveness of a 'third way'

It must have been an extremely difficult task for people living at the time of the industrial revolution to gather a reasonable perception of the extraordinary events that were taking place. Yet it really is interesting – a remarkable fact deserving to be stressed – that the first spontaneous response of the leading economists of the time to the historical events that were taking place around them was by and large in the correct direction.

Both the physiocrats in France and the Classical political economists in Great Britain did grasp the necessity of distinguishing sharply, in their analyses, between the forces behind what they called (and, for the same reasons, I continue to call here) the 'natural' features of an economic system and the 'market' outcomes brought about by the actual institutions that were at work.

But the historical events began to run much faster than the availability of analytical and conceptual tools to the practitioners of the nascent political economy *science*. Looking back now at the (in many respects) remarkable results achieved by Classical political economy, it is curious to note that, at the very end of that whole intellectual phase, i.e. after John Stuart Mill's numerous editions of his *Principles of*

Political Economy (in the 1850s–1860s), the emerging new figures heralding a really exciting, apparently decisive new era in economic science were all so opposed to Classical economics. Marxian political economy on the one side and marginal economics on the other side, which characterised the last part of the nineteenth century and the first part of the twentieth century, seemed to decree the coming to an end of Classical political economy, by giving the impression of a major jump ahead in the quality and standing of economic analysis. This impression may well be justified, but if the arguments so far presented are correct, we must admit that, whatever their analytical merits may be, they both failed to respond to the task of singling out the appropriate institutions, which the historical circumstances so badly needed. The two of them, together or juxtaposed, gave origin to a curious Marxian/marginalist phase in economic theory that nurtured two strongly antagonistic views, fixed on two diametrically opposite conceptions of the needs of the society that was in the process of coming into being. The Marxian economists picked up immediately and all too well the relevant *production* paradigm that Classical political economy had conceived, but remained far from completing it. They proceeded to concentrate on class conflict and on what they thought would have been an inevitable eventual triumph of the working class over all other classes. Paradoxically enough, those among them who realised the importance of acting on the improvement of already existing institutions were branded as 'revisionists' and were very rudely pushed out of the workers' movement, often undergoing violent persecution. The winning faction ended up by advocating a radical social 'revolution', which in their view would have changed completely the bases of society's institutions, without however succeeding in specifying exactly what the new institutions should have been. The marginalist economists, in their turn, went on developing their analyses into a theoretically beautiful but abstract construction, analytically fascinating but substantially *anachronistic*, focused on the primacy of consumers' behaviour in an ideally static, pure exchange economy, in which knowledge was supposed to be perfect and externally given, in which all resources were also given and the basic problem was simply supposed to be that of optimally allocating them. Nobody would deny that both streams of thought picked up important economic aspects that needed to be explored. But they both fell into the trap of unilateralism and hence of reductivism. They both fell short of exploring and giving us light on what would actually have been needed, at the time, in terms of the required basic institutions that the increasingly more complex, new economic systems were so badly in need of.

Perhaps only now, ex post, do we come into the position of seeing a little more clearly the paradoxical outcome of such a remarkable theoretical juxtaposition that took place and still keeps alive so many discussions.

Surely it was not easy to see clearly what kind of impasse economic science had fallen into. Even the most brilliant economists were led into open contradictions. Think, for example, of Joseph Schumpeter, who, while bringing richness of intuitions and fascination of perspectives with his original ideas on the 'destructive creation' effects of technical innovations, was at the same time so fascinated by the analytical beauty of Leon Walras's *General Equilibrium* scheme as to point it out with awe as one of the most remarkable achievements that had come to light in economic theory.[2] His assertion is not *wrong*, but is quite beside the point. What is striking is how these analytical achievements, how the jump in quality of economic investigations that took place in the latter part of the nineteenth century, failed in drawing attention to the *institutions* that would have been needed to face the extraordinarily new, relevant economic phenomena that history was bringing along.

[2] See Schumpeter, 1943; [1934], 1961.

Thus, with the social-democratic faction being rudely crushed in the Marxist camp, and hardly any criticism being advanced to the beautiful analytical scheme developed by the established prevailing academic community on the other side, the practical result turned out to be a tendency to polarise the debates concerning the institutional questions on two contrasting and ideologically loaded extremes – *laissez faire* capitalism on the one side and a thrust towards (authoritarian) centrally planned socialism on the other, without however a well-defined picture of which type of institutions each of them really needed in order to work in practice.

For decades, the challenge that Karl Marx had launched fuelled hot debates that swept through the economic, political, sociological and philosophical arena, while lack of sensible, practically satisfactory response to the challenge was contributing to enhance unprecedented social discontent and strife in employer/worker relations. Inevitable, essentially institutional, crises were simmering under the surface. They dramatically exploded in the following (the twentieth) century.

It looks almost incredible today to have to realise that, up to the Great Depression of the 1930s, the general consensus prevailing in the economics academic circles of the industrially advanced countries was for an economic theory based on perfect competition assumptions and a basically static, pure exchange, general equilibrium theoretical scheme, while the conviction of the merits of *laissez-faire* economic policies was taken almost generally for granted. On the other side, the Marxist stream of thought was gathering momentum, but with little official credit or recognition in our universities (as it was generally considered more ideological than scientific).

It was an anti-Marxist, John Maynard Keynes, who, in the 1920s (Keynes, 1926), intuited that the *end of laissez-faire* was looming in the air. But the crucial, historically marked divide came with the slump of 1929–30. The institutional failures were brought to evidence by the Great Depression of the 1930s. They definitively convinced Keynes that a major revolution was necessary in economics – not in order to destroy the existing, broadly accepted, free market economies, but in order to overturn current economic theory and most of all the economic policies derived from it, while modifying the existing patently inappropriate market institutions. It must be admitted that it was precisely the acceptance of Keynes's major challenge that finally undermined the much diffused conviction, in the academic community, that there was nothing wrong with the working of the prevailing capitalist economies (except for some possible 'imperfections' or temporary mismatches in current ways of carrying out real and monetary transactions). It was his challenge that led governments to the adoption of those various forms of Keynesian macroeconomic policies, which so decidedly contributed to save from collapse the then-wobbling construction of the Western capitalist economies and to transform them into substantially modified forms of market economies with state intervention corrections.

Meanwhile, historical events had been running very quickly. Lack of clear ideas by economic theoreticians on the one side, and lack of wisdom on the part of men in charge of governance on the other side, were overtaken by crude decisions by unscrupulous men in positions of power. As we all know, World War One was followed by a communist revolution in Russia, and World War Two led to the enforcement of communist, dictatorial regimes in the whole of Eastern Europe – through violence and imposed dramatic changes.

Thus, for quite a few decades, the twentieth century offered us two diametrically opposite groups of institutional set-ups, side by side, which were not merely in competition with each other – as it would have been interesting to see – but in really strong opposition, sometimes through crude struggles. The whole world was split into two contrasting blocs. A strong group of traditional capitalist economies on the one side struggled along and yet (after Keynes) continuously strove for adaptation. Another group of countries on the other side tried the totally opposite institutional experience of centrally planned economies with no concession to changes of any sort, with the result of being compelled rather soon to impose – by force – strict, rigid rules and at the same time inherently nurturing inflexibility and aversion to adaptation.

The confrontation went on for decades, sometimes in dramatic forms, even to the point of risking a lethal nuclear war. It came to an end, as we all know, with the collapse of the whole institutional set-up of the so-called 'real socialist' economies of Eastern Europe, a dramatic as well as sudden and unexpected event. Thus, after only six decades, the major historical experiment in central (authoritarian) economic planning ever undertaken in history collapsed. On this occasion, there was no Eastern European Keynes who could have emerged to save those socialist economies by addressing them on the way to adaptation. Whatever innovative spirit had earlier been carried by the revisionists, it had been nipped in the bud and could not be revived. There was nothing to hark back to. The general, simplistic reaction to the socialist disaster was to go back the whole way: to revert to the opposite extreme, by hastily allowing the operation of unfettered, liberalised *laissez-faire* economic practices, without even thinking of the necessity of setting up regulated market institutions, as if these would spontaneously arise by themselves. The absence of even minimal market regulations and reasonable institutional arrangements simply led to an 'unbridled capitalist' disaster: incredible chaos, corruption, rackets, which have not yet come to an end. Notice that not all socialist economies have disappeared, but those that have survived and actually can claim some success (the notable and most striking case is China) have done so by copying or trying to imitate many aspects of the 'capitalist' economies in quite different institutional surrounding, most of all with all the compulsion and repression inherited from the previous historical phase.

Can this be accepted as the final verdict of the history of the twentieth century? Hardly. The collapse of the real socialist economies in Eastern Europe, the survival of a not really idealistic socialism in Asia and at the same time the persistent struggle, through adaptation, of the capitalist economies can surely teach us many lessons, but they open up a huge set of puzzling questions as well.

One may perhaps barely draw at least a simple pragmatic conclusion. There exists no obvious institutional-organisational scheme – or at least we do not know one, in our present state of knowledge – that may help us to bring into existence what may well be conceived, on a normative level, as an ideal set of economic institutions. In point of fact, recent history has confirmed that the more the actual economies have tried to adhere to extreme institutional positions, the worse have been their actual performances. Under pragmatic compulsion, all modern societies have ended up by adopting a set of institutions that, in some way or another, is 'mixed', with sectors exposed to the free market competition and other sectors being regulated, though in different proportions, at different degrees, all varying, in relative size, from place to place, from time to time; and by no means with decisions made once-and-for-all, but actually with many decisions, after some time, being modified or reversed, sometimes with the resistance of those social groups that may have built up specific privileges meanwhile.

In these conditions, it becomes understandable that, faced with disillusionment with both extremes, so many social scientists have began to search for a third way, hoping to single it out somewhere in between the two extremes. But when put in such terms, the problem is inevitably bound to be drowned into inconclusiveness. If the appropriate solution were simply that of finding a linear combination of two extremes – even if we were to take for granted the possibility of defining two such extremes – the problem would be only too easy to solve. But the trouble is that not only are the combinations concerned infinitely many, but nobody can assure us that such combinations could be ordered in a linear way, or in any other way, *non-ergodic* or else, to take a term that has been used successfully.[3] Moreover, they may concern not two but multiple directions, and among these directions it is not easy to find a criterion for singling out the appropriate ones. Thus, as we move away from the two extremes, there appear to be infinitely many third ways that could be envisaged. To look for the appropriate 'privileged' one does not appear to be a fruitful task to embark upon and even less a sensible or helpful procedure to try. In fact, when attempted, it is bound to end up in complete inconclusiveness because of the inevitably temporary nature of each specific institutional solution, unless one is content with narrowing down the procedure to be applied in some considerably restricted sense. For example, in the narrow sense of the search for a 'third way', which may be alternative to another, earlier supposed to be the appropriate 'third way', within a numerous family of other 'third ways' that had already been chosen on past occasions and have become obsolete.[4,5]

---

[3] By Davidson, 1983.

[4] An interesting exercise was undertaken by Arestis and Sawyer (2001), who held an international conference to examine the sense in which the third way has been 'loosely used to describe the emergence of new social democracy government throughout the world' (p. 1). Their (excellent) summary, written at the end of the conference, singles out seven elements (which I do not reproduce here, but see *ibidem* pp. 3–6) that in their opinion would 'justify the description of interventionist neo-classical economics of a new Keynesian variety', which they suppose to be associated with the Giddens (2000) version of the latest Giddens/Blair 'third way'. Note the curious mixture: an *'interventionist neo-classical economics of a new Keynesian variety'* – a real monster from a conceptual point of view.

[5] Paradoxically, a clearer and in any case intuitively simpler criterion – a sort of common-sense rule of thumb – on how to search for an appropriate mixture of individually based and community-based institutional mechanisms can be found in the proposals made not by economic theorists but by moral philosophers. It may be useful to hint at least at one example of them to show how, on the matter of institutions, non-economists may offer inspiring suggestions, if not precise guidance, side by side with and sometimes even more effectively than economists themselves. In the latest pronouncements of the 'social teaching' of the Catholic Church, it is first

It is clearly the whole, crude, two-extreme type of institutional approach that at this point is emerging as misleading and in the end useless, after appearing deficient and in many ways even superficial. The terms 'capitalism' on the one side and 'socialism' on the other cover too many variants and heterogeneous contents, and if we try to look for their combination we risk adding further confusion. Much else is needed![6] We must find the way to go much deeper if we want to be in a position to disentangle economic investigation from ideology, institutional organisation from just down-to-earth pragmatic solutions.

The approach to economic analysis which is proposed here is an attempt to go in this direction. Here is where the *separation theorem* really comes to help – an analytical device to face complexity with a maximum of freedom and a minimum of self-imposed restrictions. 'Free' sectors, 'regulated' sectors, the way the 'free' sectors may need to be regulated, and 'regulated sectors' may require to be deregulated, with reference to the evolving historical events, are all subjects to be open to no pre-imposed constraints. The *separation theorem* suggests separating the investigation of those characteristics that lie at the foundations of the production economies

---

of all stated explicitly that 'the Church does not have models to propose' (Pope John Paul II, 1993, § 43), thus wisely leaving the analytical problems to economists and social scientists. Yet some guidelines on issues of social organisation are not avoided. An example is given by the so-called 'principle of subsidiarity', which may be stated as having two aspects: one negative and one positive. In its negative aspect the principle states that no social group can claim to be put in charge of tasks which may satisfactorily be carried out by smaller social groups or by single persons. In its positive aspect, the same principle implies that, whenever single persons, or (hierarchically) smaller social groups, are shown to fail to perform any given social task, then a (hierarchically) higher-up social group must be put in charge of performing it. The criterion to follow seems quite sensible and in any case intuitively convincing. Yet the substance remains vague in terms of actual applications. Surely the economists should be able to suggest more deeply founded and specific contributions.

[6] An interesting attempt carried out so far in post-Keynesian literature is the one presented by Heinrich Bortis (1997). He uses the term 'middle [rather than 'third'] way', trying to develop the concept of '*humanism*, as a middle way between liberalism and socialism' (p. 33).

(as I have tried to express by the natural economic system), which enjoy properties of substantial permanence and offer solid terms of reference and confrontation, from the investigation of the institutions necessary to deal with the particularities, in time and space, of the specific problems which are constantly raised by the 'challenge of history'.

Economic science has proceeded for too long to mix up the two stages of investigation. By not making any distinction between them, it seems to have failed on both. Time for some deep rethinking seems to be appropriate.

4. The *separation theorem* revisited

Since the present work has placed considerable weight on the *separation theorem*, it may be advisable, before closing this chapter, to face at least a few objections to it.

First objection: to enact the separation theorem is impossible because the two proposed stages of investigation are in fact inextricably linked.

The answer to this objection emerges more clearly if we rephrase the proposition. To enact the separation theorem *would* be impossible if we were to take neoclassical economics for granted. But this is not what we have been doing. We have been proposing a *break* with neoclassical economics. This also implies avoiding its impossibilities. Consider the question in a few further details. What are really the *foundations* of neoclassical economics? As mentioned already, Paul Samuelson brought them out explicitly in his masterpiece, where he claimed that the *Foundations of* (neoclassical) *economic analysis* (1948) can be reduced to a mathematical function to be maximised under constraints, which is going to be applied over and over again to all economic problems to be investigated. This conceptual scheme has an important implication. The achievement of equilibrium prices corresponding to Pareto-optimum positions (a *foundational* characteristic) can be attained by allowing all agents to be free to compete in conditions of atomistic perfect competition (a specific *institutional* mechanism). Equilibrium (optimum) prices, which is what the analysis claims to achieve, and the effects of maximising behaviour in a context of perfect competition thus appear to be inextricably linked to, and inseparable from, one another. This may well be so. But what is inseparable within such a context does not need to be inseparable in other contexts. In particular, it need not be inseparable in the context which we have been proposing of a pure production model. What our approach thus entails is the necessity of abandoning the neoclassical approach to economic theory.

Second objection: the concept of *institution* is a very wide concept indeed. There are *institutions* (a few of them at least) which seem to be so basic as to appear absolutely necessary to the foundations of any society and hence presumably of any economic system. If this is the case, how is it possible to offer a 'separation' of pure economic theory from institutional analysis?

Part of this difficulty comes from the fact that the term 'institution' has been given a wide variety of meanings and used in many different contexts.[7] Therefore phrases such as 'there are *fundamental* institutions for a society' always leave some ambiguity on where to draw a line between those institutions that are intended to be at the basis of a society and those that are not.

Despite these difficulties, it must be stressed that our separation theorem is not meant to deny the possibility of a ranking of the various types of institutions and organisations. The natural theoretical scheme is not incompatible with such a possibility. Quite the contrary, it seems to offer some room for supporting it. But the important point to stress is that, while there is nothing in the natural economic system that

[7] See, as a significant example, the objections raised by Jeoffrey Hodgson, 1994, in a discussion with the present author. On the other side, see a more favourable alternative view as it emerges from Bortis, 1997.

precludes the existence of basic institutions, at the same time it is constructed in such a way as not to depend on them. The aim of our first stage of investigation consists in offering a pure *theoretical structure* (an *evolving* structure, it must be noticed) of the natural economic system, that is set up independently of all institutions – not in the sense that some institutions are unable to affect the speed and/or the scale of realisation of the natural economic system, but in the sense that institutions (whether fundamental or not) cannot change the essence of (in the sense of the relations characterising) the natural economic system.

The question of endogeneity immediately comes to mind at this point. To begin with, if the natural economic system is independent of institutions, what can we say about the opposite chain of causation? Could institutions be derived from the natural economic system, and if so, to what extent? To answer this question, let us adopt a largely used definition of 'institution', i.e. as a set of 'rules of the game' which preside, in our case, over the working of an economic system.[8] Through incentives and restrictions, the set of economic institutions directs the behaviour of economic agents. If we accept this simple but workable definition, we may affirm that the natural economic system is not aimed at endogenising the institutions. If it did so, it would end up in a reductionist approach similar to the one criticised above. However, the natural economic system has the power to give indications for institutional blueprints. It has the power to clarify the aims to be pursued by the institutions and in so doing to set the priorities in institution building. Institutions are human-made rules, most often to achieve (or to improve the achievements of) some goals. Some of these goals emerge as very clearly defined from the natural economic system. Just to give an example, take the goal of full employment. To achieve it, we need to set up appropriate institutions. But which

---

[8] See North (1990) for a definition of institutions along these lines.

institutions are the most appropriate to the goal cannot be ascertained from the natural economic system. At the same time, it is quite possible to claim, from the analysis of the natural economic system, that some institutional rules are *not* a solution to the proposed goal. For instance, our analysis has shown how unlikely it is that full employment may be obtained through the spontaneous operation of a fully decentralised economic system, but at the same time it has also shown that there may be many different and alternative ways by which the economic system can achieve it. In other words, the theoretical analysis, while suggesting avenues of action, leaves open many degrees of freedom. Several games may compete in pursuing the same goal. To say 'many degrees of freedom' or to say 'several games' does not mean an arbitrary (even less an unlimited) number of them. Whatever the set of incentives and restrictions a society may decide to adopt (not necessarily all of a purely economic nature), the natural economic system suggests some normative restrictions that should not be violated and/or some conditions that should always be fulfilled – think of macroeconomic condition [13] discussed on pp. 285–287. Moreover, in showing the underlying relations among its variables, the natural economic system may indicate a broad band of possible directions in which incentives and restrictions can be put into place. It thus turns out to be a device to shape the directions of the institutional environment, without having the pretence of imposing any specific institutional model. Institutions *can* be changed, even drastically. The relations of the natural system are permanent. While institutional analysis may be affected by the natural economic system, the (evolving relations of the) latter will not be affected by the institutional set-up. It is in this sense that it has been claimed that the natural economic system is pre-institutional. This is sufficient to conclude that institutions cannot become endogenous to the natural economic system, and at the same time that they are neither independent from, nor totally exogenous to, it. By taking advantage of the natural economic system, it is possible to gain much clearer ideas of the boundaries and avenues within which institutions can operate.

Third objection: this is an objection that is likely to come from many sources and not only from neo-classical economists – among others, from industrial economists dealing with technical change. The objection is that the *determination* of the coefficients that characterise the natural economic system (both in its technological and in its consumption structures) may not be entirely unconnected with certain institutions, e.g. legal rules, fiscal and monetary policies, *laissez-faire* or regulating rules, etc. But there is no preclusion to the choice of particular institutions, as we have already said. We may now add that there is no preclusion to the way in which the level of technical and consumption coefficients is achieved, on the basis of the institutional setting that is in place at any point of time. It is precisely for this reason that the role of institution is so crucial for economic analysis: without institutions the natural economic system could never turn into an actual economic system. Institutions therefore, in our framework, do not only have the subsidiary role of helping the natural economic system to coming into existence, they also play the active role of contributing to determine (as best as can be achieved) the level and evolution of the variables that, in the natural system, are taken as totally or partially exogenous.

This is, in fact, a very important point that deserves ample discussion, especially with the industrial economists.

A separate but equally important point is, however, that the analytical structure of the natural economic system does not imply that all existing institutions, or all institutional mechanisms at work at a specific time, should necessarily be taken for granted. The natural economic system is a powerful device. It may well call into question institutions that have been inherited from the past, if they are no longer justified, or if they have accidentally or unjustifiably developed in entirely inadmissible directions. Some significant examples of these problems will emerge in the following pages. A particularly important one is on the theme of intellectual property, where it will be shown how commitments to alternative pure theories with different theoretical foundations may entail drastically different, in fact opposite, institutional implications.

Chapter XI

Back to the future of the Keynesian revolution

1. Recollection

We are nearing our conclusion and we may try to gather the various threads of the arguments developed so far.

It has been argued that the break with tradition – the 'revolution in economics' – that Keynes thought to be necessary and that the Cambridge Keynesians undertook to continue may well be said to have remained unaccomplished, or to have fallen into neglect. But it cannot be said to have been a failure. Indeed, it cannot fail, if we want to achieve a satisfactory economic theory that may help us to understand the new economies in which we have come to live since the industrial revolution. It has been argued that a new paradigm in economics, primarily focused on production and learning, has become necessary in order to interpret, analyse and discuss the newly emerging economic problems and to provide the institutions that are appropriate to their management.

Keynes realised – with rare intuition – that the whole construction of mainstream economics needed a radical shake-up in order to be realistically brought into line with the course of events of what he called the 'monetary production economies' of our time. The Cambridge Keynesians developed their work as a continuation of such a task. The list of features they brought together – which I dared to summarise at the end of Book II[1] – is a rough indication of the directions in which they have been striving to go. Owing to the rather personal way in which each of them has pursued their task, they have commonly been regarded as providing results that appear heterogeneous. An explanation has been given here in terms of the complexity of the 'production' economies which we are called to investigate, as against the simpler 'exchange type' of economies of the pre-industrial era. A methodological innovation has been proposed, able to simplify the investigation and to bring the works of the whole Cambridge School of Keynesian Economics into a comprehensive, unified theoretical framework. This methodological innovation relies on what I have called a *separation theorem*, to which I came back at the end of the previous chapter. It consists in separating, in our investigations, a fundamental stage dealing with the basic, permanent features of what I have called the natural economic system and a stage of investigation devoted to the *institutions* necessary to shape the real world in the direction of its 'natural', normatively grounded configuration.

It has been argued that this is the point to which one must go back, for a resumption and reshaping for the future of a so much needed Keynesian revolution. Once this radical step is courageously taken, the fields of investigations that open up become well defined, clearer and dramatically wide.

The space that remains in this book will be devoted to a series of hints on the way one may proceed, very naturally, from the solid basis of the natural economic system (itself to be completed) to explore without prejudicial constraints the extraordinarily complex institutional problems that the monetary production economies have brought to us. I shall endeavour to concentrate more on the problems that remain to be faced in the future rather than on those (as done, e.g., in Harcourt, 2006) that have been solved in the past.

---

[1] See above pp. 219–237.

2. The generalising drive of the production (and learning) paradigm

It seems reasonable to begin by considering briefly at least some aspects that explicitly bring into evidence the favourable features of the new paradigm, as against those of the old one.

One strong feature of the 'production' paradigm is given by its drive to generalisation. This point is important. The proposed change of paradigm represents a radical change. For those used to argue within a *corpus* of investigations and research as huge as that accumulated so far by mainstream economics, the prospect of a change of paradigm may appear frightening. It clearly becomes vital to know what must be discarded and what can be reabsorbed by a process of generalisation. In fact, we can see immediately here how the separation theorem plays its role.

As long as we move at the foundational stage of investigation, there can be no escape. Accepting the foundations of the new paradigm implies discarding the foundations of the old one. The Keynesian original claim began here. There can be no compromise at the foundational stage.

Yet things may shape up differently at the second stage of investigation (concerning the institutions). A lot of economic investigations which have been carried out under the umbrella of the pure exchange paradigm (especially those using particular behavioural hypothesis) may well be open to being reabsorbed into the pure production paradigm, but at its second stage of investigation. Let me say that in the new paradigm, as such, there is no preclusion, at the institutional stage, to look at the economic system even from the oldest and most ingrained of all institutional mechanisms – the competitive market mechanism – provided that it is considered in its proper setting, namely as an *institutional* mechanism.

We all know that the merits of the competitive market mechanism are by now widely appreciated. Yet they should

not be over-estimated, nor be referred to inappropriate institutional conditions. We know that the market mechanism, in
order to work efficiently, is subject to strict rules, which much
economic literature has after all been investigating at length
and with reference to specific institutional set-ups. And we
know that not only may there be 'market failures', but also
circumstances in which the competitive market mechanism
does not work at all. For example, even in the field of goods
and services, we know that the market price mechanism does
not work properly, or does not work at all, in the field of the
public goods. There is a rich literature in this field, which
may well (judiciously) be taken advantage of.

It is important to realise after all that, strictly speaking, traditionally minded economists could object and
(rightly) claim and argue their cases on the basis of traditional hypotheses, even within the newly framed production paradigm, simply because, *at the institutional stage*,
this paradigm imposes no preclusion. The new procedures
do not exclude the testing of conclusions reached on the
basis of the more traditional hypotheses – at the limit, even
straight utility and/or profit maximisation hypotheses. The
difference is that, within the new paradigm, their explica-
tive value, far from being pre-imposed in an exclusive way,
must face confrontation. They have to be set against, or else
complemented by and then confronted with, those offered
by any other hypotheses and/or any other approach. In any
case and most of all, the results have to be evaluated on
the basis of their effectiveness in reaching the normative
standards set by the configuration of the natural economic
system.

This is indeed the novelty that is proposed here, namely
to have uncovered the existence of fundamental and permanent standards of reference that are at the basis of the natural
economic system. It is these concepts that provide the terms
of evaluation and confrontation, for all results that are generated by any specific, actually working, institutional set of

organisations. Here is where the separation theorem is yield-
ing its best service. When the investigations of the natural
economic system, with its normatively marked persistent features, are carried out independently of, and in a logical sense
before, the investigations aimed at finding the appropriate
institutions that may lead to their realisation, then the following (institutional) stage of investigation – with all its historically shaped, and thus evolving, characteristics – comes
to the fore with all its merits, all its widely developing impetus, as it can be enriched with concepts and theories which
may well come from fields of analysis far outside economics,
to be used to complement it or act in its stead.

The favourable characteristic of this way of proposing the
'production paradigm' is that it emerges as a truly general
paradigm, with respect to the more traditional 'exchange
paradigm'. This is because the new paradigm appears to be
able to absorb contributions achieved within the previous one
in a truly general fashion. Many empirically founded investigations proposed originally by neoclassical economists, who
have however found themselves cut off from any connection with optimal positions – and thereby bereft of their
reliance on traditional economic welfare justifications – can
more naturally be grafted on to the new paradigm at the second stage of investigation, where they may in fact find a
stronger support by standards of reference that have independently emerged from the first (the foundational) stage of
investigation.

In this context, the attractive characteristic of the production paradigm, as it is being proposed here, is that it
can indeed rescue and thus absorb a lot of research work
which has been carried out so far by originally neo-classical
economists, especially with the characteristics that have
most recently developed, in which –with good, empirically
justified, reasons – the analysis is being carried out by
assuming conditions of non-perfect competition, non-perfect
knowledge, uncertainty about the future, strategic behaviour,

non-cooperative games, etc., and even with reference to non-market institutions.

Through this route, a considerable number of investigations, which have been carried out in the immense literature on the functioning of not so much 'perfect' markets, when they are empirically relevant, may be rescued from the neoclassical approach in which they started and, freed from their limits, inserted into that (second) stage of investigation which concerns institutional relations.

To conclude – and summarise with reference to those neoclassically derived investigations that, by adopting non-orthodox behavioural assumptions, have achieved valid, empirically solid results – the fruitful upshot of the two-stage investigation approach here advocated is the possibility of absorbing them, in a way, *i.e.* at the institutional stage, which represents a true generalisation in the sense of Kuhn of the alternative, newly proposed production paradigm.

3.   On monetary theory and policy

These are only a few notes on a huge field of investigation. The purpose is confined to identifying the point where the discussions on monetary theory and policy are fitting into the production paradigm, besides stressing the novel relations and phenomena that emerge from it and could not be perceived within the old paradigm.

In this methodological framework, the problems of monetary theory and monetary policy concern both stages of investigation, i.e. both the foundational and the institutional stage, even though – with the development of the central financial institutions that have been a very conspicuous characteristic of the emergence of the industrial economies (think of the central banks and of the many international monetary institutions) – it is the *institutional* field of investigation, especially at the macroeconomic level, that has mostly risen to topical relevance.

On monetary matters, popularity of the recent monetarist theories, as we all know, reached its highest pitch around the 1970s, in a period of unexpected inflation due to external events (mainly the international oil crisis), for which all the established monetary institutions were almost entirely unprepared. What has favoured their counter-revolutionary challenge to Keynes's economics and saved many of their elaborations from logical contradictions is the analytical property of the general equilibrium model of being framed in strictly *real* terms, so as to make it possible to add to it, from outside, a single magnitude – the quantity of money – without bothering about the whole set of already determined (real) variables. Through this exogenously introduced macroeconomic variable, the single degree of freedom remaining open in the general equilibrium scheme is closed. Nothing is changed in the already determined set of (real) economic variables (in this context, meaning the reductive assumption of 'neutral' money), and that is sufficient to determine the *absolute level* of prices. Curiously enough, this might appear as a partial application of our separation theorem, in the sense that all the relations concerning the monetary macroeconomic variables are separated from the functioning of the basic, real-quantity conceived, microeconomically based, general equilibrium scheme, which is supposed to work out equilibrium optimum positions independently of the monetary part of the economy. But the separation is a fiction, since the general equilibrium model, that is supposed to work at the micro level, keeps together its foundational features concerning supposed optimum allocation of resources *and* its institutional features of an atomistic, perfectly competitive market, able to achieve them. With this odd mixture, the monetarist macroeconomic construction – a giant with clay feet, considering its reductionist assumptions – reveals all its fragility, under the heavy weight of the institutional complexity of the monetary production economies.

Yet one might also say that the monetarist separation mentioned above, though partial, allows an analysis of monetary macroeconomic relations which, for some purposes, may well yield results that can be directly confronted with those of macroeconomic monetary analysis carried out *at the institutional level* with the production paradigm. This is true because the scheme, based on the assumption of neutrality of money, is not, *at the institutional level*, logically incompatible, as such, with an economic analysis that is lying its foundations on the characteristics of a production economy! The new paradigm is general enough as to be able even to absorb the monetarist framework (of course with the introduction of the conditions of neutral money). This could well be used as a hypothetical exercise, with the only purpose of showing the generalising property of the production paradigm that would thereby be confirmed. But it would also turn out to be a practically useless exercise (because of the monetarist reductive assumptions!).

The new paradigm, owing to the extraordinary richness of its structural dynamics foundations, would precisely be evincing the necessity of breaking out of the monetarist restrictive narrowness. We know all too well that the attack on the traditional conception of the neutrality of money was originally one of the major ingredients in the devastating attack on traditional economic theory launched in the 1930s by John Maynard Keynes, heralding an economic theory where, at the institutional level, real and monetary phenomena are inherently linked and interacting with one another, thereby singling out monetary policy as one of the tools in the hands of governments to influence the level of output and employment. This is precisely what traditional economics was unable to contemplate. Most of all, it is Keynes's intuitions and elaborations on the typical instability of the financial markets in the monetary production economies that have generated the most powerful stimuli to the development of entirely novel fields of investigations on the financial institutions.[2]

But this is not all. There is much else that the production paradigm is opening up as fields of analysis to pursue. What becomes important to stress here for our purpose is the set of new features of the industrial world that could not be detected within the old paradigm. The production paradigm precisely leads us to realise why and how entirely novel institutions are becoming necessary, precisely where the old paradigm is sadly powerless to give any guide. Even our simple, pure labour scheme (presented in Chapter II) is sufficient to make us see clearly that there is not one single degree of freedom as is the case evinced by the traditional scheme, but no less than *three* degrees of freedom that in monetary production economies open up and need to be closed from outside the foundational basis of the natural economic system. There is indeed the requirement of the choice of the *numéraire* – the only degree of freedom that could be seen from the old pure exchange model – but there also is the requirement of a choice to be made of the *rate of change* of the standard chosen for the price system (which comes down to the necessity to fix the rate of inflation) and moreover there is the external requirement of fixing the monetary rate of interest. These three degrees of freedom, that are inherent in the natural economic system, by needing to be closed, are all crying out for the setting up of appropriate newly conceived institutions.

One can see many hints and signs that Keynes himself and most of his (Keynesian) followers have for a long time intuitively perceived these problems, even if they may not have

---

[2] On these lines the American post-Keynesians have been particularly active (e.g. Minsky, 1975, 1986; Davidson, 1972.) On the same subjects, but at different levels, see the remarkable recent work by Godley and Lavoie 2007.

been able to grasp them fully. In various forms, these hints are creeping into their elaborations in terms of criticisms of the traditional positions and/or contributions to the shaping of the new monetary and financial institutions.

The completion of a fully fledged pure production model on the one side and a deeper examination and understanding of its institutional implications on the other side might well generate, in this field, a literally dramatic explosion of research, in fact long needed and overdue.

4.   Main sources of unsolved institutional problems

The particular angle of our arguments adopted in the previous section may also be helpful in the following pages as a quick device to characterise major points of strength of the new paradigm, simply due to the fact that, by being conceived with reference to the economic systems that have emerged since the industrial revolution, it immediately reveals the sources of the requirements for entirely novel institutions. This could not be perceived from within the old paradigm, since the latter referred to a reality where the new industrial features had not yet emerged. Precisely this earlier historical absence of the new features may in fact have created a kind of black hole in the old theories, where crucial problems may often have remained hidden and thus ignored, simply because it was impossible to perceive them, with potentially adverse consequences on the new institutional problems which may have remained unsolved for decades.

In fact, the main challenge to existing institutions, originally generated by the industrial revolution, came from the side of the factors of production. We had to wait until Roy Harrod (1939, 1948) to realise that the really novel features concerned what he somehow innocently called 'dynamic economics', a term specifically intended to stress the relevance of the *rates of change* characterising three major industrial economics factors: i) the growth of population, ii) the accumulation of capital (i.e. the growth of physical capital), iii) technical progress (i.e. the growth of knowledge). The crucial consequence of singling out the *rates of change* of the variables concerned, as the vital centre of attention, is that they imply no longer once-and-for-all changes (no matter how relevant) but *persistent* changes, i.e. *cumulative* movements.

The major problems lay precisely in the difficulty of grasping the need for the *new* institutions that had become necessary. To the Classical economists it seemed natural that the set of institutions which had proved efficient up till then should also be extended to the new features of the industrial production process. Nobody perceived immediately what kind of revolution the industrial take-off had really generated! A few remarks on the three factors on Harrod's list may be helpful.

Growth and structural dynamics of population

The Classical economists had become scared by the sudden explosion of population which they witnessed. The phenomenon was unprecedented and appeared all too clearly as accompanying the process of industrialisation. On considering it, they fell into the logical trap of thinking of a general 'law of diminishing returns' (Malthus, 1798, Ricardo, 1821).[3] Simplistic as this may seem, it would in fact be difficult to claim that, for more than a century, later economists have been able to see these problems in a decidedly better way. The most elegant contribution that recent economic literature has been able to produce on population in a process of economic development is a mathematical, beautifully elegant scheme on cumulative growth – the celebrated von Neumann model (1937, 1945). Fascinating as it is, this model fails completely to make us grasp the institutional relevance of the profound demographic phenomenon that had taken place. By assuming a perfectly proportional expansion of all

---

[3] For details, see Pasinetti, 1999.

sectors of an economic system, in line with a strictly proportional growth of overall population, with no technical
progress and constant (if not decreasing) returns to scale, it
prevents us, if taken literally, from realising the terrific institutional problems that have been brought into being by an
epoch-making event that has caused the world population to
multiply by a factor of ten in barely three centuries, while on
the way changing completely its age composition and structure from one country to another and from one generation
to another. The phenomenon has turned out to be extremely
complex and typically to involve many disciplines: demog-
raphy, anthropology, sociology, history and other social sciences. But economists cannot obviously call themselves out
of it, as the Classical economists understood perfectly well.
From our point of view, we can only lament dearth of economic analysis both at the foundational stage and at the institutional stage of investigation.

It is surprising, in fact, to realise how little has been done in
this field since the Classical economists. Keynes himself was
not very perceptive on this problem. He was able, though,
to point out how important it was, in the short run, to pay
attention to the *proportion* of national income that population as a whole decides to devote to consumption and as a
consequence to the proportion of it that is intended for saving, a rather obvious macroeconomic relation, on which however the economists had not focused their attention before.
The Cambridge Keynesians have felt the attraction and fascination of related Classical-like macroeconomic theories, but
more with reference to income distribution. Recently, the
life-cycle theory of savings (especially by Modigliani and
Brumberg, 1954, and Modigliani and Ando, 1957) has been a
welcome addition. The approach taken however – by relying almost exclusively on rational individuals' behaviour
of utility maximisation – has not been entirely convincing
and in fact it has been challenged, especially with reference to structural hypotheses concerning the distribution and

redistribution of assets (bequests and inheritance effects) in inter-generational relations (see, for example, the works of Mauro Baranzini (1991, 1993, 2005)). From our own point of view, in a field of investigation rather neglected by economists, it will simply be worth pointing out how the paradigm proposed in the present work does not lack suggestions of problems to investigate. First of all, it posits the question of whether there exists, at the foundational stage of investigation, the possibility of defining a 'natural' distribution of income and wealth. Second, it posits the question of which kind of institutions this feature of the natural economic system is implicating. And third, it brings to the fore the problem of whether our existing institutions are up to the task of aiming at ideal ('natural') features in this field, or – more realistically – to what extent and/or in which ways they are failing to do so.

Capital accumulation

The second basic factor of economic dynamics in Harrod's list is singularly tricky.

For millennia, humankind had produced the goods it needed by means of labour and natural resources (essentially through the cultivation of land). By the end of the eighteenth century, a new factor of production appeared on the economic scene: *capital*. As we well know, physical capital (which is what is relevant here) is a collective name that stands for a set of material goods which are instrumentally used – together with labour and natural resources – to obtain final consumption goods and also capital goods themselves, which then need to be replaced periodically.

The capitalistic transformation of production was generated by the invention and progressive use of machines operated no longer by human or animal energy but by a whole series of new sources of energy that had been and still are cumulatively developing. It did bring with it an enormous increase of overall production, but this was not accompanied by an equitable or reasonable distribution of the consequent benefits. There can be little doubt today, when looking back to that period, that the increases in wealth were concentrated in the hands of restricted groups – the capitalists – who organised the production process in the newly constructed factories. The very emerging of the factory organisational system entailed a radical change which escaped immediate attention, not merely in the actual production but also in social relations. For the 'proletarians', who did not own anything except the possibility of offering their labour, it meant a separation of the place of work from the place of their families, with the duty to go to the factories – which became the symbol of the new era – at strictly pre-determined times, in a subordinate position and, at least initially, with excessively long working hours, while wages were kept, by competition, at the limit of subsistence. It meant the formation of social classes – the capitalists and the workers – which generated a conflict between capital and labour that characterised the industrialising countries during the whole of the nineteenth century and most of the twentieth century. Through this process, the free market economies had in fact been transformed into *capitalist* economies.

There has been slowness in grasping the really upsetting institutional implications of these changes. I have myself shown elsewhere, in an analytical way, how different the impact of capital goods is compared with that of consumption goods, on an economic system considered as a whole.[4] Briefly, in the case of consumption goods the economic system suffers no consequences from the way these goods are used. The owners of consumption goods are free to make any decision they like. A consumption good can be entirely consumed, it can be hoarded for future use, it can be sold, or given away to the external world, it could even be destroyed, with

---

[4] See Pasinetti, 1983.

no consequences whatever on the actual working of the economic system. Not so in the case of capital goods! The capital goods *must* be kept in existence, they must be used for the whole period of production and then they *must* entirely be replaced as means of production, otherwise the whole production process halts! It is important to realise that the existence, and then the accumulation, of physical capital is an absolute necessity in the production process of the industrialised economies. Without physical capital there cannot be corresponding jobs for the labourers. Capital and labour are complementary (even with some – limited – margins of substitution, relevant however almost exclusively in the long run).

This means that physical capital goods – unlike consumption goods – perform a function which is *relevant for society as a whole*. They procure jobs for the labourers. We may well say that they fulfil a *social* function. For this reason, capital and labour cannot be put on the same level: they do not play a symmetrical role. Behind capital there is a particular way of using the excess of income over consumption. Behind labour there are human beings and their families.[5]

It is here that a delicate problem immediately arises. Short reflection will convince anybody that the delicate and critical point that emerges concerns the *ownership* of the means of production. While there is no difficulty in producing arguments in favour of private ownership for the consumption goods, the private ownership of the means of production is a more questionable issue, simply because in an industrial system any decision on the use of capital goods has consequences that *affect society as a whole*. Yet the problem is tricky. The source of ownership of capital goods and of consumption goods, in a free society, appears to be the same. If we find it legitimate for any single individual to decide to dispose of his/her savings in the way he/she likes, or to

---

[5] See footnote 6 below.

hoard them in the form, let us say, of gold bars, why should one object to, or interfere with, any use of his/her accumulated savings in the form of physical capital goods? A clear, uncontroversial answer to this question – a typically novel institutional question brought by the industrial revolution – has not emerged so far.

The conclusion to this short aside is in fact critical. For the special *social* status of capital goods – a novelty of the industrial era – raised the problem of how to exercise the rights of property on a factor of production, which is revealed to have a *social function* to fulfil.

The disconcerting issue is that, since the beginning of the industrial revolution, when the problem of capital as a factor of production first emerged, this institutional problem has remained with us – practically *unsolved*. At the one extreme, Ricardian-socialists, Marxists and others have argued that the means of production should be owned by the community as a whole and not by single individuals. At the other extreme, liberals or simply anti-statalists have claimed the primacy of private ownership, supported by arguments stressing the efficient allocation of resources induced by property rights. Discussions on these major institutional problems have been virulent at times.

It may also be useful to mention that more recently, in the 1980s, there has been a flourishing literature (e.g. Weitzman, 1984, Meade, 1989 and others) with proposals of new and original forms of collaboration of capital and labour, based on the participation of labourers in the risks, organisation and control of the means of production (a minimum level of wages being in any case assured).[6]

---

[6] It may be interesting to mention that, since the Catholic Church began making pronouncements on social matters on purely ethical grounds (not on grounds of economic analysis!), it has felt compelled to make an explicit stand on the conflict of labour and capital, which is worth recalling. It can be summarised in three points: i) legitimacy of private ownership, not only of consumption goods but also of the means of production; however,

On parallel lines, since the 1930s, a considerable economic literature (especially in the US) has brought attention to the development of economic institutions (the public corporations) in which a separation has taken place between (formally legal) ownership – maintained by a crowd of small shareholders – and the effective power to take decisions, kept by an elite of managers, only partially contributing to share holding.[7]

The collapse of the 'real' socialist economies has deprived of topicality – and has effectively contributed to divert attention away from – these basic issues, bringing many discussions to an abrupt interruption. It has also indirectly engendered a shift of emphasis in favour of *laissez-faire* economic policies. The whole world of international finance has been shaken by the huge recent financial scandals concerning the misbehaviour of single (well-paid) managers, aided by chartered accountant institutions supposedly created to guarantee the correctness of their activities.

One of the merits, among others, of the production paradigm advocated here is that it inevitably keeps these institutional problems – concerning the interconnections of capital ownership, labour relations, top management and economic power – well in evidence, thus persistently keeping

ii) some sort of restricted status (not specified) to be implied by the ownership of capital goods, since they have a social function to fulfil, which confers on labour a primacy over capital; iii) recognition of the fact that free market economies have historically generated an inequitable distribution of income and wealth in favour of the capitalists and that some corrections (not explicitly specified) should be made to this distortion. It may also be interesting to mention the justification that is given for the primacy of labour over capital: '. . . the means of production . . . cannot be *possessed against labour*, they cannot even be possessed *for possession's sake*, because the only legitimate title to their possession . . . is *that they should serve labour*' (italics in original, Pope John-Paul II, 1981, *L.E.*, § 14).

[7] The classical work on this problem is Berle and Means (1932). But see also John K. Galbraith (1956). Carl Kaysen was at one time so optimistic as to talk of a 'soulful corporation' – a corporation that takes care of many categories (stakeholders) of its participants, in various forms. But see now his more recent review of the present situation (Kaysen, 1996).

alive and stimulating thoughts, criticisms,[8] proposals of various kinds, even if satisfactory, uncontroversial solutions remain very far from reach.

Technical progress

Meanwhile, another, related, more recently perceived set of institutional problems (alas also as yet largely *unsolved*) has been coming to the fore with increasing strength. The problems concern the third factor on Harrod's list: technical progress. In a sense, and rather curiously but understandably, it has somewhat attenuated the once absolutely central emphasis on capital accumulation, but it has brought to the surface new institutional difficulties which again concern the same right – the right of property – but through a totally different route and in a totally different respect.

Here again the spontaneous tendency has been all too obviously to go back to reliance on that usual institution, the free market mechanism, that was inherited from the earlier trade phase of the emerging modern world. We have repeatedly pointed out how the market mechanism had quite rightly attracted the attention of the Classical economists. Adam Smith's incidental metaphor of an invisible hand, acting through the markets – though originally presented by him with qualifications (then forgotten)[9] – has become the symbol of how individuals' (selfish) behaviour could become a social device for the benefit of the whole community. But only more recently have we been realising, in a clearer way, that the market mechanism is inherently endowed with forces that, through the competition mechanism, include a multiplicity of quite different aspects, of which at least two

---

[8] See Galbraith's latest brilliantly provoking essay (2004).

[9] The symbolic – rather than real – paternity of this expression, so commonly attributed to Adam Smith, has been analysed in detail and with force by Alessandro Roncaglia (2005a, pp. 324–325; 2005b, pp. 19–20).

(mentioned earlier) are crucial to our arguments. One refers to the process of the optimum allocation of given resources (let us call it *static* competition), the other refers to the incentive to inventiveness, in a typically evolving setting (let us call this *dynamic* competition). The Classical economists had perceived the existence of both aspects (though underestimating the second), but were unable to produce a formal analytical scheme for either.

Neoclassical economists have been analytically more successful, but they have done so at the price of concentrating on only one of them (the static one), excluding the other. It was only in the last few decades of the twentieth century that a whole spate of economic research developed, focusing on the *dynamic* aspects of market competition. This shows (incidentally but quite clearly) that the relevance of the free market institution is much wider than simply that of the optimum allocation of given resources (the only one on which neoclassical economists could concentrate). At the same time, the upshots of research on the dynamic aspects, now that they are emerging, reveal that they do not match with the upshots of research deriving from the static general equilibrium scheme. Institutional requirements that are essential to reach (efficient) results within the static approach (think, for example, of perfect competition) are often in contrast with institutional requirements that are revealed to be necessary to reach (successful) results within the context of the second (the dynamic) approach.

The institutions that at the beginning of the twenty-first century we have been able to set up in order to deal with these problems are represented by a panoply of anti-trust legislation, of committees and authorities of various kinds that are mainly compelled to rely on judicious pragmatism and historical cases, rather than on a (still lacking) overall clear theory of a supposed overall efficiency (or lack of efficiency) of the (not so free) market institutions.

All this has thereby added further complications by increasing the interdependence of economic analysis at its institutional level and a particularly specific one of the other social sciences – law.

5.   Clash of the institutional implications of different paradigms

We are led to face, at this point, a very significant instance of how two different paradigms (the traditional pure exchange paradigm on the one side and, in our terms, a newly conceived production paradigm on the other side), once accepted at the foundational level, may inevitably lead to entirely different directions and to actually different practical prescriptions on the type of institutions to adopt.

Social scholars in general (especially lawyers!) had envied the economists who can claim the availability of an elegant tool of analysis such as the general equilibrium scheme. The attraction and beauty of this scheme is that one can show it to lead to optimal positions by merely requiring two clear institutional ingredients: perfect competition and property rights enforcement. This economic model, however, was essentially conceived with reference to material goods, within a static framework. Whether the same model can preserve the same optimality properties when extended to include immaterial or intellectual goods was not initially questioned; it was not even thought to require a proof. But in fact this is precisely what *should* have been proved. So far, nobody has produced this proof.

Indeed, there is a crucial difference between tangible, material goods and immaterial, intangible goods. It has by now generally been perceived that there are two properties normally associated with public goods which become relevant also for the problems concerning *knowledge* (i.e. the factors behind technical progress). These are the property of non-rivalry and the property of non-excludability.[10] Normally, tangible, material goods are both rivalrous *and* excludable. These are precisely the two characteristics for which the assignment of property rights fulfils the social function of efficiency, by inducing, through the competitive price system, an optimal allocation of the given resources. But intangible, immaterial goods are different. They are generally both non-rivalrous *and* non-excludable. In our societies non-rivalry is still largely a technical characteristic, while non-excludability (or excludability) is increasingly becoming a characteristic regulated by law (i.e. an institutional characteristic). More specifically, a public (non-rivalrous) good, such as knowledge, can be made excludable 'artificially' by making it so by law, i.e. by the assignment of copyrights or/and patents. However, in this case, we cannot invoke the same efficiency function which is associated with the case of material goods.

It should be clear, to begin with, that from a welfare economics point of view, excludability imposed by law on immaterial goods generates social waste. This is because an intellectual good, once available, can be offered to many other consumers at almost no extra cost. For instance, the fact that any person can listen on the web to Beethoven's Symphony Number 9 does not prevent millions of other people from listening to it as well, at no cost, or almost no cost. Yet in spite of this, i.e. in spite of these technical characteristics, other people may be *excluded* from listening through legal means – the imposition of copyright fees. Hence, the increasing importance of the intellectual goods in our economies

---

[10] As is well known, a good is said to be 'non-rival' when a unit of that good can be consumed by one individual without detracting from the consumption opportunities available to other individuals for that same unit. A good is said to be 'non-excludable' when, once it is provided, its benefits are available to all. For details, see, for instance, Cornes and Sandler (1986, p. 6).

has produced a new branch of property imposed by law – *intellectual* property. This new type of property aims at making intangible goods excludable through legislation, so that the legal owners of these goods can charge consumers a price.

But what justification can there be for this? The argument is that bringing excludability in, through legal means, has the effect (and thus the justification) of introducing incentives to inventions and innovations. It has been claimed that there may be some inventions that would never have been obtained if their inventors could not have been protected by patents. This is not entirely convincing, nor historically proved. One must realise, in any case, that such a protection also creates a monopolistic position, since the owners can charge prices or fees well above the cost of the research that has led to the discovery of the intellectual goods and so often far beyond, both in quantity and in time, what can be justified by any incentive motive.

From all this, one can certainly conclude that the assignment of property rights for immaterial goods – on the mere basis of the incentives that these property rights might stimulate – represents, in economic terms, a much weaker justification, to use a mild expression, than the traditional justification associated with tangible goods, for which property rights, under proper conditions, may fulfil the economic function of inducing an efficient allocation of resources. At the same time, research on the already mentioned dynamic aspects of competition have produced many interesting factual results, but have not produced any sufficiently strong analytical scheme(s) for giving us a satisfactory framework for welfare-based decisions. To begin with, the existence of incentives following from the possibilities of gaining property rights is not always a necessary condition for promoting innovations. Many inventions – in the applied fields and not only at the level of pure science – are normally achieved without the protection of patents, as has been pointed out in many reports. The inventor may well have been stimulated, and then be satisfied, simply by the recognition of his/her paternity of the idea.[11] Moreover and most importantly, a justification for assigning intellectual property rights can in any case be argued only on a *temporary* basis, i.e. for a limited period of time. In a society in which innovations and inventions are taking place rapidly, it appears reasonable that the lengths of time for which copyrights and patents fees are assigned should become increasingly shorter than they have usually been in the past, especially on the international scene.

In this respect, it may be helpful to recall the enormous importance of the subject of knowledge diffusion in international economic relations. It is usual, when we talk of acquisition and diffusion of knowledge, to think in terms of the most advanced economies. But we should not neglect, and even less forget, the situation of the poor countries. These countries are, at present, facing the huge problem of catching up with the living standards of the advanced world. Contrary to what traditional economics has upheld, the ability of poor countries to close the gap that divides them from the rich countries no longer depends so much on lack of savings or massive capital accumulation (as Marxian literature strongly stressed until not so long ago and in general continues to stress even now), but rather on their ability to catch up with overall knowledge and educational standards. Not surprisingly, to the developing countries, the problem of intellectual property appears to be an obstacle to their economic (and also cultural) development. It is becoming increasingly evident that, while it is not impossible for them to catch up with

---

[11] There is an important aspect, which is quite separate from the intellectual property strictly considered as a source of income, that should not be neglected in this respect. Obviously any person who has invented something has a right to the recognition of the authorship of his/her original ideas, quite independently of any commercial exploitation that may derive from it. The patent system itself may well be of help in fulfilling this function, jointly with appropriate normative rules concerning how to establish priority of publication or of availability. (This is, of course, a field to which lawyers may have a lot to contribute.)

the living standards of the developed world, their chances are crucially dependent on their ability to catch up with the available global education standards and the world state of technical knowledge, which in fact means, to a large extent, with the capability of the world as a whole to build up the appropriate set of national and international institutions. I think that it is not unreasonable to feel that, in the twenty-first century, precisely these institutional problems are going to emerge as crucial and in bad need of solutions that should be characterised by a consensus as wide as possible. They not only concern economics; they require interaction among all the other social sciences (and in fact not only among the social sciences).

Even more importantly for our purposes, they imply institutional problems that need to be faced differently according to whether our analysis has taken its first steps from within one of the two paradigms we are considering or within the other. The clash between the two paradigms, which emerged in our previous arguments at the foundational stage of investigation, reappears here but right at the core of the second – the institutional – stage of investigation. In other words, the clash becomes much wider, including institutional implications in terms of conflicting directions and recommendations for the type and character of institutions to be arranged or even for those in need of being newly invented. More specifically, a confrontation and clash may break out between deductions and institutional prescriptions following from the pure exchange paradigm and deductions and prescriptions following from the pure production paradigm.

This whole field of evolving knowledge is thus emerging as the most topical and stunning novelty of all, in an evolving industrial society, if it leads to a straight clash between the two paradigms, not only at the foundational stage but also at the institutional stage of investigation.

We have already stressed the damage caused in the past by (unwise) simplistic extensions of concepts and categories coming from the old pure exchange paradigm to the problems concerning the new realities of the (industrial) economic systems. In a similar way, new disastrous effects may be caused by equally simplistic extensions to the case concerning the learning processes and the diffusion of knowledge.

6. The rationale behind conflicting institutional directions

When we recalled earlier the *foundations* of neoclassical economic analysis, elegantly presented by Paul Samuelson in his *Foundations*[12] – namely in terms of a mathematical function to be maximised under constraints – we unveiled how the scheme is inextricably linked with a very specific institutional set-up, represented by a free market economy, that relies on private property of existing (given) resources to be traded on perfectly competitive markets. But we have also pointed out that this theoretical scheme was typically conceived with reference to a traditional environment of material goods. The evolution of a society in which intellectual goods are becoming of paramount importance is changing the whole economic environment.

What has been the reaction of mainstream (neoclassical) economists? To answer the question, we must go back to consider the properties of knowledge, briefly summarised in the previous section. Clearly, non-excludability and non-rivalry of intellectual goods do not match the strict requirements of an efficient allocation function for the free market institution. The reaction of mainstream economists to these sheer facts has been, and is, quite clear, logical and very significant. It has not been that of acknowledging the obvious 'market failures', when knowledge becomes the predominant factor. This would have implied a consequent need to search for alternative institutional solutions. To avoid this, efforts have persistently been pursued in the opposite direction.

---

[12] See above p. 323.

The special character of knowledge is indeed recognised, but mainstream economists forcefully propose to build – and have become strong promoters in building – *an artificial legal system* aimed at making knowledge what actually it is not: namely a private or quasi-private good. In other words, the solution that is being pursued follows a simple but powerful logic: let us not change our free market institutions. Instead, let us go down to the foundations of the new phenomena and *artificially* change the characteristics of knowledge itself by making it excludable by law, so as to fit it into the pre-conceived institutional framework, based on private property and the market price mechanism.

The advantage, it is claimed, consists in transforming knowledge into a normal tradable good. This would (artificially) remove it from the exposure to the inherent 'market failures'. The illusion is to be able to extend to the production of knowledge those Pareto-optimal properties that are typically associated with material goods. Given the basic features of non-excludability and non-rivalry, the effort of turning knowledge into a private good is bound to ramify in many directions: by setting up a costly panoply of administrative and legal measures to deal with an artificially invented institutional (legal) phenomenon.

First, enormous efforts are made at strengthening and *extending* intellectual property rights and the patent system of protection (which in the US now includes also typically immaterial goods such as software). This is obviously a system of man-made, highly artificial protection. Ideas can fly from head to head and be used by many people, without the need to sign a legal contract of ownership. Among other things, when payments of property rights are imposed, in order to allow the actual application of an idea, transaction costs dramatically increase, depriving knowledge of many – in most cases of almost all – of the vast potential efforts that could come from its diffusion. Among other aspects, the enforcement of a legal system of protection for intellectual property may prove very costly indeed, given the immateriality of knowledge, much more costly than the simpler and immediate procedures allowed by the rivalry characteristics of material goods.

Second (at least formally), widespread efforts must be made to break up monopolies (since the formal proofs of allocative market efficiency pre-suppose perfectly competitive conditions) in those sectors that depend heavily on the improvement of knowledge. Anti-trust laws have been strengthened, authorities specifically devoted to monitor market competition have been set in place or further expanded. The purpose is clear: to try to preserve, or rather to pretend to preserve, the free market mechanism even in those cases in which the spontaneous organisational tendency is towards a monopolistic market structure (mainly because of decreasing costs of knowledge-based products).

But it is at this point that we cannot avoid the crucial question. Is this the only possible approach – as mainstream economics is taking for granted – to the institutional problem raised by the accumulation of knowledge? Should the tide of the market institutions be considered so overwhelming as to submerge all market-adverse aspects of knowledge? Our proposed production paradigm suggests that further investigation has become necessary. The question is almost obvious: which possibility is there to look for alternative solutions?

We should begin to open our eyes and start to perceive the fact that a pure market approach to the process of human learning and diffusion of knowledge, especially when it is artificially created, is bound, in the long run, to throw the economic system into disarray. It is certainly bound already to impose a series of constraints in the short run and most of the time to give many more troubles than advantages. An increasing share of our social time is bound to be devoted to legal disputes concerning intellectual property rights. Quite apart from the huge sums (how far justified?) that lawyers are making out of these legal battles, it would be difficult to consider all this a positive-sum game for society as a whole, even if we take it for granted that our economies should remain market-oriented (but appropriately so). Far less can such a prevailing trend be considered a factor of economic growth. On the contrary, it patently appears a very serious obstacle indeed to the diffusion of knowledge and thus, inevitably in the long run, to economic growth.

But let us now come to the vital question: what are the alternatives? We must begin at the very basis. What are the constraints, imposed in terms of alternative institutions, associated with the production paradigm? The answer here is striking: no specific one! No constraint; complete freedom. It is up to us to investigate which institutional mechanism is the most appropriate in any specific historical circumstance.

But at the same time, what an abundant richness of deductions, of suggestions are potentially flowing from the foundational stage of analysis that the new paradigm can offer!

A realisation of the very nature of knowledge, of the effects of its improvements and of its diffusion, of the consequences on the working and development of economic systems, and on the choice it may suggest on the appropriate institutions to be set up: all this represents an immense field of analysis, a field of investigation that the whole traditional economics has (perhaps inadvertently or unconsciously) tended to leave aside, to avoid, or even to suppress – neoclassical economics much more so, because of the incompatibility pointed out above with its foundational assumptions. (Classical economics was also lacking, but as an effect of underestimation and absence of awareness – not as an effect of foundational incompatibility.)

7.   Innovative features: learning as a human right and free communication of achieved knowledge as a social duty

Growth and diffusion of knowledge (rather than simply technical progress) should have been the name given to the third factor on Harrod's list. He did not imagine (and certainly it took time for us to realise) what a revolutionary factor this is: both for society as a whole and for the economic analysis that is necessary and worth being set up to investigate its implications.

When fully brought to the centre of our economic investigations, at the foundational level and at the institutional level as well, it may strikingly break out as being so pervasive as to invest and change the perspective also of the other two features of dynamic economics (population growth and capital accumulation). The early idea of considering population as a kind of reservoir of workers, to be fed in order to be used as mechanical clogs in the machinery process of factory production, is bound to (and should perhaps already have) become obsolete. The idea itself of workers is taken over by a wider concept, namely that of human activity in general; indeed, endowed with the most marvellous of all powers: the human mind. Physical capital itself may be considered as the expression not only of intermediate commodities but of *hyper-integrated* labour, and thus again, by transposition, of hyper-integrated human activity.

What used to be feared as the scourge of the 'mouths to be fed' of Malthusian reminiscence may increasingly be seen as the potential richness of a higher number of, and better trained, human brains, endowed with the possibility of innovative, original ideas and new intellectual conceptions.

The above-mentioned process of hyper-integration is giving analytical substance to these concepts. Within this perspective, the pure labour model briefly recalled in Chapter IX above may be seen as something that transcends its initial appearance of a device for simplifications and emerges as a really fundamental tool of economic investigation.[13]

---

[13] I cannot refrain from recalling here another of Keynes's flashes of intuition: 'I sympathise . . . with the pre-classical doctrine that everything is *produced* by *labour*, aided by what used to be called art and is now called technique . . . It is preferable to regard labour, including of course the personal services of the entrepreneur and his assistants, as the sole factor of production' (Keynes, 1936, *italics* in original, pp. 213–214). These ideas (and intuitions) of Keynes's seem to me to find their analytical expression precisely in those concepts of vertical hyper-integration

The consequences of putting ourselves into this perspective may now appear almost obvious – a pressing necessity to search harshly for the type of institutions that are really appropriate to the new tasks. At the same time, the social implications may emerge daunting to the traditional mode of thinking and almost obvious on the evidence of recent events. The social duty for a community as a whole to provide a basic education for everybody, mentioned in Chapter IX when presenting the pure labour model, might emerge as only the first step of a reasonably preliminary public duty in all societies based on increasing knowledge.

The human right to learn and the symmetrical duty to freely communicate existing knowledge may well be going to revolutionise the institutions to be invented and set up as the bases of our legal and political and economic systems of the very near future.

8.   An international claim for a resumption of Keynes's *revolution in economics*

A final note on a wider worldwide perspective is perhaps due. It is probably going to be on the international scene that the present institutional set-up and consequent approach to the process of economic growth and diffusion of knowledge is raising, and will inevitably continue to go on raising, the most serious problems. In the near future, technical progress, in the more extensive sense of a persistent growth of knowledge, is likely to turn out to be (if it is not already!) the crucial source of general well being, not so much in terms of overall economic growth as mostly in terms of the quality and character of the evolving composition of our production and consumption, within a natural environment requiring to be defended and preserved. Especially for those countries that

(of production sectors, of labour coefficients, of productive capacities) as already hinted at above (on pp. 278 and 302) and as developed in detail in Pasinetti, 1973, 1981, 1988.

are lagging behind and have a huge gap of technical knowledge to surmount, the challenge is tremendous.

Historical circumstances have so far favoured the concentration of knowledge in the developed world. The worrying
question is: what could be the result of artificially making it
a privately owned good on a global scale? The poor countries
that could take advantage, at no extra cost for anybody, of the
acquisition of the knowledge already in use in the advanced
world could no longer be allowed to reap these advantages
if, following the indications coming from the now dominant
economic paradigm, the present process of legal privatisation
is kept on going (which in social terms would actually mean
erecting obstacles by means of legal exclusion). They might
be (and in fact they have been already) asked to pay heavy
royalty fees for the use of existing and well-established and
widely available knowledge, no longer entailing any cost for
any country (except for minor adaptations). How far could
all this be justified? Presumably, in the advanced world, the
interested majority will continue to argue that higher royal-
ties mean higher incentives to research and innovation, and
hence to economic growth for all. But the other side of the
coin may keep on becoming heavier and heavier. The risk may
be increasing of building up an artificial knowledge barrier
that might force the majority of the world population into
permanently lagging-behind conditions. This could hardly
be justified.

Questions of this kind should probably force economists
(and not only economists) to look at the institutional problems raised by the process of human learning and most of
all at the international diffusion of knowledge from a radically different point of view and from strikingly different
perspectives. The real challenge is to get rid of the old ways
of thinking and accept the fact that the characteristics of
knowledge (of which technical knowledge is only a subset)
are really peculiarly new and require the necessity of looking
into the possibilities of a broader set of institutional devices

and mechanisms, more appropriate to the acquisition and diffusion of knowledge for the benefits of the whole world community, including the developed countries themselves.

It may sound upsetting, but this is not going to take place if economists and policy makers stubbornly and firmly remain convinced of the irreplaceability of the now prevalent economic paradigm, proudly associated with neoclassical economic theory.

It is precisely on this point, i.e. on a radical change of the current dominant paradigm, that Keynes's 'revolution in economics' may find a dramatically forceful, earlier unexpected, vigour and regain the lost strength for a decisive resumption of what began with wide expectations and awed fascination but has remained a 'revolution' still unfulfilled – a revolution still needing to be accomplished.

References for Book Three

Arestis, Philip and Sawyer, Malcolm, (2001), *The Economics of the Third Way: Experiences from around the world*, Cheltenham: Edward Elgar Publishing.

Arrow, K. J. and Debreu, G., (1954), 'Existence of an equilibrium for a competitive economy', *Econometrica*, vol. 22, pp. 265–290.

Baranzini, Mauro, (1991), *A Theory of Wealth Distribution and Accumulation*, Oxford: Clarendon Press.

Baranzini, Mauro, (1993), 'Distribution, accumulation and institutions', in Heertje, A., ed., *The Makers of Modern Economics*, vol. II, Aldershot: Edward Elgar, pp. 1–28.

Baranzini, Mauro, (2005), 'Modigliani's Life-cycle Theory of Savings Fifty Years Later', in *BNL Quarterly Review*, vol. 58, pp. 109–172.

Berle, Adolph A. and Means, Gardiner C., (1932), *The Modern Corporation and Private Property*, New York: Commerce Cleaning House.

Bortis, Heinrich, (1997), *Institutions, Behaviour and Economic Theory: A contribution to classical Keynesian political economy*, Cambridge: Cambridge University Press.

Bortis, Heinrich, (2003), 'Keynes and the Classics: Notes on the Monetary Theory of Production', in Rochon, L. and Rossi, S., eds, *Modern Theories of Money*, Cheltenham: Edward Elgar, pp. 411–474.

Collison Black, R. D., Coats, A. W. and Craufurd, D. W. Goodwin, eds (1973), *The Marginal Revolution in Economics: Interpretation and Evaluation*, Durham, North Carolina: Duke University Press.

Cornes, Richard and Sandler, Todd, (1986), *The Theory of Externalities, Public Goods, and Club Goods*, Cambridge: Cambridge University Press.

Davidson, Paul, (1972), *Money and the Real World*, New York: Halsted Press.

Davidson, Paul, (1982–83), 'Rational Expectations: A Fallacious Foundation for Studying Crucial Decision Making Processes', *Journal of Post Keynesian Economics*, vol. 5, Winter, pp. 182–199.

Friedman, Milton, (1957), *A Theory of the Consumption Function*, Princeton N.J: Princeton University Press.

Galbraith, John Kenneth, (1956), *American Capitalism, The Concept of Countervailing Power*, Cambridge, Mass: The Riverside Press.

Galbraith, John Kenneth, (2004), *The Economics of Innocent Fraud*, Boston: Houghton Mifflin Co.

Giddens, Anthony, (2000), *The Third Way and its Critics*, Oxford: Polity Press.

Godley, Wynne, and Lavoie, Marc, (2007), *Monetary Economics – An Integrated Approach to Credit, Money, Income, Production and Wealth*, London: Palgrave Macmillan.

Harcourt, Geoffrey C., (2006), *The Structure of Post-Keynesian Economics – The Core Contributions of the Pioneers*, Cambridge: Cambridge University Press.

Harrod, Roy F., (1939), 'An Essay in Dynamic Theory', *The Economic Journal*, vol. 49, pp. 14–33.

Harrod, Roy F., (1948), *Towards a Dynamic Economics*, London: Macmillan.

Heckscher, Eli F., (1955), *Mercantilism*, 2 vols, London: Allen and Unwin.

Hodgson, Geoffrey M., (1994), 'A Comment on Pasinetti', in Delorme, R. and Dopfer, K. eds, *The Political Economy of Diversity: Evolutionary perspectives on economic order and disorder*, Aldershot: Edward Elgar, pp. 46–50.

Hodgson, Geoffrey M., (1999), *Evolution and Institutions*, Cheltenham: Edward Elgar.

Hodgson, Geoffrey M., (2005), '"Institution" by Walter H. Hamilton', *Journal of Institutional Economics*, vol. 1, no. 2, pp. 233–244.

Kaysen, Carl, ed., (1996), *The American Corporation Today*, New York: Oxford University Press.

Keynes, John Maynard, (1926), *The End of Laissez-faire*, London: Hogart Press; reprinted in *Essays in Persuasion*, 1931, London: Macmillan and New York: Harcourt, Brace & Co., pp. 312–322.

Keynes, John Maynard, (1936), *The General Theory of Employment, Interest and Money*, London: Macmillan.

Kirman, Alan, (1989), 'The Intrinsic Limits of Modern Economic Theory: the Emperor has no Clothes', *The Economic Journal*, vol. 99, pp. 126–139.

Kirman, Alan, (1992), 'Whom or What does the Representative Individual Represent?', *Journal of Economic Perspectives*, vol. 6, no. 2, Spring, pp. 117–136.

Laidler, David, (1999), *Fabricating the Keynesian Revolution: Studies of the Inter-war Literature on Money, the Cycle, and Unemployment*, Cambridge: Cambridge University Press.

Landes, David, (1998), *The Wealth and Poverty of Nations*, London: Little, Brown & Co.

Malthus, Thomas Robert, (1798), *On the Principle of Population*, London: Joseph Johnson.

Meade, James Edward, (1989), *Agathotopia: the economics of partnership*, Aberdeen: Aberdeen University Press.

Mill, John Stuart, (1848), *Principles of Political Economy with some of their Applications to Social Philosophy*, 1st edition, London: Parker and Co.

Minsky, Hyman, (1975), *John Maynard Keynes*, New York: Columbia University Press.

Minsky, Hyman P., (1986), *Stabilizing an Unstable Economy*, New Haven: Yale University Press.

Modigliani, Franco and Brumberg, R., (1954), 'Utility analysis and the consumption function: An interpretation of cross-section data', in Kurihara, K. K., ed., *Post Keynesian Economics*, New Brunswick: Rutgers University Press, pp. 388–436.

Modigliani, Franco and Ando, A., (1957), 'Tests of the life cycle hypothesis of saving: comments and suggestions', in *Bulletin of the Oxford University Institute of Statistics*, vol. 19, pp. 99–124.

North, Douglass C. (1990) *Institutions, Institutional Change and Economic Performance*, Cambridge: Cambridge University Press.

Pasinetti, Luigi L., (1962), 'A multi-sector model of economic growth', a Ph.D. dissertation submitted to the Faculty of Economics and Politics of the University of Cambridge, September.

Pasinetti, Luigi L., (1965), 'Causalità e interdipendenza nell'analisi econometrica e nella teoria economica', in *Annuario dell'Università Cattolica del S. Cuore, 1964–65*, Milan: Vita e Pensiero, pp. 233–250.

Pasinetti, Luigi L., (1973), 'The Notion of Vertical Integration in Economic Analysis', *Metroeconomica*, vol. 25, pp. 1–29.

Pasinetti, Luigi L., (1977), *Lectures on the Theory of Production*, London: Macmillan.

Pasinetti, Luigi L., (1980), 'The Rate of Interest and the Distribution of Income in a Pure Labour Economy', *Journal of Post Keynesian Economics*, vol. 3, Winter 1980–1981, pp. 170–182.

Pasinetti, Luigi L., (1981), *Structural Change and Economic Growth – A Theoretical Essay on the Dynamics of the Wealth of Nations*, Cambridge: Cambridge University Press.

Pasinetti, Luigi L., (1983), 'The Accumulation of Capital', *The Cambridge Journal of Economics*, vol. 7, pp. 405–411.

Pasinetti, Luigi L., (1986), 'Theory of Value – A Source of Alternative Paradigms in Economic Analysis', in Baranzini, Mauro and Scazzieri, Roberto, eds, *Foundations of Economics – Structure of Inquiry and Economic Theory*, Oxford: Basil Blackwell, pp. 409–431.

Pasinetti, Luigi L., (1988), 'Growing Sub-systems, Vertically Hyperintegrated Sectors and the Labour Theory of Value', *The Cambridge Journal of Economics*, vol. 12, pp. 125–134.

Pasinetti, Luigi L., (1993a), *Structural Economic Dynamics – A Theory of the Economic Consequences of Human Learning*, Cambridge: Cambridge University Press.

Pasinetti, Luigi L., (1993b), 'Contribution' to the discussion, in Tsuru, Shigeto, *Institutional Economics Revisited*, 'Raffaele Mattioli Lectures' (Milan, 1985), Cambridge: Cambridge University Press, pp. 126–130.

Pasinetti, Luigi L., ed., (1998), *Italian Economic Papers*, vol. III, Bologna: il Mulino and Oxford: Oxford University Press.

Pasinetti, Luigi L., (1999), 'Economic Theory and Technical Progress', in *Economic Issues*, vol. 4, part 2, pp. 1–18.

Pasinetti, Luigi L., (2000), 'Critique of the Neoclassical Theory of Growth and Distribution', *Banca Nazionale del Lavoro Quarterly Review*, vol. LIII, pp. 383–431.

Pasinetti, Luigi L., (2003), Letter to the Editor, in 'Comments – Cambridge Capital Controversies', *Journal of Economic Perspectives*, vol. 17, no. 4, Fall, pp. 227–228. (A comment on Avi J. Cohen and Geoffrey C. Harcourt's 'Cambridge Capital Theory Controversies', *Journal of Economic Perspectives*, vol. 17, no. 1, Winter, pp. 199–214.)

Phelps, Edmund S., (1994), *Structural Slumps – The Modern Equilibrium Theory of Unemployment, Interest and Assets*. Cambridge, Mass: Harvard University Press.

Pope, John Paul II, *Laborem Exercens*, 1981.

Pope, John Paul II, *Centesimus Annus*, 1993.

Quah, Danny, (2001), 'The Weightless Economy in Economic Development', in Pohjola, Matti, ed., *Information Technology, Productivity, and Economic Growth*, Oxford: Oxford University Press.

Quah, Danny, (2002), 'Matching Demand and Supply in a Weightless Economy: Market-driven Creativity with and without IPRs', *De Economist*, vol. 150, no. 4, October, pp. 381–403.

Ricardo, David, [1821], (1951–73), *On the Principles of Political Economy and Taxation*, 3rd edition, 1821, vol. I of *The Works and Correspondence of David Ricardo*, Sraffa, Piero, ed., with the collaboration of Dobb, M. H., Cambridge: Cambridge University Press.

Roncaglia, Alessandro, (2005a), *The Wealth of Ideas: A History of Economic Thought*, Cambridge: Cambridge University Press.

Roncaglia, Alessandro, (2005b), *Il Mito della Mano Invisibile*, Bari: Laterza.

Salvadori, Neri, (2003), *Old and New Growth Theories – An Assessment*, Cheltenham: Edward Elgar.

Samuelson, Paul A., (1947), *Foundations of Economic Analysis*, Cambridge, Mass.: Harvard University Press.

Schumpeter, Joseph Alois, (1943), *Capitalism, Socialism, and Democracy*, London: George Allen & Unwin.

Schumpeter, Joseph Alois, [1934] (1961), *The Theory of Economic Development: an inquiry into profits, capital, credit, interest, and the business cycle*, Cambridge, Mass.: Harvard University Press.

Smith, Adam, (1976), *An Inquiry into the Nature and Causes of the Wealth of Nations*, edited by Campbell, R. H. and Skinner, A. S., 'The Glasgow edition of the Works and Correspondence of Adam Smith', Oxford: Oxford University Press (originally published in 1776).

Sraffa, Piero, (1960), *Production of Commodities by Means of Commodities – A prelude to a critique of economic theory*, Cambridge: Cambridge University Press.

Stiglitz, Joseph E., (2001), *Financial Liberalization: how far, how fast?*, in Caprio, Gerard, Honohan, Patrick and Stiglitz, Joseph E. eds, Cambridge: Cambridge University Press.

Sylos Labini, Paolo, (1995), 'Why the Interpretation of the Cobb-Douglas Production Function must be Radically Changed', in *Structural Change and Economic Dynamics*, vol. 6, pp. 485–504.

Von Neumann, John, (1937), 'Über ein Ökonomisches Gleichungs-system und eine Verallgemeinerung des Brouwerschen Fixpunktsatzes', in *Ergebnisse eines Matematischen Kolloquiums*, Vienna, vol. VIII, pp. 73–83, transl. as 'A Model of General Equilibrium,' in *The Review of Economic Studies*, vol. XIII [1] 1945, pp. 1–9.

Weitzman, Martin L., (1984), *The Share Economy: Conquering Stagflation*, London: Harvard University Press.

Index